SHADES

of

COLOR

INNOCENCE OF A CHILD

AN UNEQUALED LEGACY

SHADES

of

COLOR

INNOCENCE OF
A CHILD

———

AN UNEQUALED
LEGACY

CLIFTON SAVOY, PH.D.

SAVOYHOUSE PRESS

Cover: Western Oklahoma Sunset.
Courtesy, Dr. Paul Reed of Guymon, Oklahoma.

Building: Fine Arts Building, Northwestern Oklahoma State University.
Courtesy, Northwestern Foundation & Alumni Association.

Book cover and interior design by The Book Cover Whisperer:
OpenBookDesign.biz

978-1-7376498-2-3 Hardcover
978-1-7376498-0-9 Paperback
978-1-7376498-1-6 eBook

Printed in the United States
FIRST EDITION

CONTENTS

ACKNOWLEDGEMENTS

The encouragement by my wife, Judith, and friends—sometimes pulling and pushing—has been invaluable. If not for them, I wouldn't have overcome the many obstacles to complete this writing project. Truly, it has been an adventure, and I am extremely blessed.

Many, whom I shall never forget, stepped through the door at the right moment. A few should be mentioned publicly: Kathlyn Carter Smith, Jim Schroeder, Kenneth Strunk, Mary (Williams) Nichols, Tommy Griffin, Bill Bixler, Curtis Thompson, Dale Swiggot, Kim Hudson, Judy Wolgamott, Milt Basset, Jim and Bonnie Bostwick, and so many at Northwestern OSU; especially, Dr. Janet Cunningham, President, Allen 'Skeeter' Bird, and John Allen.

To the contributors, who sat for long periods of time for interviews and were courteous to respond to return phone calls and emails—endless questions, it will forever be my honor to have the privilege of bringing life to their true stories. Unfortunately, many have passed away before publication. They will never be forgotten. Special thoughts of appreciation and gratitude are extended to them and to their families, and may each story live forever as well.

Appreciation also is extended to Robin Pearson for sharing artistic talents: http:artistatplay01.wixsite.com/artwork

Above all, special gratitude is extended to the Lord God, who opened doors, introduced me to people, characters, and ideas; and who patiently walked with me up and down the hills of this journey—one tremendously richer and wonderful than I could imagine.

Clifton Savoy

INTRODUCTION

What occurs when a person never learns history, forgets it, or never had it presented? … Jesus of the Bible addressed something along this line when He said, "…you will know the truth, and the truth will set you free!" Bible, John 8:32. If grounded in the scriptures, individuals would have freedom from what we describe today as 'world viewpoints and spin.' … Are you, we free today?

In a way, this question raised its head when former athletes from the 1960s of a small university in Oklahoma had a fifty-year weekend reunion. I was one of them. We looked at old annuals, photos, and news clippings, and recalled memories. Talk of a teammate no longer with us brought sadness and tears. We also mentioned how rules had changed. In football, most of us would be ejected for roughness.

We noted how life had changed—family, technology, vehicles, life-pace, and daily impacts of world viewpoints, like political correctness, and 'spin.' We were disturbed how our history and relationships were either purposely or incorrectly portrayed. Why? We had some warts, yes, but nothing to hide or alter.

Shades of Color resulted. It reveals our relationships and addresses such issues. It's based on true stories which occurred in a university setting in the 1950s-60s. Major national news was presented in dormitory TV lounges to reveal the impacts on daily life. Tough questions were raised, and the findings reveal a stunning truth—we are just shades of the same color!

Specifically, this literary work is about the first students of color—primarily, Native-American and African-American—to attend Northwestern Oklahoma State University, which is located near the center of the United States on the Salt Fork River on the northwestern border of Oklahoma. The families in this area and to the west were mostly white as were the students. Based on national news reports of racial hostility, similar results might have been expected at Northwestern. In fact, its 1962 enrolling class was required to study To Kill A Mockingbird for student orientation.

To put the 1960s in proper perspective, the decade was one of the most divisive, violent, and bloody in United States history; maybe second, only to the 1860s divided Nation in the Civil War with the assassination of President Abraham Lincoln and some six hundred thousand war deaths. Assassination after assassination occurred, including: President John F. Kennedy and civil rights leader Dr. Martin Luther King, Jr. At times, hundreds of thousands protested in Washington, D.C., as Congress struggled with Vietnam War issues, as well as its longest filibuster in history—one to block the Fourth Civil Rights Act. Marches, protests, and sit-ins were frequent and met with inflamed resistance—even university doors were blocked, and some protestors were killed. Bomb blasts of houses and churches killed others. The one hundred years and the lynching of thousands of blacks, as well as white sympathizers, by the KKK in the push-back against Lincoln's Emancipation Proclamation; and the Thirteenth, Fourteenth, and Fifteenth Amendments to the Constitution; and 'separate but unequal' were coming to a head. The escalation of the Vietnam War added more dissension and violence. Some protestors even set themselves on fire and died. Many university and college campuses also were hotbeds of anti-war sentiment, which boiled over into clashes with authorities. And, Indian tribes from the east remembered the Trails of Tears, forced land allotments and dark times without tribal leaders. Such news events dominated TV lounges and made lasting impressions.

What was it like for the first few Indian student-athletes to enroll and play a sport at Northwestern? ... Or, the first few Blacks? ... Relations with other athletes or students? ... Sharing dressing\locker room facilities? … Playing side-by-side, or being asked to room or even bunking together on road trips? … How did it feel on a sports road-trip to walk into a restaurant with the coaches at the door along with a white owner, who just months previously said, "You can't eat here (because you are black)?" … How did it feel to watch teammates walk by, just feet away, into an eating place as you and your brother stood outside after being told, "We don't serve coloreds here?" … What reaction occurred upon being called into the coach's office and asked if "Had any problems with a couple of black guys rooming with you on the sports road-trip (or vice versa)?" … Did it affect you when the dining and dance club shut the door and denied entrance for a long-planned fun night? … Why would a young, college age white girl stop to ask if a black stranger wanted a ride to the Northwestern campus? How did it feel to be called the N-word? Was it some sort of white racial guilt trip that elected you homecoming queen? … Did that white guy merely pretend to kiss you in front of that mostly white crowd? … Were there conditions to attend that white church? Was there a 'lynching party' if you stepped out of line? Date a person of another color? Have any white friends? Why were you called 'Uncle Tom' and other names in sports competitions? How did it feel to travel with a white guy to his home-town and be one of the first to stay the night?

Additional questions about national historical events are provided on page one of the Appendix section. These compel an honest examination of one's racial and political views.

Was the 'Promised Lands' vision of civil rights leader, Dr. Martin Luther King, Jr. a reality at Northwestern? Were the relationships a picture of his dreams? Did Northwestern have an unequaled legacy? Let these stories speak for themselves. A gauntlet of emotions will occur—laughter, sorrow, tears, and joy. As the final word is read, you'll also discover hope for 'Freedom' and the future of our Nation.

Clifton Savoy, Ph.D.
Northwestern Class of 1967

LIGHTS ALONG THE PATH

"…you will know the truth, and the truth will set you free!" Jesus to believers. *Bible, John 8:32.*

"…God created man in His own image…" *Bible, Genesis 1:27 ESV* Numerous verses repeat or refer to this truth.

"We hold these truths to be self-evident, that all men are created equal, that they are endowed by their Creator with certain un-alienable Rights, that among these are Life, Liberty, and pursuit of happiness…" *Declaration of Independence*, signed by the fifty-six individuals who represented the Thirteen United States of America. July 4, 1776.

"…I have a dream that my four little children will one day live in a nation where they will not be judged by the color of their skin but by the content of their character." Dr. Martin Luther King, Jr. August 28, 1963, Lincoln Memorial in Washington, D.C.

"Skin may differ, but affection dwells in black and white the same." … "We have come a long, long way but we still have a long, long way to go." … The answer is, "the Agape Love of God." … Dr. King, Jr. March 17, 1966. Southern Methodist University. Dallas.

"…I have seen the Promised Land and we get there!" Dr. King, Jr. April 3, 1968. Church of God in Christ, Memphis, Tennessee. Reference to Moses and the scripture verse, *Bible, Deuteronomy 34:1-8).*

SCENES

1 ~ 77

1.

DR. MARTIN LUTHER KING, JR. INTERRUPTS BIG BEN'S GAME

March 18, 1966, Vinson Hall and Big Ben
Northwestern Oklahoma State University

"That fool's going to get shot one of these days!" lamented the man about Dr. Martin Luther King, Jr. The comment could've been made during any of the many 1950s and 1960s civil rights protests King led across the South, Washington, D.C., and northern cities.

For certain, could've been during the violence and deaths of the bombings in Birmingham, or 1963 church bombing that killed four girls, or bloody Sunday during the 1965 Selma to Montgomery march, or while King looked through the bars of jail, or some other violent\ non-violent protest.

This time, though, it was in Spring 1966 in Vinson Hall on the campus of a small university in Northwestern Oklahoma located on the Salt Fork River. "That fool's going to get shot one of these days!" Big Ben Smith repeated in a frustrated tone. His back was to me, but I sensed he knew I'd stepped into his room to see what his fuss was about. He mumbled, as his massive, black hand slapped the side of an old radio, "Can't pick up anything but Martin Luther!" Sounds squawked in and out, as he moved the tuning dial, "…all men are created equal…"

Ben's favorite pastime was baseball and he knew all the player stats.

His favorite team was the Los Angeles Dodgers, but would settle for second choice—Harry Carey and the St. Louis Cardinals. Ben and his brother, Glen, laughed when one said, "Wind had to blow just right, but usually could pick up one on the radio."

Not today, though, as parts of King's 1963 "I Have a Dream" speech made the airwaves. "…that one day, little black boys and black girls will be able to join hands with white boys and white girls as sisters and brothers."

I lived across the basement hallway, in four-story Vinson Hall, with two other jocks. Our doors were open to let any breeze move about since Vinson had no air conditioning. Other male students and jocks also lived in one of its three wings.

Vinson Hall, a male-only dormitory, except its house mom, viewed from the southwestern side. Courtesy use from Northwestern. Student athletes would storm out the exits, like ants to a picnic dinner bell, shortly before practice, and hustle to Perceful Fieldhouse located to the west across a large parking lot where several cars and pickups could be observed with nearly flat tires until break of some kind to travel home. That is, unless hitchhiking.

The bareness of Ben's room always shocked me. Looked almost like no one lived there. Dim light from two ceiling fixtures filled the room in a dull-yellow hue, as they reflected off a polished concrete floor. Two windows, but no curtains. Three beds, but each covered only with a sheet. Three pairs of perfectly pressed jeans hung in a single closet. A well-used clothes iron sat on the top shelf. Couple clothes chests; a hair trimmer lay on top of one of them. Couple study desks, with a few books and papers and two worn-out pinochle decks. An old radio, which had been salvaged from a trash pile and barely held together by its broken case, was perched on a window sill. A wire tethered it, like a last life-line, to a rusty window screen for a makeshift antenna. The glow of its big tubes seemed to pulse with excitement in being given new life, and radiated into the shadows of the night.

In comparison to my roommates and me, our room probably looked like a mansion, although we didn't come from well to-do families. Standing in Ben's doorway, I reflected back three years earlier to the first time I laid eyes on Ben and Glen. It was August 1963, as we began pre-season football practice. I'll never forget my wonder about life. *How could the Big Guy above be so unfair to bless one human being so much more over another? Not fair!*

2.

NORTHWESTERN'S FIRST BLACK STUDENT-ATHLETES, PRE-SEASON FOOTBALL AND DORMITORY\CAMPUS LIFE

August 30, 1963, Pre-season, Two-a-Day Football Practices
Northwestern Oklahoma State University

Pre-season football practice signaled the campus was about to come alive with students for the fall semester. Seasoned lettermen, excited recruits, and hopeful walk-ons arrived. Other students converged on campus a few days later, like hungry critters called to the dinner bowl.

"Those newbies and walk-ons won't know what hit 'em," laughed a senior letterman to a teammate, as they scanned the football practice schedule posted just outside the entrance doors to the dressing rooms.

First day: Shorts, Ts, and helmets. Stretch and 5-minute jog, calisthenics, 2-mile timed run, position drills, directional sprints, iron mule, and specialty drills.

"Yeah," the other letterman agreed with a deep belly laugh, as they passed through the entrance doors. "Wonder how many'll drop out after they meet, Juice (Coach Walter Johnson) and the iron mule?" His next words faded away, as the doors closed, "Or discover they're 'red meat' for our scrimmages?"

I followed close behind them. I was a beginning sophomore, but it was my first season out for football. A joyful bounce was in my step, as I entered the large, horseshoe-shaped room, with dressing stalls around the walls, showers in the middle, and rehab/prep-tables on the side. Sweaty-body odors already filled the air and hit my nose, as if I needed a reminder of the competitive journey I was about to travel. The scene stopped me in my tracks. *Wow!* New helmets sitting on new shorts and Ts and shoes in front of each locker was a fantastic sight! Names written on white tape were on each helmet.

Happy thoughts reverberated in my head. *After all, Head Coach Art Parkhurst surely was delighted to have a walk-on, whose high school team had lost only three games over three years, and collected two state championships.* My reasoning, though, didn't acknowledge the team record probably would've been the same without me.

I scanned the names in the first dressing area: Kippenberger, Foster, Mitchell, Barnett, Stephens, Garrison, Sweat, Waljie, Ward, Brooks, Anderson, Dominico, Hornung, Massey, Boyle. *Where's Savoy?* My emotions were getting the best of me. *Not here!* It quickly dawned on me. *I am just a walk-on. My first year. I shouldn't expect to be with seniors and lettermen.*

On to the back dressing area. My frustration rose, as I scanned the names: Hiner, White, B. Smith, G. Smith, Strunk, I. Campbell, L. Campbell, Pipestem, Davis, Myers, Amerin, Estep. *Where's Savoy?* ... Then, I saw it. ... "What's this? ... With two other names at one locker? And ... where's our helmets?"

My sky-high emotions crashed to the earth, and the impact hit me full force. ... *Coach Parkhurst wasn't impressed, after all, when I checked last Spring about coming out for the team. I'd forgotten how he laughed and almost fell over in his chair when I said, "I can help your team." And I followed that with, "How about some scholarship monies?" How did I mis-understand when he didn't mention any money and was slow to approve my being a walk-on?*

There wasn't enough room for three players to share a locker. *They must expect some to quit.* My inherited determination boiled over. *Well ... that's not going to be me!*

The call of "Savoy, Savoy, come to the equipment room," momentarily distracted me from my distress. Both dressing areas were now abuzz with players getting ready for practice. "You Savoy?" asked a big, burly guy behind the counter and, as I nodded, he asked, "Size?"

"...Uh, 71\4th I think."

He thrust a well-used helmet into my hands, and barked, with a nod, "Get a chinstrap out of that box over there." He turned towards other players wanting help, and bellowed, "Next?"

A used helmet? A beat-up, scarred one at that? Not sure how long I stood there feeling sorry for myself. *Where's my new helmet?* When my senses tapped me on the shoulder, like an impatient person in line, to move along, I sulked back towards my shared locker but, before reaching it, I encountered one of those crossroads of life.

Rounding the corner of the showers, I came face-to-face, inches away, with something I'd never seen up close. It was a black guy—a big one!

No experiences with black people? Nope! None, and I didn't have a sheltered childhood. No black people lived where I grew up in the small rural town in Western Oklahoma, in the Panhandle—an area once called, "No Man's Land." In that vast Great Plains area to the Rockies, blacks were few. Only time I saw one in person, up close, was when I was about age eight. He was operating the elevator at our hotel in Oklahoma City. I remember being curious at his darkness. My only other experience with a person of color was in high school, but this was only playing a team or two with a few Indians. That was it.

What little I knew essentially was observations from four places: As a freshman spectator when Northwestern played basketball against predominately black Langston University; the 1950-1960s civil rights protests on TV; black sports persons on TV like, Wilt "The Stilt" Chamberlain, the Globe Trotters, Floyd Patterson, Prentis Gaut of Oklahoma University, and Jim Brown; singers like Fats Domino,

Chubby Checker, and Nat King Cole; and movies like *Gone With the Wind*, *To Kill a Mockingbird*, and the *Little Rascals*.

Indeed, I was plowing new ground, as this big, black guy towered over my 6'0" height by 5" or 6"—my forehead to his chin. Simultaneously, we stepped to the same side to let the other pass. Chin-to-forehead again! Instantly, both back the other way. I bumped his big belly this time! I'm sure we looked rather comical in our do-si-do moves. Just needed square dance music.

After I reached the security of my shared locker, I peered back at the big guy I'd just met. His big belly gave him an appearance of bird-legs. *What position does he play?*

Then, out from behind the big guy, another black guy appeared. I learned later they were brothers, Ben, the first big guy, and Glen Smith. Glen stood naked, in only his glory, except for a jockstrap. Looked about 6'2" maybe 6'3" and 225 lbs. I couldn't believe what I saw—muscles galore! And their contours were even more impressive, with what seemed to be a 30" waist! It was like looking at Jim Thorpe, Jesse Owens, and Jim Brown all mixed together in one body! *Michelangelo couldn't have chiseled it any better!* I looked down over my own body, gulped, pulled my T-shirt on, and muttered under my breath, "Not fair, dear Lord! Just not fair. I could never develop muscles like that no matter how much or long I trained!"

Over the next four years, a friendship with Ben and Glen developed, and I learned of some gut-wrenching moments and racial hostilities they'd had prior to attending Northwestern. It broke my heart to learn, after fifty years of our university days in the rearview mirror, they'd also had a few similar experiences while representing the university in athletic competition.

"Be on the field in 15 minutes!" bellowed one of the student graduate coaches. As I turned to finish dressing, I discovered the other two guys arrived—one had a new helmet. I had to sit on the floor to tie my shoes. *Just great!*

I looked away, though, as the burly equipment manager interrupted my self-pity. "Pipestem! Pipestem! Where are you?" he bellowed from the entrance to our dressing room. Suddenly, I saw Pipestem. *An Indian, and bigger than the big black guy. Must be 285 lbs., and ... his head. It's the biggest I've ever seen!*

"Try this on," the manager said. A slight grin came to my face, along with a comforting feeling I had company in my misery, when I noticed it was a well-used helmet. "Biggest one we could find," the manager continued. Pipestem pulled it on, but it was obviously too small. "Good. Use it until your new one arrives."

New helmet? My eyes crossed in frustration, as I'd soon be alone in my misery. I looked down at my beat-up, well-used helmet, as I headed to the practice field, and made a mental pact. *Savoy, put everything in high gear! Get in the game—whatever it takes. Play any position!*

Freshmen brothers, Ben and Glen Smith, and transfer junior F. Browning Pipestem. The Smiths were the first two black athletes to play a sport at Northwestern. Courtesy use, 1963 Northwestern.

3.

The moment of death was near. Whispers of pity from two friends standing in the background of a dimly-lit bedroom faded, as the 1939 movie scene panned to a close-up of the bed and 88-year-old Chips, teacher and headmaster of the British boarding school. "…you said it was a pity, a pity I never had children. But you're wrong! I have! Thousands of them … thousands of them, and all boys!"

Petite Annabel Griggs wiped a tear away, as the scene slowly darkened, before turning her small B&W TV off. Her face, surrounded by a head-full of neatly groomed gray-black hair, had a warm glow about it, as if she just shared precious memories with a dear friend—Mr. Chippings of *Goodbye, Mr. Chips.*

Actually, in a way, she did. As the Residence Mom of Vinson Hall of Northwestern, her apartment and the office were in the middle of the building. She developed a rapport, like Mr. Chips, with the boys who came under her wings. No, she didn't have 59-years like he did, but they lived all around her for several years. Sadly, her "boys in men's bodies," as she described them, would leave at the end of each academic year. Some never returned again due to graduation, dropping out, or transfer. Also, like Mr. Chips and World War I, she had another reason—the escalating Viet Nam War—some would never return, even to their own home.

"My boys," Mom Griggs always assured Dean Capel, "didn't do it!" Whether it was the Vinson Hall basement flooded from a water fight or putting that mummified calf's head in the student's bed, "They're just not those kind of boys!"

A new crop of "boys" always brought joy, but the 1963 Fall seemed to be extra exciting. *Hmmm, three black athletes. First time for those. Ben and Glen Smith, football, and H. L. Brown, basketball. How did Coach Parkhurst put it? "Same floor with other jocks?" So, basement, same room.* She continued down the list. *And two Indians—Bill Mitchell returns and new player, F. Browning Pipestem. What's the 'F.' stand for?* After a few moments of study, she muttered, "It'll be an interesting year."

Loud voices from a large group of her football boys entering the building jolted her thoughts. *They'll be tired from their first day practice.* She knew their habits. *They'll check their box for mail that hasn't yet arrived, sit a moment in the TV lounge, and then hit the bed before the early-morning practice.*

Her 'Mom' instincts to make the place like home moved her to action. She hurried the few steps to the TV lounge across the hall. Flipped on a few side lights and the TV. She didn't have time to wait until the tubes warmed up, so she set it on one of the four channels they received. *News time anyway. Need to replace this old Philco B&W with one of those 23" color ones.*

As the office door closed behind her, her football boys came around the corner. All checked mailboxes. A few complained, "Nothing?" And, to Mom's surprise, all quickly entered the TV lounge, as "oohs" and "whistles" sounded from it.

She frowned. *What's going on? Bonanza, Combat, or Beverly Hillbillies not on. It's news time.* After more "oohs" and "whistles," she tip-toed down the hall and peeked into the back entrance of the lounge, more "Oohs" and "whistles" sounded. ... *Aha! ... So, that's why!*

Los Angeles — News special: a series of photos of Marilyn Monroe blended in and out on the TV screen—most in skimpy clothing and suggestive look—red heels and smo-o-kin'! ... "It's been a year now," a voice sounded in the background, as the picture switched to a cemetery scene and then panned to reveal people coming and going near a monument. Some carried flowers. "It was August 5th 1962, when the buxom blonde reportedly overdosed on sleeping pills. They've come to remember her."

The TV picture displayed other photos of Monroe, and stopped on one of her, on a street, in a white skirt that was blown, suggestively, above her knees and a part over her head by a breeze...

The football players erupted in all kinds of "Oohs" and "Whistles." The shuffle noise of players squirming in their seats to give private parts more room was obvious.

"The model-turned-actress had a busy, but short life. She was only 36." The next picture was of the December 1953 issue—the first—of *Playboy* magazine. "She was the 'Sweetheart' of the month, and..." The image shown was an intentionally blurred nude photo of Monroe. ". . . She bared it all in the centerfold."

"Awe, come on!" exclaimed several players loudly. Boos erupted from the rest.

"I've seen that *Playboy*," one bragged.

"Me, too!" ... Another added.

"I have that issue! ... Got it from an uncle. ... Cost him fifty cents."

"Give you a dollar."

"Get serious!"

"How'd you like to have been the photographer?"

Everyone erupted, "Yeah!"

One followed with a tease, "You all been like deer in headlights—dumbfounded!"

The TV picture faded to a scene of Monroe on the arm of baseball star, Joe DiMaggio. "Monroe and DiMaggio had a whirlwind romance, and married January 1954. They divorced 274 days later in October."

"One night with me," someone yelled, "wouldn't have divorced me-e-e!" a player boasted.

"In your dreams," a rebuttal came from across the lounge.

A player quipped, "DiMaggio probably discovered they were silicone implants!" The lounge erupted, "Yeah!"

The picture scene returned to the cemetery. "Yes, she's gone now, but she may have mesmerized every male who wasn't blind!"

Mom Griggs admonished her boys, "Shame on you." She paused for a moment to let the words register. "Your Moms wouldn't approve." None responded, and she headed to the office.

Over her shoulder, she heard faintly, "We're just getting an early start on Louie B's (Bouchard) Human Anatomy course. Maybe, it's Anna B's (Fisher) class." The lounge erupted in laughter, and Mom Griggs chuckled, as she closed the office door behind her.

Oxford, Mississippi—A voice sounded, as photos of the University of Mississippi faded in and out on the TV screen. "The campus of Ole Miss is quiet now, but for nearly a year it's been a turbulent, deadly environment of racial riots and killings, with hundreds of U.S. Marshalls present 24-hours a day, 7-days a week to ensure the safety of Air Force veteran, James Meredith. He made history as the first Negro to attend and graduate on August 18, 1963."

A Northwestern player mumbled, "I'm done here," as he struggled out of his chair, and headed to the exit. "Me, too," added another, with a deep yawn, as he stood up. Chairs were immediately pushed every which way, as at least three-fourths of them stampeded out the door.

"Hey, leave it there," a player piped up quickly, as another was about to change the channel. "They're going to talk about those killings."

Air Force veteran, James Meredith, tries to enroll at Ole Miss

The TV picture was one of Mississippi Governor Ross Barnett, and the voice continued, "The journey started when James Meredith, an Air Force veteran with good grades from Jackson State University, applied to Ole Miss for the Fall 1962 semester. University officials denied his enrollment, and Governor Barnett stood in the doorway to prevent his entrance."

There was a momentary shot of the Supreme Court, as the voice continued, "In 1954 and *Brown v. Board of Education*, the Supreme Court ruled that "Separate but Equal," segregation, in public schools was unconstitutional."

The scene returned to the Governor and then a scene of the Ole Miss campus. "Nonetheless, Governor Barnett publicly vowed to keep the university segregated..." The TV faded to a scene in the Oval Office of President John F. Kennedy with his brother, Attorney General Robert F. Kennedy. "The Attorney General ordered 500 U.S. Marshals to ensure the security of Meredith. The President hoped legal means, along with the U.S. Marshals, would persuade the Governor to comply. Armed protestors also were a concern. The Governor had responsibility for civil order and would allow Meredith to enroll."

An outside scene of a dormitory building appeared on the screen. "Sunday, September 30th, Meredith was escorted quietly by Mississippi Highway Patrol into a room in Baxter Hall."

A reporter spoke, "The 500 federal marshals were assembled on campus, and were supported by the 70th Army Engineer Combat Battalion from Ft Campbell, Kentucky." The scene moved to a crowd of students, "Of course, the presence on campus of patrol and marshals drew attention. Rumors had spread of a Negro (Meredith) being turned away from enrolling, and it was easy to speculate the massive security on campus that efforts to de-segregate Ole Miss were afoot."

Massive, on-campus security.

A growing crowd appeared on the screen, "1,000 quickly formed, but the highway patrol maintained control until it was withdrawn in early evening, despite the Governor's apparent opposition, by a State Senator. The crowd quickly swelled to over 3,000 and broke out into a full riot on the campus."

"When the marshals ran out of tear gas and could no longer control the violence, President Kennedy sent reinforcements—Military police,

Border Patrol, and the Mississippi National Guard. He also sent Navy physicians and hospital corpsmen attached to Millington Naval Hospital. All were under command of Brigadier General Charles Billingslea."

Riots and deadly assault!

A scene of Baxter Hall, where Meredith was housed, appeared again. "Rioters discovered Meredith's location, and started an assault." A burning car appeared on the screen. "The white mob attacked General Billingslea's car as it entered the university gate in the early morning, and set it on fire. Billingslea and two others escaped from the burning car, then crawled 200 yards under mob gunfire to safety. The army didn't return fire."

Morning light appeared. Next day, October 1st. "166 of the 500 marshals were injured, and 40 soldiers and National Guardsmen were wounded in the 12-hours since Meredith arrived."

A scene of a violent crowd and then two bodies being loaded into an ambulance appeared. "No injuries to the crowd are known, but two outsiders were killed, in what law officials described as "execution-style murders." Sometimes reporting is dangerous.

Execution style murders!

A journalist had a gunshot wound to the back of the head. The other was a young white repairman in the wrong place at the wrong time. A bullet wound was in his forehead."

The TV picture faded to a black man surrounded by security personnel. "Meredith became the first Negro student on October 1st to be enrolled at Ole Miss. He graduated August 18, 1963. To the end, hundreds of marshals provided security 24 hours a day."

Demonstrations by black people were shown, followed by a photo of Dr. Martin Luther King, Jr. "President Kennedy strengthened relations in assisting Meredith to graduate from a previously segregated university, but there was a perception Kennedy's administration had not lived up to its 1960 election promises of justice and freedom in the democrat-controlled southern states and northern urban cities. "It's tokenism," King said of Kennedy's race policy."

Military planes appeared on the screen. Then missiles blasting off, followed by a nuclear mushroom cloud, and a photo of USSR Nikita Khrushchev. "Events since Meredith's enrollment last October 1st reveal Kennedy had more to worry about than the 1964 election and obtaining the Negro vote or the democrat-controlled vote across the South. His center stage was filled with Russian missiles in Cuba and all-out nuclear war through the 1962 Fall. Involvement in Vietnam also was growing."

Cuban Missile Crisis, Atomic War, and Vietnam!

As the Meredith-Ole Miss special ended, the lone football player still watching flipped off the TV and lights, but he didn't hear Mom Griggs's quiet, "Good night" over his shoulder, as he headed off to sack out. … just like all her other boys.

4.

August 31, 1963, Pre-season, Two-a-Day Practices Continue
Northwestern Oklahoma State University

There's something about the dawn of a new day, its panoramic awesome beauty that excites the soul and kindles new hope, energy, and resolve. Birds sing greetings in cheery delight, as night shadows slink away into hiding and dew drops nourish the thirsty. So it was, on the Northwestern campus, as August two-a-day football practices moved along.

Western Oklahoma Morning Sky Courtesy Desiree McGuire of
Slapout, Oklahoma—Northwestern Class of 1986

Sleepy-eyed footballers suddenly poured from Vinson Hall, and headed to the multi-purpose fieldhouse across the large parking lot. "I needed more sleep," mumbled sophomore Ken Strunk to nearby players, as he yawned deeply and stretched his body.

"Me, too," another added his two-cents-worth.

"Awe, you guys are just wussies," laughed junior Mike "Roids" Garrison. "Why, we'd have a half-day's work done already out in Northwest Texas."

"Roids," a player teased Garrison, "think you've been smo-kin' that paoti stuff!" As the others laughed and hee-hawed, he added, "Besides, you're just a city-slick-a."

By that time, their walk had taken them by a 2-tone pink, 2-door hard-top '55 Chevy. It'd left its better days in the rearview mirror. One of its bald tires was flat. Roids' 2-tone red-black '55 Plymouth was in the next parking spot. "Whose is this?" asked a player.

"Saw Glen and Ben Smith, the black freshmen recruits from Crescent, drive up in it."

"This is theirs?"

"Yeah. Should've seen the smoke blowing from the tailpipe!"

Laughter broke out on hearing, "Must've been burnin' drip."

"Been there," said one.

"Guilty," quipped another.

"Probably all Roids uses in West Texas," teased another.

Ignoring them, Garrison inquired, "Did you know Ben and Glen will be the first blacks to play a conference sport at Northwestern?"

"Is that right?"

"Yeah, and Coach Keith Covey, new basketball coach, brought a black freshman with him—H. L. Brown. Supposed to be a playmaker, really good—Oklahoma All-State."

"Coach Covey? Our assistant football coach?"

"Yes, and heard he has some other good freshmen, too."

"Oh, Lord, have mercy on those round-ballers!"

"Speaking of blacks, what'd you think of the TV news special on James Meredith and those riots at Ole Miss?"

"Something, huh? Thousands rioting, and killings, and hundreds of police with him a full year to keep him safe until he graduated just a few days ago."

"Can you imagine? Ole Miss top dog administrators wouldn't let Meredith enroll, and the Governor of Mississippi stood in the doorway. President Kennedy and his brother and the military had to get involved."

Another player added excitedly, "They'd hung Meredith if they could've gotten to him!"

"Think you're right if the tear gas wasn't everywhere!"

"Bet he was one scared guy. Can you imagine a violent mob of 3,000 around Vinson Hall and this parking lot and then all the military and marshals between them and the building?"

"Yeah, Meredith probably soiled his britches a couple times. What a difference between Ole Miss and Northwestern! No one here's paid much attention to Ben and Glen Smith. At Ole Miss, their '55 Chevy would've been a pile of charcoal by now! ... And, have you even seen any cops here at Northwestern?"

"Who's James Meredith?" a couple players asked.

Before anyone responded, a car drove past and parked near the entrance to the athletic center. Coach "Juice" Johnson stepped out, looked their way, hitched up his pants, and bellowed in his usual seemingly angry drill-sergeant voice, "If you're not on the field in 10 minutes, you're going to run extra sprints!"

As they skedaddled towards the dressing rooms, a grin crossed Coach Johnson's face, "See you at the Iron Mule." Players who'd earned the right called Coach Johnson "Juice," but never to his face until they graduated. Even then, no one was sure what "earning the right" meant.

It was the first day in full pads. Started out with a short jog up and down the field and stretching sore muscles and joints, followed by calisthenics. "Make sure you work those necks to strengthen them," barked a graduate assistant trainer! "Don't want any neck injuries!"

Everything moved into high gear after separating the squad into position groups. "Run in place," barked another graduate assistant. "Forward! ... Back! ... Hit the turf! ... Up and running!" Then with a grin, he'd repeat the torture.

About the time it appeared the best of the players was about to fold and half a dozen had barfed part of their last meal, the grad assistant blew his whistle, and yelled, "Break into your position groups!"

Meanwhile, Head Coach Art Parkhurst and Assistant Coaches Johnson, Covey, and Philips walked around, checking out the squad, and making notes of player skills.

Ends, halfbacks, linebackers, and defensive backs ran pass routes, with each defending as well to learn moves. Interior linemen worked on stances, run and pass blocking, defensive play, and footwork. After a time, they'd hit each other one-on-one, two-on-one, and five-on-five. Tempers flared, and a few fights broke out. Quarterbacks were pampered, of course, and worked on signal calls, snaps, hand-offs, pitches, and passes.

Today, practice included offensive and defensive plays against meat squads holding dummies. Soon, dummies would be tossed aside; and blood, bruises, and injuries would be constant visitors. Wind sprints followed, with a visit to the Iron Mule, and a 200-yard cool-down walk unless involved in special teams snapping, kicking, or receiving.

"I hate two-a-days," moaned an exhausted junior lineman to no one in particular, as the group approached the Iron Mule.

"This'll be your last day if you don't buckle down and show some leadership!" barked Assistant Coach Junior Johnson, as he hopped on a huge iron tube contraption that looked more like it should've been on the front of a big Caterpillar pushing boulders from a mountain roadway bed. There were five vertical 6" thick-gauge steel tubes spaced apart like the spacing of players on the line, welded together on steel runners like a sled. A player pushed it with his shoulder, just like blocking.

"You five—Mitchell, Kippenberger, Garrison, Sweat, and Pipestem," Juice bellowed, "show the other linemen how to push this Iron Mule."

They could barely move the mule, but Juice motivated all of us in his intimidating way to push it for what seemed like hundreds of yards. "Come on, those others did better!" Our calves and thighs quivered and begged for mercy. "A few more yards, and you'll reach where those wimpy half-backs reached." That made us dig a little deeper, but we'd be so weak, standing upright was almost impossible. "Next—Dominico, Davis, Ward, Gregory, and Stewart," Juice barked. "Don't let those other wimps outdo you!" Juice left a permanent mark on each of us.

As each day passed, players fought, sometimes literally, to move up the depth chart. A scrimmage game at a nearby college was scheduled near the end of two-a-days, but the travel squad would be limited to only 2-deep by position except quarterback. The good news: there'd be one less two-a-day practices. Hallelujah!

Football Head Coach Art Parkhurst (L) and Assistant Coach Walter Johnson. Courtesy of Northwestern, 1964 Ranger Annual. Both were veterans of WWII: Parkhurst in Marine assaults of Pacific Islands and Johnson with Patton's 3rd Army.

5.

August 31, 1963, Evening News Special, TV Lounge of Vinson Hall
Northwestern Oklahoma State University

The Saturday evening sky was ablaze in fabulous reddish colors from the setting sun—something often observed on the Oklahoma western plains. Summer heat lingered, as the last day of August pushed against the coming coolness and colors of Fall.

Western Oklahoma sunset. Courtesy Dr. Paul Reed of Guymon, Oklahoma

"Quiet here," Big Ben Smith muttered to brother, Glen, as he swatted a gnat from his face. They slowly walked the 150-yards up the hill towards Vinson Hall, after downing the evening meal with other footballers in the campus cafeteria. "N'body here 'cept the guys."

Sweat beads glistened on their black foreheads, but they gave them no mind, as they were accustomed to working outdoors in manual labor on the family 80-acre farm southwest of Crescent, Oklahoma. Grandparents managed somehow to acquire it in the early 1900s, and parents, with eleven children, scratched out a subsistence living, like that championed by George Washington Carver in his *Forty Acres and A Mule*. Ben and Glen were heard to say, "Swimming in a pond was their only way to cool down."

"Yeah," Glen nodded, "but two-days'll be over soon." After a few more steps, he added, "Hope those girls enroll like coaches thought they would." His eyes mellowed, as he reflected a moment, "Maybe the one I met on my recruiting visit'll return."

The mention of girls brought some pep to Ben's step and excitement to his voice. "Hot number? Remember her name?"

"Dorothy something, I think."

Ben pressed for more, "Where did she live? Classes?"

"Didn't talk about that."

A pained looked crossed Ben's face, "You're worthless," he teased, as he threw a backhand to Glen's shoulder. He nodded toward their car, "Flat tire. Couldn't take 'er out anyway."

"Saw it. Didn't matter. No money for gas."

"Have to fix by Thanksgiving."

"We'll pump it up, but have to hitch a ride if no gas."

Ben's lips tightened and he grimaced, as he moved to another subject, "Glad no practice in the morn'un."

"Me, too!" Glen agreed, as they trudged into Vinson Hall.

Faint sounds from the TV lounge down the hall grabbed their attention. A news special blared to an empty room. "It's that march on Washington," Ben expressed. "King's there."

Washington, D.C.—the TV picture panned the front of the Lincoln

Memorial. A crowd of people, mostly black, stood on the steps, around a speaker's podium. The faint sound of a song by Peter, Paul, and Mary—"How many roads does a man walk down, before they call him a man?"—could be heard, as the picture zoomed slowly in on the face of Lincoln's statue in the background. Then slowly, the picture panned out across the mass of people stretching to the Washington Monument. The singing faded as a voice sounded on the TV speakers.

"A quarter of a million people led by Roy Wilkins, Dr. Martin Luther King, Jr., and other Negro leaders, converged on the nation's capital last Wednesday, August 28th. They marched for 'Jobs and Freedom.' It was the 100-year anniversary of President Abraham Lincoln signing the Emancipation Proclamation in 1863."

"They came by cars and chartered buses, trains, and airplanes. Some airlines, however, were grounded by bomb threats." ... "Some traveled all night long to attend. Speakers addressed the issues of racial and economic inequality and injustice." ... The scene of King speaking to the mass in front of the Lincoln Memorial appeared on the screen. "Attendees expressed the speech of Dr. King was the highlight of the day and inspiration for the movement."

"President John F. Kennedy gave hope to the Civil Rights movement by gaining support from republican leaders On June 11th, followed by a TV explanation to the nation. He sent his bill to Congress on June 19th, saying, "Action was imperative." That same day, though, Mississippi activist Medgar Evers was murdered in his own driveway."

The picture faded to marches in Little Rock, then Baltimore, then

Birmingham, then the Governor blocking the entrance to Ole Miss, then back to an empty Lincoln Memorial. "Some organizers faced bomb and assassination threats. One west coast paper was even threatened to be bombed if it didn't publish an article of President Kennedy as a Nigger Lover. A Kansas City man threatened to put a hole between King's eyes. Roy Wilkins was threatened with assassination if he didn't leave the country."

The Lincoln Memorial appeared and the scene panned slowly across the area where the 250,000 rallied. "They are gone now, but Lincoln and Washington remain to remind us of the cost of freedom. ... Only time will tell if these marchers for Jobs and Freedom were successful in rallying support for their cause from people across the nation. . . . Only time will tell if they've been able to persuade the Democrat-controlled Congress to take up and pass the Civil Rights legislation put forth by President Kennedy. ... Only time will tell if they've improved their economic condition, and civil rights and freedoms portrayed in King's speech."

The picture faded back to August 28th and King on the Lincoln Memorial steps, speaking to the 250,000 and millions of others watching by TV:

"Five score years ago, a great American, in whose symbolic shadow we stand today, signed the Emancipation Proclamation. This momentous decree came as a great beacon light of hope to millions of Negro slaves who had been seared in the flames of withering injustice. ... But one hundred years later, the Negro still is not free. One hundred years later, the life of the Negro is still sadly crippled by the manacles of segregation and the chains of discrimination..."

"...I have a dream one day this nation will ...live out the true meaning of its creed: "We hold these truths to be self-evident, that all men are created equal."

"...I have a dream that my four little children will one day live in a nation where they will not be judged by the color of their skin but by the content of their character."

The picture panned to a close-up view of Dr. King and revealed the massive crowd. "…I have a dream … that little black boys and black girls will be able to join hands with little white boys and white girls as sisters and brothers."

"When we let freedom ring … from every state and every city, we will be able to speed up that day when all of God's children, black men and white men, Jews and Gentiles, Protestants and Catholics, will be able to join hands and sing in the words of the old Negro spiritual: Free at last! … Free at last! … Thank God Almighty, we are free at last!"

Dr. Martin Luther King, Jr. and the rally on August 28, 1963 in Front of the Lincoln Memorial in Washington, D.C., Photo National Archives

6.

September 2, 1963, Coach Parkhurst Cautioned Ben and Glen
Northwestern Oklahoma State University

Coach Art Parkhurst looked up from his desk at the light knock of Ben and Glen Smith. "Wanna see us, Coach?" They asked in a nervous tone, as if trouble was ahead.

"Yes, come in," Parkhurst replied, as he stood quickly and motioned, "Take a seat." He closed the door, and inquired, "You men getting settled?"

The brothers shot a look of concern to each other, and Ben replied in a weak voice after a moment, "Yes ... sir."

"Room, and meals, and practice?"

Both nodded up and down, but read the other's thoughts, *What's Coach getting to?*

Coach Parkhurst noticed the concern written on their faces, "There's no trouble. Just wanted to know if you're getting any negative, racial treatment anywhere?"

They shook their heads back and forth. "No sir," Glen responded softly.

"How about the team? Practice? Sometimes in the heat of competition something like that'll come out."

Both shook their heads back and forth again, "No sir."

"Well, I suspect you'll get a little of that, but anything major, I want to know. Now, playing on the road might be different; especially, when it comes to games." Parkhurst tapped his pencil on the desk, and continued. "Players on other teams will do lots of things to get a good player out of the game. Fellas, they'll call you a name or say something about your Momma you won't like and do it with some rough play. Anything to get you angry and out of control enough to take a swing at them in front of a game official. You have to be ready for those!"

Ben glanced at Glen, then back to Coach Parkhurst. "Coach," Ben replied, "heard stuff like that all our lives. We were cautioned to beware of trouble when away from home."

"Okay, I just wanted to have this talk. Get ready for practice. Your counselor will help you to register and obtain books and supplies. Make sure you go to registration."

"Yes sir," Ben replied.

As they were about to walk out the door, Coach added, "Hold on! ... Couple more things. On our road games, players will need to be at least four to a room. Any problem with a couple white guys with you?"

Both shook their head back and forth.

"Good. Another thing, let's stay on campus for a while until your pictures and names get in the paper. Okay? Don't expect any problem with the town folks, but let's get down the road a piece. ... Understand?"

Ben and Glen nodded, and hustled out the door to dress for practice.

7.

September 5, 1963, End of Two-a-Days in Pads
Northwestern Oklahoma State University

The miserable August heat—the kind that hits 100 in the shade, creates mirages on the Oklahoma plains, and dries clothes in about five minutes on an outdoor line—muscled into early September. Wasn't much thought given, though, to its effect on Northwestern's afternoon, 2nd-of-the-day, football practice, except to move starting time back an hour as if that'd help.

Nothing was going to stop the last major scrimmage of the two-a-days practices. One could opine the coaches used the near unbearably hot conditions to see which players would stay engaged and productive when the going got hot and heavy. After all, what was a little heat compared to assaulting Pacific island after island, as a Marine Corporal in WWII, like Head Coach Parkhurst did or Assistant Coach Johnson who was with General Patton's 3rd Army in Europe, fighting through France, Germany, and on for hundreds of days? Casualties by the thousands occurred. Nonetheless, the two ice breaks probably prevented team mutiny.

Didn't take long for the rivers of sweat off foreheads and faces to become mere trickles because body water was gone. Every uniform was saturated and soiled with dirt and grass stains. Bruises, cuts and blood attested to a player being unlucky, in the wrong place at the wrong time, or to determination at one more chance to prove, "I belong in the 2-deep listing."

One player had two teeth missing in his front upper set. Savoy had a busted upper lip. Myers, a promising freshman receiver, sustained a separated shoulder. A few had ankle and elbow sprains. Blood splattered and wiped on pants was a norm. Tempers flared, and fist-fights did as well. Eager subs played any position, "I'll do anything at a chance to impress a coach!"

A couple of Northwestern professors, sports fanatics, didn't let a little heat deter them, though, and watched eagerly from the sidelines. They, too, fought in WWII, and the heat discomfort was insignificant compared to anything they experienced.

The Thursday evening scrimmage seemed like it would go on forever, as exhausted players pushed their bodies to run or defend a play to the satisfaction of coaches. Yells echoed across the campus. "Come on," barked a coach to the offense line. "You're letting those wimpy guys whip you!" Coaches on defense said the same. "Air it out!" admonished Assistant Coach Keith Covey to the defensive teams when they failed on a play, "Run, touch that (baseball) scoreboard."

A frustrated player grumbled under his breath, barely audible for teammates, but no coach, to hear. "Crazy! Offense or defense wins on each play. Half the coaches never happy."

A defender whispered to a quarterback, "Run a sweep. Everyone pull to that leaky water sprinkler near the sideline, and we'll hold off from tackling until then." The sweep occurred, and all rolled into the shallow pool, like a bunch of hogs finding a bit of cool heaven.

A loud whistle blew. Usually it was from an assistant coach correcting how the play was run. It was Coach Art Parkhurst, though, and he motioned the squad around him. Players were gleeful, as he seldom blew his whistle. Meant practice was about over—except for running short sprints. "Only helmets, shorts and Ts both practices tomorrow," he reminded them. "Travel squad list for the scrimmage against Dodge City'll be on the board tomorrow evening, as you come in from practice. Be on time to leave on Saturday. And," he paused, as he looked around the group, "Better buckle your chinstrap. Dodge City already has half-dozen guys committed to a Big 8 school next season—four good ones on offense."

He motioned everyone to line up. "Ready?" he asked gleefully, like he'd relished this moment of torture all day. Exhausted players toed the lines. "Ready?" This moment was one of the worst mental times for a player. It was gut-check time because few had any fuel left in the tank. Anyone 'dogging it' often had to run additional sprints. Sometimes, it included the whole team. Coach Parkhurst yelled again, "Ready?" After a moment he yelled, "Everyone to the showers!" The squad erupted in childish-play and sounds, like each had been given a Christmas toy. Sprinklers suddenly started, but players just trotted or walked through them, as they provided relief from the hot Oklahoma day.

8.

September 5, 1963, End of Two-a-Days in Pads
Northwestern Oklahoma State University

"Take plenty of salt tablets," a trainer admonished the exhausted athletes, who slowly made their way into the dressing rooms. Most plopped down on their bench and leaned back against their locker. A pungent, stinky, sweat aroma quickly filled the rooms, as pads were pulled off and players hit the showers. The trainer made a mistake by standing by a large wash basket as he repeated the salt tablet warning. Within moments a couple of foul, sweat-soaked t-shirts bounced off the back of his head. Laughter filled the air along with expressions of, "Not me!"

"What was that yelling with the offense today?" a guy asked to anyone within hearing.

"Oh, it was the Indians," replied Mike 'Roids' Garrison, with a roll of his eyes. He noticed the puzzled look as he turned to fellow lineman, Don Sweat, to pull his shoulder pads off. "They were on the warpath against each other."

"You stink!" Sweat exclaimed with a wrinkled nose, as he removed his cleats.

Roids retorted, with a throaty laugh, "Here's a little cologne for you," and he rubbed his sweat-soaked t-shirt on him.

"Creep!" Sweat and his brother, Ron, fired back as they threw their own t-shirts back at Roids. Instantly, everyone nearby was dodging sweat-soaked t-shirts, jock-straps, and socks.

1963 Northwestern Football Game Program, Courtesy Northwestern

"Indians?" Offensive end, Ken Strunk, asked with a puzzled look, as he dodged a sock. "Who's the other one besides Browning Pipestem?"

"Mitchell," blurted out Ron Sweat, identical twin to Don. He continued in a 'where-you-been' tone, "You've been lining up beside him in practice."

"Huh?" Strunk's mouth gaped, and a frown crossed his brow. "Bill Mitchell?" he muttered as he looked Mitchell over a couple of spaces down the bench. "No way! Don't believe it!"

Bill 'Buster' Mitchell photo (L) from 1963 Northwestern Game Program; Sophomore Class Photo of Ken Strunk from 1964 Annual Courtesy Northwestern.

Mitchell nodded, as their eyes met. "It's true." A few moments passed, but he could sense Strunk's disbelief. He reached into his locker. "I have a photo of my Mohawk Lacrosse team on the Reservation in Northern New York."

Strunk studied the photo, looked back at Mitchell, then back at the photo. "All I see is a bunch of young Mohawks and a white guy with black hair," he responded in a doubting tone.

"That's me. Really," Mitchell replied. He glanced around to other teammates for support. A couple, including Kip (Jack Kippenberger), a lineman and good friend, nodded in agreement.

Still skeptical, Strunk pointed to the photo's backside, "The name here is Buster. You're pullin' my leg. It's somebody else."

Mitchell was a little agitated by now. "No, that's me, honest. They called me Buster in my young days."

Roids Garrison and Mitchell also were close friends, and Roids interrupted. "I'll tell you the REAL story how Mitchell got the name, Buster." Roids gave another deep laugh.

The comment caught Mitchell off-guard, and he was curious in what way Roids would spin the yarn. Others nearby listened, too.

"Some coaches back East had a connection to Dodge City College," Roids explained, "in Kansas, and knew Mitchell was a good football player. Got him a scholarship. He lived in a boarding house with five or six other guys, and a woman like Mom Griggs of Vinson Hall."

"Yeah," Mitchell added, "That's right. It was a large house owned by a widow, who fixed our meals. She didn't have much." Mitchell added some levity to the truth, "Think the only meat we had was road-kill the guys found."

The group laughed, as one of the Sweat twins quipped, "Oh, yeah. Sure. It was probably a neighbor's cat."

Roids continued, "Mitchell nor his folks had enough to pay for him to come home to the Mohawk Reservation, so Mitchell stayed in Dodge

City and did work for the widow and for farmers and ranchers around that area. He did the same when he arrived at Northwestern, too."

A guy further down the bench made a wise crack, "Ya' could'a put on one of those 10-gallon hats and impersonated Wyatt Earp in those Boot Hill shoot-out enactments."

"No way." Another laughed, "Couldn't find a gun belt big enough!"

A lineman added gleefully, "He'd probably been another Matt Dillon and spent all his time in the saloon with Kitty."

Mitchell chuckled in agreement. Garrison added, "Mitchell was deathly fearful of western snakes, like our rattlers. One day, while building fence, he reached down and grabbed a stick to move it. Turned out to be a snake." Mitchell nodded, a pained look on his face. Roids enhanced the spin with a deep belly laugh, "Heard he nearly had a heart attack."

"It's true," Mitchell added. "Think that day I looked for another job. Just don't like snakes!"

By now, every player in the room stopped and listened to the story. "Well, as many of you know, Mitchell has a quick-trigger, defensive reaction with his forearms and upper body if someone spooks him from behind—he'll blast you. Friend or foe, only happens to you once in football before you learn it."

Several nodded they'd experienced Mitchell's 250+ lbs. body and quick arms. Mitchell added, "Reacted that way, long as can remember."

Roids continued the yarn. "Well, seems there was a girl once, who learned of Mitchell's fear of snakes. She had one in her hands—wrapped around her arms. Decided to scare Mitchell. A friend yelled to warn her just at the moment she tapped Mitchell on the back and thrust the snake into his face. "Watch out! ... Don't!" ... Too, late. Mitchell re-acted abruptly. His forearms busted her out cold." Roids grinned, "and that's why he's called Buster."

Laughter exploded across the room and drowned out Mitchell's reply, "Girl and snake story's true." His attempt to explain where his nickname originated also went unheard.

"Okay," Strunk acknowledged to Mitchell, "You're a Mohawk. You the first Indian to play a sport at Northwestern?"

"No," Mitchell quickly replied. "There were a couple just finishing up before me—Benny Smith, a Cherokee, and Wayne Postoak, a Choctaw. I don't know much about them since this is only my 2nd year at Northwestern. Maybe a junior or senior, like Billy Foster, who's played 3-4 years or Coach Parkhurst or Coach Johnson can tell you something about them. No idea if there were any Indians before them."

A player later asked Roids, "You mean, Mitchell's been home only once, maybe twice in his 4 years of college?"

Garrison replied sadly, "That's what I know."

9.

September 5, 1963,
2nd Dressing Room, Last two-a-Days in Pads

In the other dressing room, players were exhausted as well. "Hey, give me a hand," Ira Dale Campbell asked his brother, Larry, for help in pulling off his shoulder pads. As the pads slipped off Ira's head, body steam exploded from everywhere, like a train engine blowing steam.

"You smell like a hog!" Larry exclaimed with a puckered face.

Ira tugged off his sweat-soaked t-shirt, and then helped Larry with his shoulder pads. When Larry looked away, Ira slapped the sweaty shirt over his head and laughed as he took off to the showers. "I'll get you!" Larry promised loudly.

Big Browning Pipestem, whose locker was next to the Campbell's, sat in his practice gear, cooling down, and taking in the amusement. "Need a pull?" Ira Dale inquired after his shower, and both he and Larry jerked the big guy's pads off.

"Hey, watch the ears!" Pipestem complained, as the Campbells acted like it was accidental.

A few lockers down, big Ben Smith sat on the bench and leaned, exhausted, against a locker. "Where you been?" he asked brother Glen, as he sat down to undress and shower.

Glen leaned over and spoke where only Ben could hear, "Coach Parkhurst was glad we got enrolled. Thought there'd be some tutors in Vinson. He'd check if we wanted."

Ben pursed his lips, thinking about what he said, "Veldon Zollinger offered to help with math. Maybe need help on some other class." His mind was somewhere else, though, "Anything more about those girls?"

"Not yet, but saw Dorothy (Dodson). Said three other black girls were enrolled. Maybe meet on the week-end. Two from Tulsa: Wanda Randle and Rosa Thompson; and Vera Dodson from Ft. Smith."

"Need to get our car tires fixed."

"Won't matter," Glen replied with a discouraged tone. "No gas and no money. And we have that Dodge City scrimmage."

Ben shrugged his upper body and grimaced, as he thought on their practice performances. "You'll be on the list, but not sure me."

"We'll know tomorrow. Let's hustle, and maybe we'll run into the girls at the cafeteria.

Across the room, a player asked a buddy, as he stripped to shower, "You see the new cheerleaders trying out in the gym?"

"Yeah." He grabbed a towel and headed to the shower. "Got my eye on one already."

"You can forget those," another teammate yelled, "They like lettermen. Besides, I'm telling 'em you have to get a bedtime story every night from your Mommy!" Laughter chased the guy into the shower.

Another added in an eager tone, "Let's hurry. The cheerleaders may still be out front. If not, we'll go early to the cafeteria, and check out the new girls."

Meanwhile, highly-touted running back transfer, Ed 'Butch' Amerine dressed quietly only a few lockers away. A look in his eye seemed to warn, *I have a beauty, Barbara Watson, already picked out, and you guys better stay clear of her!*

10.

NORTHWESTERN'S FIRST INDIAN
STUDENT-ATHLETES

September 5, 1963, Northwestern's First Indian Athletes

"Coach Johnson," Mitchell called out when he noticed the coach walking by, "hold up, please." The coach tossed his practice clothes into the wash basket and turned to see who called his name. "Have a minute?"

"Why, yes, I suppose," Johnson replied in his normal gruff-bark but, this time, with an inquisitive look on his face.

Mitchell looked around at Garrison, Strunk, Don and Ron Sweat, and a few other players still dressing. "We've been talking about the first Indians to play at Northwestern. Said I wasn't the first. Know of two others before me. Benny Smith and Wayne Postoak were here a couple years ago. Were they the first?"

*(L-R) Benny Smith, Cherokee Nation, and Wayne Postoak,
Choctaw Nation, Courtesy Northwestern Ranger Annual*

Johnson nodded no. Mitchell continued, "Heard you've coached and played here since the early 1950s, and you'd know them and any others during those years."

Coach Johnson nodded yes, this time, and hitched up his pants. A distant look crossed his face, as he began to talk. "Benny and Wayne were here about the same time—1959 I think to 1961, maybe 1962. About the time Tom McDaniel, Larry Windsor from Thomas, Crowder, and Stewart Authors—Dr. Authors son. The one in the English Department. Good players.

"Benny's a Cherokee and Postoak's a Choctaw. Coach Parkhurst recruited Benny for football. Played on all special teams, an end on offense and linebacker on defense—a few times both ways. Remember him with two interceptions in the 1959 Homecoming game, and we won it. Caught a TD pass in 1960 Homecoming game and we beat Central Oklahoma State. He also played on my basketball and baseball teams."

Coach Johnson again had a faraway look like he was tapping deeper into his memory. "Think Benny helped to start the rodeo team with Ken Blue, a high jumper on the track team, and Veldon Zollinger. Might have been couple others." He paused to clear his throat. "Coach Parkhurst wasn't happy with the rodeo action. Didn't want them hurt."

Johnson paused as a hint of a smile appeared. He looked at Mitchell and gave a subtle tease, "Benny even looked Indian."

"Hey, coach," Mitchell laughed, "you know I'm Mohawk."

Johnson followed with one of his rare, visible chuckles. "Benny married a paleface, Cheryl Faye Parks from Alva." At this, loud laughter broke out among the players listening to the talk, with a few razzes directed to Mitchell.

Johnson continued, "I recruited Postoak and Don Berlin, a 6'10" center, for basketball from Butler Jr. College in Kansas. Postoak also played football one season here at Northwestern. Caught lots of passes in one game, and led the conference in receiving until getting hurt. Think one of the conference leaders end of season."

Coach Johnson's gruff, take-no-prisoners demeanor changed as he shared another smile and account with the players.

"Benny and Postoak came with war paint on their faces once. It was the homecoming game with Central. It fired up the team, and we won. Each caught touchdown passes." Coach Johnson reflected a moment. "Good players. And Postoak also married a paleface—a girl from Beaver, Oklahoma. Virginia Curfman, I think was her name."

A nearby player had a go at Johnson, "Heard some wild, off-field stories about Benny and Postoak. Know any others?"

Coach Johnson reflected for a moment, "You'll need to ask Gary Wolgamott about Benny—they roomed together a couple years. Gary's now a graduate student at Oklahoma State University, but he's out front today helping Coach Bud Mathews give an exhibition to recruit new athletes for the gymnastic team. The Coffman twins, Kay and Vicki, also are helping out."

Johnson nodded towards Billy Foster down the bench, and continued, "As for Postoak, Foster over there and Carl Lemon, who just graduated and went into the Marines, probably knew as much as anyone at Northwestern. They'd play Postoak and Berlin a domino game called Moon on our basketball road trips." Johnson chuckled, "Lemon belly-ached that "Postoak and Berlin believed anything was fair. No one could beat them because they had signals or something. Whoever played them, suspected it, and they knew others knew. Finding out was the allure of the game with them. The goal was to figure out how, but no one ever did."

Mitchell returned to the first question, "Coach, were Benny and Postoak the first Indians to play a sport at Northwestern?"

"No. As I recall, Turner Bear, Jr., a Muscogee-Creek from Checotah, played 1951-52. Another player at that time, Bruce Hough, looked Indian, but not sure. Turner wasn't big, but he was fast. Played football, basketball, and baseball here two years. Quarterback in football. Threw a TD pass in freezing weather against Central Oklahoma State, and we beat them." Johnson paused for a moment, "Wind was really blowing—still feel that cold."

Coach Johnson paused again as he reflected on the memories. "Couple of interesting things about Turner: his Dad was appointed by President Dwight Eisenhower to be Chief of the Muscogee-Creek Nation. He also served as head of the Council of the Five Civilized Tribes.

"Turner was dedicated to coming to Northwestern. His parents would only drive as far as Sand Springs, just west of Tulsa, and he had to hitch hike the 175 miles the rest of the way. He visited Coach Dick Highfill a couple of times after he left."

Coach Johnson looked into the eyes of the players, and asked gruffly, "Any of you want to play badly enough to hitch hike 175 miles to do it?"

————

Author Note: Northwestern alumnus, Tom McDaniel went on to obtain a law degree but, after a lengthy career, he returned as Northwestern's president. Later, he answered the call of Oklahoma City University to be its president. In time, a city-, county-wide call for further public service to help develop the commercial district of Oklahoma City. McDaniel finally retired, but continues various services. He contributed greatly to the compilation of this Northwestern story: *Shades of Color: Innocence of a Child-An Unequaled Legacy.*

As for Turner Bear, Jr., he's going strong, as shown in the photos: nearly seventy years apart. He even had both his letter jacket and sweater. We listened in delight to hear about his cherished time at Northwestern and family life of service to the Muscogee-Creek Nation, other Nations across Oklahoma, and the Seminoles of Florida. President Dwight D. Eisenhower certainly recognized leadership. It was an absolute blessing the trails of these former Northwestern athletes crossed. … Additional information of Turner Bear Jr. is provided in the Appendix.

1952 Northwestern offensive team: Backs: 00 Bruce Hough, 12 Ronnie Holmes, 25 QB Turner Bear Jr., 28 Troy O'Hair. Line (L-R): RE Charles Steele, RT Bob Wells, RG Joe Harrison, C Benny Benson, LG Chris Humphrey, LT Joseph Cashmere Vincent Abramavage, LE Jim Reed. Courtesy Turner Bear, Jr.

Clifton Savoy, Turner Bear, Jr., Ken Strunk, and Jim Schroeder (L-R). October 2019 photo courtesy Kathlyn Carter Smith of Broken Arrow, Oklahoma

11.

GYMNASTICS EXHIBITION, BENNY SMITH, CHEROKEE. RESCUE FROM DEATH

September 5, 1963, Gymnastics Exhibition
Northwestern Oklahoma State University

"Oh, wow!" Gasps and cheers sounded from the on-lookers at the gymnastics exhibition, as, just graduated, nationally ranked Northwestern gymnast, Gary Walgamott, completed two flips and one and a half twists before landing perfectly on the trampoline mat.

Gymnastics Coach Bud Matthews beamed and exclaimed, as the cheers continued, "You'd probably won that national meet in Dallas, if you'd made that jump, there!"

"Yeah," agreed a joyous Walgamott, as he hopped to the floor, shrugged his shoulders and raised an eyebrow, with an ear-to-ear smile. "No pressure. No stumble."

"Well, I really appreciate you coming back to help out today," Matthews commented with an affectionate tap on his former star's shoulder.

"My pleasure, coach. Glad to help. … Any time."

With that exchange, Walgamott walked to the side, and Coach Matthews turned to introduce two other gymnasts to the crowd. "These are freshmen twins, Kay and Vicki Coffman, of Alva. They began their gymnastics interest under Ray Chinn, who was gymnastics coach at Northwestern from 1952 to 1956."

NORMAN D. MATTHEWS
Instructor of Physical
Education

Ray Chinn

Gary Wolgamott, Norman 'Bud' Matthews, and Ray Chinn. Courtesy Northwestern and Ray Chinn

Gary meanwhile walked to the other end of the gymnasium where the cheerleaders were working on routines with Dr. Yvonne Carmichael. His sister, Judy Walgamott, was new on the squad. "Hi, sis," he called out with a sly grin, as he glanced momentarily at some footballers nearby. "Special audience?" he teased.

YVONNE CARMICHAE
Instructor of Physical
Education for Women

Dr. Yvonne Carmichael and the 1963 Northwestern cheerleaders; L-R front: Gloria Metcalf, Lynn Hammer, and Donna Riley; Back: Mary Ann Roepke, Judy Wolgamott, and Sharon Boruff, Courtesy Northwestern

"Oh," Judy retorted in a tone and expression of, 'I'll punch you when I get the chance.' "They're just waiting around to talk to you."

"Me-e-e-e?" Gary responded with a puzzled look.

"Yes, you. Heard you are friends with Benny Smith, and they wanted to ask about him."

12.

September 5, 1963, Benny Smith—Cherokee Indian

"Benny Smith, the Cherokee? Yes. Know him well." Wolgamott replied to the questions. "We started in 1959. He was a good athlete. Roomed together in Vinson's basement two years. Studied and double-dated together. … Best man in my wedding." Gary paused and a warm smile filled his face as memories came back, "Called me 'Wogie,'… great guy."

As questions were asked, Gary continued, "Benny was raised in the old traditions of the original Keetoowah Society of the Cherokees." He recognized the same bewildered look on their faces as he had when he first learned of Benny's background.

A player asked in a tongue-in-cheek tone, "Does that mean he dressed in buckskin pants, went bare-chested, wore body-length head-feathers, and screamed blood-curdling yells?"

Gary laughed in his disarming way. Others gathered around. "No, that's only in the movies. . . Benny dressed like most other guys—blue jeans, a plain shirt, and a short haircut." He paused for a moment, "Don't get me wrong, though. Benny looked Indian, and was proud of his Cherokee heritage."

"Whadda ya mean?" a player asked in a slow drawl.

Gary paused again to ponder the question. "Well, Benny's father and grandfather were medicine men and Chiefs. His grandfather is recognized for reviving all the old traditions and customs. On a trip to Benny's home once, I learned that many people came to him for treatment, including black people living nearby."

His comments were met with puzzled looks from those listening. "I've learned bits and pieces from Benny and indirectly from talks with his father. Only a few become a Cherokee medicine man, as it's a spiritual calling. Information learned slowly over a lifetime is passed to only those in the next generation, who have demonstrated the highest human values and self-initiative to learn and allow the spirit to be manifested in life."

By now, more students and players had joined the group listening to his fascinating description of Benny Smith's Cherokee heritage. One asked, "Is Benny a Chief?"

"I don't think so. I'm ashamed to say I really don't know."

"Is he a medicine man?" another asked.

This one was even more difficult, and Gary paused for a long time, reflecting on his experiences. Cautiously he answered, "I never heard Benny claim to be one. But he was raised in the old traditions—honored ways and culture of the Cherokees. I remember how Benny described it: 'I had the honor to learn prayers, rituals, and blessings for various events.' He also learned how to read, write, and speak the Cherokee language, in the system developed by Sequoyah. Benny is fluent in the language. And, get this, his 1962 Master's degree thesis was titled: *The Keetoowah Society of the Cherokee Indian*. You can go over to the Northwestern library, and obtain a copy."

He looked slowly around the group, and followed with a question, "If you consider all those characteristics, can you make the case that Benny might be a Cherokee medicine man?"

"Tell us more about your trip to Benny's home."

Gary glanced at his watch then at his Sis, Judy. She knew that he was thinking he needed to get back on the road to his wife, Sandy, in Stillwater, which was several hours away.

Another warm glow, however, came to Gary's face, as his memory floated back in time. "I'll never forget my visit. Two small log-cabins connected by a hallway, deep in the woods and across some streams,

CLIFTON SAVOY

in eastern Oklahoma, near Vian. There was a bearskin on the wall. Benny's dad was the only one there, and later I learned Benny's mother had passed when he was a youngster. I had a great time, and I really enjoyed talking to Benny's father. On the way back to Northwestern, I asked him how he would say his name in Cherokee.

"Benny gazed at me, smiled, and answered softly. "My Cherokee name isn't Benny. It's Red Bird. In Cherokee, it sounds like, Do Tsu Wa, and it's spelled, Λ. ꟙ. Ᏻ.

"Huh? I remember asking him. What do you mean?"

"I'm named for my grandfather, Red Bird. The name doesn't mean, red or bird, though. It's a title given to red bird, the cardinal, which means: Of real beauty.

"I teased him. Always knew you were a beauty." The listeners to the story laughed.

"Benny ignored me. He said his father's name in English is Stokes. In the Cherokee language, it's, "Ꮝ. Ᏽ. Ꭺ." It sounds like, "Ga Ge Di."

Gary's focus returned to the group around him. "Benny had a good relationship with everyone I can recall at Northwestern and in town. He always seemed to look at things through a prism of Cherokee wisdom. He said it reminded him of a couple of old Cherokee sayings:

"All to hold hands no matter how far we have to reach."

De tsa da do yo hi ni Ge s do

Ꮪ Ꭺ Ꮈ Ꮴ Ꭿ Ꮎ Ꮁ Ꮄ Ꮼ Ꮧ

"We cannot find reasons to let others go as in giving up or turning your back on them."

Gu wa Li tsv Di tsa da yo hi s di e tse he vdi

Ꭱ Ꭺ Ꮅ Ꮳ Ꮅ Ꭺ Ꮈ Ꭿ Ꮎ Ꮼ Ꮧ. Ꭲ Ꮴ Ᏸ Ꮼ Ꮧ

Gary continued, "Benny mentioned the quality of our lives was linked to all others; even the weakest among us. He lived that philosophy.

"We're only as strong as the weakest teammate!"

E ga Li go Sv Wa ni ga lo Sv Na s quu Yi ga dla ni Yi da
ᏍᏍᏆᎡ ᎠᎮᎦᏍᎷ ᏔᎶᎠᎥᎢ ᏦᏍᏍᏋᎯᏴᏓ

Gary paused, and a voice in the group inquired, "Tell us about Benny bringing that guy back to life in Vinson Hall."

13.

Spring 1961, Basement Restroom–Showers of Vinson Hall

Gary's face turned pale, as his mind turned back a couple years to the scene in Vinson Hall's basement restroom and showers. "It's something I'll never forget! Benny found a water soaked body face down on the bathroom floor. He was calmly trying to revive him, even though each second was critical.

"It was spring, but," he paused as a smile crossed his face, "Northwestern star high jumper, Ken Blue, who had somewhat of a 'James Dean' rebel-type personality and always wore a t-shirt and blue jeans, Veldon Zollinger, and couple others enticed Benny Smith and a few others to try riding bulls and starting a Rodeo Club at Northwestern."

He added a side note as he remembered, "Football Coach Art Parkhurst wasn't fond of them doing that — 'Get hurt, and you'll lose your scholarship.'"

Gary continued, "It was a Friday night, I wasn't there in the early moments, but here's how the event was described to me.

"Benny knelt beside a body surrounded by frantic onlookers. One, who was in the back of the crowd and could barely see the top of Benny's head asked, 'Is he dead?'"

"Can't tell!" exclaimed one with a better view.

"He's not breathing!" informed another.

"What's going on?" inquired a student who'd just entered the basement through the southwest entrance steps.

"Guy drowned in the shower!" Blue replied, as he nodded toward the crowd, bunched around two figures on the bathroom floor. "Benny Smith's trying to save him."

"Bunch had been out on the town," Veldon Zollinger added, "and we were down in the room. Benny, Larry Weiser, John McCoy, Berry Brown, Blue, and me were there. Others were coming and going. Blue challenged any takers in who could throw rope half-hitches the fastest around a bed post."

"Well, Tommy (fictitious name) accepted Blue's challenge, but said, "Hafta go to the head first." It was obvious he'd had a lot to drink. Was gone a long time, and Benny went to check on him. Water was spilling over into the main floor from the shower, and Tommy was face down on the shower floor. Apparently, he'd stepped under one of the showers with his clothes on to sober up, passed out, and fell on the drain. Benny drug him out of the water, and has been trying to revive him."

"I arrived soon after that," Gary explained, "And news spread rapidly down the basement halls and to other floors of Vinson Hall. Before it was all over, the crowd even bulged out the southwest exit to the parking lot."

"Did he live? Was he all right?" asked one of the ever growing group now listening.

"It didn't seem like he would," Gary replied. "Benny had Tommy on his stomach and face to the side, and gently pushed upward for a moment on his ribs. Then it looked like he blew air into Tommy's mouth or nose, I couldn't tell which, for a few moments. Then he pushed and blew quickly again." He stopped as he relived the scene in his mind. "What struck me was how calm Benny was all this time. Think the rest of us were on a super adrenaline, frantic high." Gary paused again, then added, "Time was critical to get oxygen to the brain!

"After a moment, water bubbled and then gushed from Tommy's mouth, and he began coughing and then threw up. Next day, he was weak and groggy but, mentally, seemed okay."

Someone in the crowd commented, "Lucky that Benny went to check on him."

"Yes," Gary responded, "a few seconds later, and he'd be pushing up daisies today." He glanced at his watch. *Oops, need to let Sandy know I'll be late.* "Also, Tommy was fortunate Benny knew how to revive him. But," he paused to let his next comments sink in, "I learned Benny never had any mouth-to-mouth training to resuscitate anyone. So, where did that knowledge come from, and ... what about his calmness?"

———

Author Note: The fledgling Northwestern Oklahoma State University rodeo team grew from the few individuals in the early 1960s to one of the top in the U.S. with over a hundred athletes and several National Champions by 2019. And, as for Northwestern's bull rider and star track high jumper, Kenneth Lancaster Blue, he later married Charlene, of the Navajo Nation. They were blessed with three daughters: Sierra, Virginia, and Hannabah. They raised their family on the Navajo Reservation in New Mexico, where Blue taught for many years. Unfortunately, his lovely wife passed away in 1991, but Blue is still going strong. ... Don't think he high jumps over barbed wire fences anymore, though.

As for Benny Smith and Gary Wolgamott, they each had meritorious lives as teachers and mentors. Benny at his beloved Indian Nations' University in Lawrence, Kansas, and Gary at Southwestern Oklahoma State University located in Weatherford, Oklahoma. Both mentioned during the interviews for this literary creation, their journeys "began with Northwestern and its feeder-communities, and each would attend Northwestern all over again." They also expressed, "how excited they were to share their stories." Sadly, both passed away before publication, but some of their Northwestern story survives and inspires our lives. They will be missed beyond description and, no, Benny never disavowed being a Cherokee Medicine Man.

Kenneth Lancaster and Charlene Blue and daughters: Sierra, Virginia, and Hannabah. Charlene was of the Navajo Nation, and the family served the Nation as educators.

Benny and Cheryl Smith Family. Benny was of the Cherokee Nation, and had a life time of educational service at Indian Nations University located in Lawrence, Kansas.

14.

PLAYER HEARTBREAK, HAPPINESS, AND FIRST GAME

September 6, 1963, Last Two-a-Day Practice
Northwestern Oklahoma State University

It's a party! And with cake and ice cream! Everyone's going. No one wants to be left off the *Invite List.* It would be the same for the Northwestern football scrimmage against Dodge City College, and the player travel list would be posted for viewing after practice.

"Savoy. Hey, Clifton Savoy," a player called out as he trotted towards me. "Coach Parkhurst wants to see you."

I was with the defensive squad on one end of the practice field going over schemes and signals. "Me?" I mumbled with restrained excitement from suddenly being singled out. To put it bluntly, the attention was shocking, after being sent to what it seemed outer darkness and playing with every scrub "meat team" against the top offense and defense teams in the preseason two-a-days. *Must've been that bell-ringer collision with another player that got me noticed.* Assistant Coach Johnson gave a nod that I could go.

Apprehensive thoughts filled my mind, as I trotted to the other end of the long field. With each step, though, my confidence grew, with an equal puff of my chest.

Yeah! Coach Parkhurst wants to tell me in person I'm on the travel squad list for the scrimmage. After all, I'd sized up the competition at the three positions coaches had me playing most. Some of my abilities I thought were better or as good as the others, and I've had some really good plays on both offense and defense. Yeah, that's it! Coach wants to tell me in person!

So, with a Cheshire Cat grin, I stopped by his side. "Yes, Coach?" I questioned.

"Savoy," he replied, while keeping his eyes on the offense as it ran a play. "Glen (Smith)," he hollered enthusiastically, "that's the way to use your body to block a defender! Remember that when you go up high to catch a pass over the middle!"

With the play over, Coach Parkhurst momentarily looked my way, "Savoy. Coaches have noticed you have a good leg."

Leg? I'm sure my face had a puzzled look, but Parkhurst had already turned away. Yes, I kicked off for two years in high school, but what's this all about?

Parkhurst headed to a huddle to discuss another play, and instructed over his shoulder, "Stick around after practice, and work out with the kicking specialty teams."

"That's it?" I grumbled, as my mountain-top emotions crashed and left my guts in turmoil. "Stick around for kicking practice? Nothing about the travel squad?"

Practice soon was over, and only those players working out with the specialty teams were on the field. Glen and Big Ben Smith were among them. I joined the group. *Is there nothing these guys don't do?*

Actually, I'd planned to delay going into the dressing rooms, so I'd be alone when I read the names on the scrimmage travel list. So, staying with the kicking teams fit that plan.

When I approached the bulletin board, my heart pounded, beating two, maybe three times its regular pace. My eyes skipped down the names: Amerine, Anderson, Barnett, Boyl, Brooks, both Campbells, ... Massey, Mitchell, Pipestem, both Smiths, Stephens, Strunk, both Sweats, Woltje, Ward. ... *No Savoy.*

An emotional low hit like a ton of bricks dropped on my head. *No Savoy? I must've skipped over it!* My eyes flashed upward. … Reality hurt deeply, as I agonized. *Savoy's not there.*

Seemed like a joyous party in the dressing rooms, when I entered. Felt like everyone'd been invited but me, as players were laughing and busy packing their scrimmage gear. Ben and Glen were laughing and the Campbells and Pipestem were teasing each other as usual. Only things missing were ice cream and cake. I hustled straight to my street clothes, gathered them up, headed quickly to my basement room in Vinson Hall, and shut the door. Immediately, an emotional release slid me to the floor where I sat against the door in a fog for a long time.

Laughter and voices outside my door in the hallway, after what seemed like hours later, jolted me to my senses. Someone exclaimed, "H. L. (Brown), we'll beat you next time!"

"No, Ben. You and Schroeder'll never beat Glen and me."

"Don't be too, sure, Little Man," Big Ben replied.

"Says you," retorted H. L. "We're ping pong champs!"

Jim Schroeder changed the subject, "Make sure you tell Larry Procnau and Bob Drake and any other freshmen to come work out with us tomorrow morning. Darrell Inman, Marvin Miller, John Altramura, Bob Herbig, Virgil Beasley, and others are showing up. Informal. No coach, yet. Just us."

"Will do. Thanks for inviting us to the Baptist Student Union. Fun time. We'll be back."

As the sounds faded down the hall, I had a heart-to-heart talk with my inner voice about my football prospects. "Coaches had me no higher than third on the depth chart at any position."

"You're better than that ranking!" my inner voice exclaimed.

"Yeah, I believed so, too, but don't forget, it's the coaches who do the ranking, and Coach Parkhurst has final say."

"Well, what's next?"

"I know I can make the travel squad to do the kick-offs."

1963 Northwestern Basketball Squad (L-R) Front: Bill Massey, H. L. Brown, and Marvin Miller. 2nd Row: Junior Kelley, John Streich, Darral Inman, John Altamura, and Robert Herbig. Back: Assistant Coach Chirold Epp, Bob 'Wings' Drake, Larry Prochnau, Jim Schroeder, Virgil Beasley, and Head Coach Keith Covey. Glen Smith, not pictured, also was on the team. Courtesy of Northwestern.

"Is that enough? ... Being only on specialty teams? It's playing, but...?"

"No!"

"Well, here's a suggestion. You were out for the basketball team last year until you broke an ankle. Why don't you shoot around and scrimmage with them tomorrow morning?"

Mid-morning, the loud voice of Assistant Coach Johnson blasted across the gym, "SAVOY! ... WHAT ARE YOU DOING?"

I left the basketball scrimmage and hustled down to Johnson, who spoke in a deeply angry tone, as he nodded toward the football players carrying gear behind him, "We have a football scrimmage, and we're about to leave!"

I felt like all eyes in the building were on me, to watch my humiliation, as I replied, "Coach, my name wasn't on the travel list."

"Oh?" he questioned with a stunned look. He gazed at me for a moment, then quickly turned without a word and disappeared back into the coaches' offices.

As I returned to the basketball scrimmage, I noticed the quietness. Indeed, everyone in the huge gym area had followed the exchange.

Within a few minutes, Coach Johnson's voice bellowed again throughout the gym, "SAVOY, COME HERE!"

I felt frustrated and embarrassed, as I trotted towards him. I was angry. *What do you want this time? You know my name wasn't on the travel list!*

He barked, "A player is sick. You have five minutes to grab your football gear and get on the bus." ... It took me four!

15.

FLEDGLING NORTHWESTERN RODEO
TEAM. BIG BEN ON A HORSE?

September 14, 1963, Big Ben and Zollinger, Math Tutor
Northwestern Oklahoma State University

The large basement room of Vinson Hall must've been built like one of those animal or fish traps that allowed entry but no exit, as it always seemed to have more students in it than beds no matter the time of day.

Ken Blue, one of those who actually roomed there, looked up from repairing a bull-rider's rigging to see a large body in the doorway. "Come on in, Ben," he gave a shout out in his laid-back voice, as all heads and eyes looked toward the door. "Nobody knocks here."

"Ya'all," Blue continued with a look around, "Ben Smith and his brother, Glen, live at the far end of the hall around the corner. Their other roomy is H.L. Brown, who's a basketballer."

Ben was greeted promptly by each of the seven or so guys in the room. Veldon Zollinger, who Ben came to see, expressed, "Give me a minute, and we'll get on that math."

Blue teased with a chuckle and in his laid-back way, "Ben and Glen are on the football team, but the real reason they came to Northwestern was because of so many black girls."

"Yep!" Ben laughed along with everyone else and added, "All four of them."

"Grab a seat."

As Ben started to squat his big behind on a trash bucket near Blue, Russ Wine, a Northwestern golf star and one of Blue's roomies shouted, "Not there, Ben! ... That's a spittoon."

"Maybe something there that'll bite you in the butt," laughed a guy sitting on a wood bottle crate near the door. "Take this one," he suggested, as he handed Ben the crate. "It'll hold ya."

Another guy held out a pack of soft-chew, and laughed, "And this'll keep the bites and roaches away."

Ben grinned, ear-to-ear, "Not big enough yet."

Blue grumbled about the bull rigging, and a new guy, a city-slicker, asked, "What's the purpose of that bell?"

A tongue-in-cheek sounded before Blue could respond, "It's ring lets the bull know he's losing. Cowboy's still there."

"Naw," retorted the guy throwing half-hitches with a rope on the bed post. "It lets the cowboy know he's still alive after the bull's kicked and gored him in the head, stomped on his chest, ripped off his manly parts, and trotted away."

Hoots and laughter filled the room, and Blue joined in. "Some truth there, but I can tell you, 8 seconds on a bull is a long time."

"Amen!" exclaimed several others.

"Ben, join the rodeo team," invited a guy squatting on his haunches and helping Blue. "We're puttin' one together."

"No thanks," replied Ben with a laugh. "I'll stick to football. Never get me on a bull!"

"Could do other things, like Zollinger, who bulldogs," one suggested.

"Three problems with that," blurted out the guy throwing half-hitches. "Ben probably couldn't find a horse big enough to carry him. If he did, it wouldn't be able to run fast enough to catch the steer, and besides ... Ben'd crush the steer."

Ben nodded, with a sheepish grin, as they all laughed. "Don't think rodeo's for me."

Zollinger said to him, "Tough loss in that football game last night, 7 – 13."

"Yeah," Ben replied as a frustrated look twitched his face, "Should'a won or at least tied it. On 2-yard line twice more and didn't score."

"What ballgame?" asked a guy half-asleep across the room.

"The one at Southwestern Kansas, dummy!"

"Northwestern play on a Friday night?"

"Yes. This one time. It was on the radio. Listen next time."

Blue asked, "Ben, how'd you and Glen do? … Start?"

Ben shuffled his body, in a nervous sort'a way, and replied slowly. "Glen started on offense. Played whole game. Caught a few passes." After a pause, "I was in for only a few plays. Coaches told me that I need to get in shape."

As football talk subsided, Dale Swiggett, a pitcher for Northwestern, made eye contact with Big Ben. "I was in a baseball game against you back in high school. Lahoma and Crescent. You pitched. We had a runner at first. I was supposed to bunt. Swung away instead, for a triple. Remember the game?"

"Yeah, I do." Ben replied with a deep belly laugh and an ivory-white smile that was accentuated by his black face. "Felt sorry for you, and tossed you a softy."

As the laughter subsided, Zollinger added, "Ben, Swiggett's a math major, maybe he should be the one to tutor you."

"Oh, not so fast," teased a guy in the room. "Hear Swiggett can't even calculate his own pitching ERA." After the laughter, he added, "Besides, can't trust anyone from the fourth floor."

"Speaking of baseball," Swiggett interjected, "Who's going to be in the World Series?"

"Not sure about the National League, but it's the New York Yankees in the American League," one guy opined.

"Yeah," another agreed, "And the Yankees'll win the World Series for third time in a row. Probably in four games!"

"Who'll play against them?"

"Won't be the Los Angeles Dodgers," one guy stated matter of factly, "They choked last year and are doing it again."

As a new guy to the bunch, Ben struggled to keep his composure. He was a Dodger fan, through and through.

Zollinger asked, "St. Louis Cardinals are one game behind, and you think it'll be Cards?"

"Yep! They're hot: won 19 of last 20! And they'll whip the Dodgers in a 3-game series starting Monday."

Zollinger noticed Big Ben was quiet through the whole give-and-take, "Ben, you're probably the most rabid baseball guy here. Whadda ya think?"

"Dodgers all the way!" Ben exclaimed in an emotional defense of his team, and he grinned and nodded as each come-back sounded.

"You're dreaming!"

"No!" Ben fired back. "Dodgers are the best! Plain as day, Dodgers are the best team. Cards can't keep hot streak, and..."

"Hold your horses! Cards are gonna cool off and Dodgers heat up? You're delusional!"

Ben laughed, as he deflected the verbal punch, "No! Dodgers just in a little slump. They have the best pitchers. Last game, Dodgers won in that long game; only 2 to 1. Dodgers'll win 2, maybe all 3, be 3 or 4 ahead of the Cards with 9 games left. They'll beat the lowly Mets to clinch. No way St. Louis can catch 'em. Dodgers'll then whip the Yankees for their second championship in 5 years. ... Just watch!"

"Wrong! Wrong! Wrong, Ben! Cards'll win but, if not, no way L.A. is better than the Yankees an' all those big hitters."

Ben enjoyed the sports banter, but a look of enough-is-enough covered his face, as he explained. "Yankees and Dodgers have about same record. Yup, Yank's Ford (Whitey) and Bouton (Jim) have more than 20 wins. Dodgers only have Koufax (Sandy) but Drysdale (Don) has 19. The ERAs of Koufax and Drysdale, 1.88 and 2.63, are better'n Ford and Bouton at 2.74 and 2.53. Koufax is the strikeout king in the pros with 300 and Drysdale is not far behind. The Yank pitchers just rely on its big bombers to win."

Ben was on a roll now and his grin was ear-to-ear. "…And no team has a reliever like Ron Perranoski with 16 wins 3 losses 21 saves. Get in trouble, here comes 'Noski!"

Not all guys in the room were convinced, as one challenged, "Just takes one or two big Yankee hits to blow the game up!"

Ben turned to the voice and grinned, like he had been waiting for the hitting comment to come, "Yup, Yank's Howard (Elston), Pepitone (Joe), Maris (Roger), and Tresh (Tom) with over 20 HRs each and Mantle (Mickey) usually but he's been hurt. Played only about 60 games, a third. An' they have other big hitters. Dodgers only have Howard (Frank) above 20, but Davis (Tommy) has 16 and his .326 BA is better'n the Yanks. Also, Wills (Maury) has .302 and 40 stolen bases. Dodger runners'll keep Yank pitchers so busy, they'll throw one up for hit after hit." Ben chuckled with delight as he delivered the knock-out, "And the Dodger pitchers'll mow down the Yank big bombers 'cause they'll swing for the fences!"

At that point, there was silence, as no one offered a rebuttal to Ben's statistics. Soon, Zollinger spoke. "So, Ben, what's the problem you're having with math?"

Ben shrugged his shoulders. "Just can't keep up with all those numbers!"

16.

NEWS SPECIAL: FOUR BLACK CHILDREN
KILLED IN CHURCH BOMBING

*September 18, 1963, News Special, TV Lounge of Vinson Hall
Northwestern Oklahoma State University*

"I'm late! I'm late! For a very important date! No time to say hello, goodbye! I'm late! I'm late! I'm late!" Try to talk for a moment with a student on campus in the early days of a semester, and you might think you've bumped into the rabbit in the 1951 Disney movie, *Alice in Wonderland*.

The Vinson Hall boys of Ma Griggs were no different, and she'd often find the TV on and the lounge empty. As she reached to turn it off this evening, the scene of three coffins appeared on the screen along with the words, *Funeral of Three Killed in Church Bombing!*

News Special — Birmingham, Alabama: The TV scene panned across the front of a large, predominantly black audience where three coffins were positioned in front of a podium. A man stood behind it. "Dr. Martin Luther King, Jr., gave the eulogy today for three of the four young girls who were killed in the bombing of the 16th Street Baptist Church of Birmingham early last Sunday morning, September 15th."

Civil Rights struggle, bombings, and death!

Dr. King spoke, and the scene panned backward to reveal the eight thousand present. "... We gather to pay our tribute of respect to these beautiful children of God. ... They are now committed back to that eternity from which they came. ... These children were victims of one of the most vicious crimes ever against humanity. ... Martyred heroines of a holy crusade for freedom and human dignity..."

The TV faded to exterior smoke and dust filled scenes of the church building, as the reporter's voice returned. "Around 200 people were present in Sunday school before the 11:00 worship-service when the bomb exploded and caved in interior walls."

"Most of the parishioners survived," the reporter stated as the scene was filled with emergency vehicles and church members moving about covered in dust, some stumbling about, and others frantically digging through the rubble. "But the bodies of four girls under age fourteen were found in a basement bathroom beneath the rubble. Another with them lost an eye, and more than twenty people were injured in the blast."

The scene switched to an earlier view of the church before the bombing, "This church has long been a meeting place for civil rights organizers like Dr. King, and many of the marches in Birmingham began at these steps."

A scene appeared of the massive crowd in front of the Lincoln Memorial. "It's been less than a month since Dr. King and hundreds of thousands rallied August 23rd in Washington, D.C. for jobs and freedom, and left in hope since no major incidents or violence occurred. But this bombing," the reporter continued, as the scene returned to the dust and smoke filled view of the 16th Street Church, "is the third to Negro homes and churches in Birmingham in the last eleven days after a federal court order mandated desegregation of Alabama schools."

"The next view was a photo of the Alabama Capitol. "Governor George Wallace has been an aggressive foe of de-segregation, and it's ..." The TV faded to human figures wearing white robes and

Court ordered school desegregation and the KKK!

hats covering their faces, "rumored the Ku Klux Klan in Birmingham is one of its strongest and violent chapters."

The TV faded to the front of the 16th Street Church. A large crowd was outside. "Thousands of angry black protesters gathered after the bombing and violence broke out across Birmingham when Governor Wallace sent the state patrol and police, under Commissioner Eugene "Bull" Connor, to break it up. Two young blacks were killed before the National Guard restored order."

As the scene returned to the coffins and large crowd, King's voice resumed, "So, in a sense these girls have something to say to each of us in their death.

"… To every minister of the gospel who has remained silent behind the safe security of stained-glass windows.

"… To every politician who has fed his constituents with the stale bread of hatred and the spoiled meat of racism.

"… To a federal government that has compromised with the un-democratic practices of southern Dixiecrats and hypocrisy of northern Republicans.

"… To every Negro who has passively accepted the evil system of segregation and who has stood on the sidelines in a mighty struggle for justice.

"… To black and white alike, that we must be concerned not merely about who murdered them, but about the system, the way of life, the philosophy which produced the murderers

"God has a way of wringing good out of evil… Character for color!"

"So my friends, they didn't die in vain. God has a way of wringing good out of evil. … The innocent blood of these little girls may serve as a redemptive force that will bring new light to this dark city. … The death of these little children may lead our whole Southland from the low road of man's inhumanity to man to the high road of peace and brotherhood, and these tragic deaths may lead our nation to substitute an aristocracy of character for an aristocracy of color.

"… To the bereaved families, I hope you can find some consolation in Christianity's affirmation that death is not the end. Death is not a period that ends the great sentence of life, but a comma that punctuates it to more lofty significance. Death is not a blind alley that leads the human race into a state of nothingness, but an open door which leads man into life eternal. Let this daring faith, this great invincible surmise, be your sustaining power during these trying days."

"Death is not the end…"
"God will lift you up…"

"… If one will hold on, he will discover God walks with him, and is able to lift you from the fatigue of despair to the buoyancy of hope, and transform dark valleys into sunlit paths of inner peace. …And the eternal meaning of love. This is a beautiful thing for all generations."

As Ma Griggs returned to the office across the hall, she heard faint voices outside the closed door. "Ben and Glen Smith. Must be coming from the cafeteria after football," she mumbled. Then as the seldom-used front door closed with its irritating clang, another voice sounded. "H.L. Brown. Why'd he come in that way?"

"Hey, where you been?" Big Ben asked, his weariness evident in his voice.

"Baptist Student Union."

"Still champ?" Glen inquired.

"Yeah, but it was mostly a service. Had some good snacks, though."

"Lucky we weren't there," Ben teased, as they headed to their basement room.

The voices faded as they walked down the hall. H.L. retorted, "Dreaming."

After viewing the news report, Ma Griggs was worried. *Did they know of that Baptist Church bombing last Sunday and the six deaths? … Have they experienced any of those things? Hopefully, not at Northwestern!*

17.

HOMECOMING WEEK REFLECTIONS
AND EVENTS: WW II NAZI POW CAMP
AND MEMORIES OF A FORMER POW.
"WHY DID THOSE TWO COMMIT SUICIDE?"

October 12, 1963, Homecoming Day
Northwestern Oklahoma State University

"What's that noise?" Big Ben Smith asked with a groan in his light sleep, as he pulled a pillow over his head to muffle the sound that echoed around Vinson Hall. "Sun's barely up." *Rooster hasn't even finished crowing.* After a few hopeless attempts to shut out the sound, he remembered. *It's Ma Griggs reminding her boys to finish Vinson's Homecoming display.*

"Parents and visitors will be here soon," she warned.

Homecoming was one of Northwestern's most exciting weeks, and everything peaked on Saturday with a parade, football game, crowning a queen, and big-name entertainment. Also, related activities occurred off-campus. "For a small woman," Ben grumbled weakly, like he was waving a white-surrender flag, "her voice sure can carry!"

No hope for a reprieve, he rolled over slowly and sighed, deeply, and looked across the room at brother Glen and roomy H. L. Brown. *They're awake.* "Gotta get goin'," he expressed in a weak-struggling tone, as he climbed out of bed. "Coach said pre-game meal by 9:30. Hafta get that car runnin'."

In seconds, they were headed out of the building, where the early morning coolness reminded them, they couldn't wear only a t-shirt much longer. "Look at the barricades!" Glen pointed out just steps away. "Already around the parking lot and road." They were for the football game on Newby Field and for the Big Show that evening in the fieldhouse. Crooner Mel Torme' was the headliner, with a performance by guitarist Roy Clark.

Ben, Glen, and H.L. had other plans, though. They heard the Ernie Fields Band, a black nationally known band from Tulsa that played swing in a rhythm and blues style, would be at the VFW Club, just south of campus. They'd arranged to pick up the four black girls on campus and go to the dance event.

Glen popped the trunk of his 2-door, hard-top, 2-tone pink '55 Chevy, and tossed a bicycle pump towards H. L.

Parents, visitors, and alumni already were pouring onto the campus. A few gawked and slowed their walk, as they passed the three athletes. H. L. noticed, as he paused to wipe sweat from his brow. *They must not'uv ever seen a black person up close.* His mind flashed back to early childhood in Geary, Oklahoma when it was segregated.

Seen THAT look before! ... In myself, when I saw a white person for the first time. What was it? So unusual, like when I saw a zebra or panda bear for the first time.

He quickly turned his attention back to the work. " Pump those tires up with this?" he challenged the other two. "Not me? You're bigger! Stronger!"

"Yup!" Big Ben replied firmly, "But we have a game to play, and YOU ... DON'T!"

H. L. pumped, but muttered doubtfully, "Sure this tire holds air?"

Before an answer, his skepticism continued, with another up-down thrust on the pump. "Battery's dead. Only a couple gallons of gas. Don't think we'll get'er runnin' in time, with you guys playing a football game. Can't do all myself!"

"She'll run," Glen responded sternly. "Just pump!"

Ben added, "Girl's dorm, two, maybe three miles from the club. All we need is go six to seven miles." His eyes met Glen's; a concerned look furrowed his brow. "We do have that much gas? Right?"

"Yep," Glen assured them, but put the ball back in Ben's court. "(Veldon) Zollenger and (Ken) Blue still comin' to jump-start the motor?"

Ben nodded, as Blue's pickup—one that'd also seen its better days—pulled up. "Here now. Good guys! Right on time!"

H. L. glanced up briefly and mumbled a greeting, and returned to pumping. Suddenly his head jerked up. A delightful look had replaced the doubtful frown on his face, and his eyes sparkled with anticipation as a realization hit him. Three *guys and four girls. Glen driving, Ben in shotgun because of his size, and one girl between them. Three girls and me in the back seat!* Suddenly, he pumped with vigor and sang in a happy tone, "VFW Club. ... Here we come!"

18.

---

*October 12, 1963, Northwestern Homecoming—A long
Journey from WWII and the Nazi Officer Prison of War
Northwestern Oklahoma State University*

On the Oklahoma Plains, U.S.A., the afternoon homecoming football game of Northwestern was soon to begin. A seasoned professor (Fictional Character) of history enjoyed the warmth of the sun rays as he watched the young players from the spectator stands. He noticed in the game program the description of the Big Homecoming Show that evening. *Glad my party of four has a dinner reservation at the club.* It was a reference to the old VFW, which was the U.S. military officers' club during WWII days as part of a prisoner of war encampment for captured Nazi officers and soldiers. "Every place in town is going to be full," he mumbled as he continued to reflect on the history of the large military prison.

Located just south of the Northwestern football field—near the airport. Understand there were five thousand or so POWs—nearly a thousand officers. Nothing left except the club. Been less than twenty years. Some would still be alive. Where are they today? … Understand some, like Colonel Wolf, was given a second military life in NATO. Wonder if he recalls his time in this POW prison?

Thousands of miles to the East, Colonel Werner Wolf, former WWII Nazi SS-Officer of the Afrika Korps 10th Panzer Division and later a POW in Oklahoma, just south of the town of Alva and the Northwestern campus, might've stepped out from NATO Headquarters at Brussels, Belgium, into the October 1963 evening.

His thoughts and comments might've been something like the following:

"Brr," he murmured, as the coolness of the approaching darkness surprised him. Colonel Wolf might've looked around the sky, slowly, for signs of colder weather. Then his gaze focused on the fading sunlight reflections in the west, like at different times over the last twenty years when he relived days of war and being a POW at Alva, Oklahoma. "Seven hour difference," he muttered to no one. "Early afternoon there." He reflected for a moment and added, "Hotter, too. Wonder what's happening there at this minute?"

He relived those memories over the years. *Morning roll-call, then our own officer reports and drills to stay fit. Then our soldiers would be about their camp duties.* His thoughts diverted momentarily, as a person exited the NATO building. Mentally back in time in Oklahoma, he sighed in exasperation as the memory of management overkill took center stage. *Officers passed reports up command. Had one thousand in the five thousand POWs there—four soldiers to each officer. ... How many times did each of us walk those fences and look up at the guards watching our moves?* A comforting grin momentarily crossed his face as he recalled, his escape. It disappeared quickly, though, as he remembered the agony of being re-captured. "At least," he mumbled, "almost made it across the Rio Grande."

As he walked from the NATO Building, other World War II thoughts and questions may have come to mind. *Our Panzer tanks were better than theirs. How'd we lose the war? Lack of supplies? ... It was heart-breaking when the Afrika Korps, many thousands strong, surrendered May 1943.* And that boat trip across the Atlantic to New York and long train ride in boxcars to Oklahoma was humiliating. He might've salvaged some of his and their German and soldier dignity when they proudly marched in step, looking straight ahead instead at those Alva villagers, up 7th Street and around that college. With a mumble, "Can't believe they had one out in nowhere" as they marched to the POW camp South of town.

Colonel Wolf likely recalled the size of the POW camp, over 100 buildings and 1,800' by 700' (548.64 m by 213.36 m). *Knew every inch of the place. Are there any parts of the camp left? I'll have to go back and look around some day.*

As he walked, music reached his ears, and he probably remembered the musical sounds and laughter from the U.S. Officers Club; especially from Saturday nights. *One of the best constructed buildings there, it wouldn't surprise him if it was still standing.*

————

Author Note: After WWII ended, Colonel Wolf likely reflected back to his POW days south of Alva, Oklahoma. Perhaps his thoughts included dreams like this one:

Colonel Wolf tossed and turned all night, haunted by the memories of WWII and the Oklahoma POW camp. He rose early, but the memories stayed on his mind, as he showered and dressed. *Glad the POW survivors were brought home. ... Germany should've brought back home those who died there, too. They're heroes. ... Did (Erwin) Grams and (Erich) Schindler really hang themselves, or were they murdered for some reason? Schindler knew, like all of us, Germany surrendered May 1945. Why would he commit suicide within a few weeks of all the POWs being shipped home? Grams' hanging and the execution of Erwin Rommel, accused of being involved in the assassination attempt on Hitler, were within days of each other. ... Any connection? ...* Colonel Wolf mumbled, as he looked in the mirror to finish his tie, "Maybe, best leave as history, but..." he paused for a moment, "I wonder, though, how much those Oklahomans remember, or ever knew what took place there?"

19.

October 12, 1963, Homecoming Evening
VFW Club, Alva, Oklahoma

A trail of smoke and dust followed Glen Smith's '55 Chevy and the seven excited black Northwestern students, as they pulled into the drive leading to the VFW Club and parked. The dance evening had finally arrived!

Sounds of history still echoed back and forth, although faintly. "You mean to tell me," one of the girls asked, as Glen's car door closed behind her, "This building was the Officers' Club, twenty years ago during WWII when a large Nazi POW camp was all around here?"

Music from the Ernie Field's Band suddenly filled the air. It was a rhythm and blues version of Glenn Miller's *In the Mood*. The POW question was forgotten, as the group cheered and hustled toward the building. H. L., light-heartedly entertained with some of his dance moves, as the group approached the steps to the entrance. "You want some of this, huh?"

"You wish!" one of the girls retorted with a laugh.

"Going to be a fun night," another gleefully added. "Look at the cars. A packed house!"

"Yeah!" agreed Glen. "Did you know the club also had shuffle board and pool tables?"

"Two dance floors and full dining menu, too, I heard," Ben added. "Friend said they even have shrimp cocktail appetizers."

"Not on our budget," cautioned one of them.

"Maybe they'll play Chubby Checker's *The Twist*."

"I wanna hear Ray Charles, *Can't Stop Lovin' You*! And maybe something by Louis Armstrong and Elvis."

Just as Glen pushed the entry button on the locked door for admittance, one of them quipped in jest, "Better throw in a cowboy song or two for H. L."

All but H. L. laughed as the door opened. A big white man stepped through, looked the group over, and then spoke to Glen, who started to hand their pooled cover-charge money to the man. "This is a private club, for veteran members only."

Glen froze, and his mind momentarily relived Ben and his life. *This was just another version of what they'd experienced all their lives! We've stepped into a café and immediately told, "We don't serve coloreds here." My stomach'd cramp, and I'd want to double over, and cry out, "Why?" Made us feel like a half man! ... God didn't make any junk!"*

As Glen started to respond, "But..." the entrance door closed. All had heard, no further explanation was needed. They stood silent and unmoving, like statues, while minutes passed. Dreams of a fun night shattered in seconds.

"Hey, what you all doing?" a friendly voice came from the bottom of the steps. It was Northwestern basketball lettermen, Marvin Miller, date, and Darrel Inman with cheerleader Donna Riley. They were coming to enjoy the Ernie Fields Band. "Music's wasting out here."

A faint smile crossed H. L.'s face, momentarily, when he saw his basketball teammates.

As the four passed through, Inman paused next to Ben, "Tough football loss today, 14-16."

"Yeah." Ben responded in a quiet, frustrated tone. "Should'a won it. Think coach'll be makin' offense changes."

Took only seconds for Glen to share what just happened to them and, as Miller and the other three passed through the door, he whispered to Glen, "I'll explain to the Club Commander that you, Ben and H.L. are athletes at Northwestern and all of you are students there."

A few minutes later the door opened, and the black students joined Miller and the others inside the VFW Club, laughing and enjoying the Ernie Fields Band. Soon, there were cheek-to-cheek moments. ... And, before the night was over, one of them got their wish—Chubby Checker's, 'Let's Twist Again, like we did last Summer!'

20.

TWO BLACK BODIES WOULD BE
DEAD ON THE FLOOR IF...

October 19, 1963, If Looks Could Kill
Central Oklahoma State University Game Road Trip

If looks could kill, a couple of black bodies would be dead on the café floor this day. It happened on a 1963 road-trip of the Northwestern Oklahoma State University football team against Central State University, located in Edmond just north of Oklahoma City.

As the team bus rolled to a stop in front of a café for the pre-game meal, Glen Smith, quickly raised half-way out of his seat, and shot a questioning look at his brother, Ben, seated a few rows back. *Do you see where we're stopping?*

The Smith brothers knew this café quite well from agonizing experiences in their younger days, as they grew up on a 40-acre mule farm located a few miles southwest of town. Glen recalled the last time just last spring when they thought things would be different. As they entered the café, though, they were immediately told in a loud voice where everyone could hear, "We don't serve coloreds here!"

Glen thought back to that day last spring. *My stomach cramped. I wanted to double over, and cry out, "Why?" It made us feel like a half man. God didn't make any junk! Then, as if that wasn't bad enough, the café manager whispered quietly, as we walked out, "Come to the backdoor."* So, today, what's he gonna do?

The owner excitedly greeted each player, as the team filed through the café entrance. He had a facial expression of, *Money in the bank!* But it changed instantly when he made eye-contact with Ben, and then Glen, who had ear-to-ear grins, walking just ahead of the coaches.

There was an aggressive, back and forth, albeit silent communication sent through the eye contact of Glen, Ben and the café owner.

I know what you're thinking and that you know that we know, Glen thought, as the glow of his smile pulsed brighter on his face, with each look exchanged.

Don't grin at me! You know you're out of place. You're not to come in here! Remember? We don't serve coloreds! The owner's face reddened as he realized he couldn't force the issue.

Glen fired back *We're not leaving! We're with the team!*

The owner's eyes conveyed a threat. *There'll be another day, boy-e-e-e!* Then he turned his attention to serving the meals.

As the players slowly loaded back on the bus afterwards, Ben leaned towards his brother and whispered jubilantly, "I'll never, ever forget this day!"

"Me either," Glen replied jubilantly. "One of my best memories." Then after a long pause, he continued, with a forced, sarcastic laugh, "Guess the Northwestern money talked."

Soon, the bus slowly picked up speed and the café disappeared behind them. Glen sighed deeply, and glanced around at the other players. "They don't have a clue," he mumbled with the ear-to-ear grin still on his face. "Don't have a clue at what just took place."

21.

DAD OF MOHAWK, BILL MITCHELL, TO VISIT NORTHWESTERN

October 21, 1963, Bill Mitchell's Dad to Visit Northwestern

The first-year Northwestern football player lamented to an old farmer from his home town, "Think we could be a good team, but seem not able to win. Lost 2 games by 6 points. Another by 2, and tied another. ... "Really frustrating!"

The wise farmer, a neighbor, tapped his pipe on the heel of his shoe, as he slowly responded, "If there's cream there, it'll rise to the surface." He paused and looked into the face of the young player to make sure he was listening, "Remember, though, it takes time for it to rise."

This wisdom was prophetic of the 1963 Northwestern football team. A few offensive changes, like the safety, Bill Massey, moved to starting quarterback, were beginning to gel. Players were noticeably upbeat, even after the Central Oklahoma State University game played over the weekend—a 20 to 9 loss—where players felt robbed of a chance to win.

"That (Central) player didn't score!" agonized one of the Northwestern linebackers, as players dressed for the Monday afternoon practice.

"Same thing Savoy said, too," expressed another. "That we tackled the guy at the half yard line, but he rolled into the end zone. Ref couldn't see as he was behind him (Savoy). Still, ref signaled a touchdown."

"Our defensive players tried to talk to the refs, but they were having none of it."

"Might sound like sour grapes," Mike Garrison grumbled, "But we had the momentum. After they scored, little time left. But if not, the way Massey was passing and our running was clicking, think we'd score. Worse case, it'd be a 13 to 9 loss."

"Nothin' like home cookin'," piped in a player down the bench. "Need something like a camera replay.

"You're dreamin'," replied a player in a skeptical tone. "Maybe in 40-50 years."

"Where ya been?" Garrison asked his fellow lineman, Bill Mitchell who'd quietly entered the room and began to dress for practice. "Waited at Vinson for you before coming."

"Phone call from my Dad," Mitchell replied, as he slipped on his shoulder pads and turned to Roids, "Pull my jersey on."

"Why you all broken up?" Garrison asked in an unbelieving tone of what he saw — eyes red and puffy. He probed deeper, "Something bad happen?"

"No! My Dad, Alex, is coming to see me play a college football game," Bill replied happily, but with teary-eyes again. "Saved enough to catch a bus all the way from our Mohawk Reservation in Northern New York State to Northwestern and Alva, Oklahoma. Never seen me play. My last year," he continued, as he grabbed his helmet and they headed to the practice field. "Northwestern has a Parent's Day, and Dad wanted to be here. Took a while to save the money."

"A bus that far?" Garrison asked in a tone of amazement. "What kind of work?"

"Yes, long ways, I know. Dad's an aluminum millwright in a plant in Massena, New York. "Iron-work lured many Mohawk kids out of school, but Mom and Dad had bigger dreams for me than to be an iron-worker on the St. Lawrence River. ... I'd questioned them, though, "Why stay in school when I could make more as an iron worker?"

Garrison asked, as they stepped out on the practice field, "So, what made you stay in school and go to college?"

Mitchell stopped in his tracks and expressed, "Mom said, 'Because I said so!'"

Garrison replied with a laugh, "I've heard that a few times myself!"

"Well!" A gruffy voice sounded behind them. As they looked over their shoulder, Coach Johnson added with a wishful grin, "You jolly sons can tell your Moms about a different kind of iron-experience, the Iron Mule, if you don't get a hustle on down to the team!"

The Northwestern team never lost again that 1963 season. There was doubt, though, when it trailed at half-time 27 to 7 at Eastern New Mexico University before a miracle rally and win.

22.

1963: RENOWNED FOLK SINGER, LEON BIBB, AT NORTHWESTERN

October 28, 1963, Leon Bibb at Herod Hall
Northwestern Oklahoma State University

Four shrill rings echoed from the public wall phone down the hall-ways of Vinson Hall basement. "R-i-n-g! R-i-n-g! R-i-n-g! R-i-n-g!" The sound penetrated through walls and doors, and pillows pulled over heads didn't deter it. Only those who'd developed the knack of tuning out the world were immune to its irritation.

"Somebody answer that!" yelled a student behind a closed door in a voice that sounded like he was about to explode.

"R-i-n-g! R-i-n-g! R-i-||"

"Hello," a passerby answered in a voice like he'd drawn the short straw. "Want Ben? Ben Smith? I'll check," he replied. He turned and yelled down the hall, "Ben!" ... "Ben Smith! Telephone!" No response, so he hollered at the top of his voice, "Ben!" ... "You down there?"

Several doors opened and heads poked out, including Glen Smith, to see what the fuss was all about. An inquisitive look crossed his face as he mouthed, "Who?"

"It's for Ben!" ... "Some dame is on the phone for him!"

Glen turned half-way into the room, and started to say, "B," as

Ben rushed past him and headed down the hall before he finished, "en, it's for you."

The phone receiver dangled down the wall, as whoever'd answered was nowhere in sight. Ben gathered himself, spoke slowly, and paused in between. "Hello." ... "Yes, it's Ben." ... "Yes, we'll talk more of Bibb's performance tomorrow night. Looking at one of his flyers right now. It's tacked on the bulletin board here. Looks like Vinson Hall is a co-sponsor of the event."

Leon Bibb to perform at Northwestern Oklahoma State University
October 28, 1963, 7:00PM, Herod Hall

Nationally-known Leon Bibb is to perform at Northwestern on October 28th 7:00PM in Herod Hall. Bibb is an emotionally-moving folk singer, actor, and TV talk-show host. In recent years, he has performed on tours to packed auditoriums around the U.S.

Bibb grew-up in Louisville, Kentucky. His stunning baritone voice landed him on Broadway in New York City in 1946 in the chorus of "Annie Get Your Gun," with Ethel Merman. His a cappella vocals blend his classical, spiritual and blues culture and life experiences/credits are many. Include: performer at 1959 Newport Folk Festival, the soundtrack to the 1960 film The Young One, his own NBC television talk show, and featured singer on The Ed Sullivan Show.

He has several music recordings:

    1 Discography
    1.1 Studio albums
    1.2 Live album
    1.3 Collaborative albums
    2 References
    3 External links

Leon Bibb Sings Folk Songs (Vanguard, 1959), *Tol' My Captain* (Vanguard, 1960), *Leon Bibb Sings Love Songs* (Vanguard, 1960), *Leon Bibb Sings* (Columbia, 1961), *Oh Freedom and Other Spirituals* (Washington, 1962) *Co-sponsored by the Vinson Hall Students.*

———

"No," Ben replied over the phone, "I didn't know Bibb marched last Spring with Dick Gregory and other entertainers in Mississippi and the South against racial segregation." ... "No. No idea that Harry Belafonte and Joan Baez were some of those." ... "Did see Baez sing at that big rally Martin Luther King led in Washington, last August" ... "No, wasn't aware Bibb and others were blacklisted for their stand."

Laughter suddenly broke out around the corner of the basement hallway near the southwest entrance leading to the parking lot.

Ben's caller asked, "What's the noise?"

He replied with a deep laugh, "It's Dale Swiggett and another from their hometown of Lahoma. They just returned from a weekend trip, and a few of their so-called friends came to help carry in their stuff. ... Probably because they usually have some of their Mom's baked goodies. But," Ben laughed again, "Swig's been known to spike them with chocolate Ex-Lax."

As the noise faded down the hall, Ben continued where they'd left off, "At least, Bibb can still tour and perform at places like Northwestern." ... "Okay, I'll tell 'em."

Roomies, brother Glen and H. L. Brown, peppered Ben with questions the moment he walked through the door. He exclaimed, "Hold on! Hold on!" as he tried to maintain a sad-face. "I have bad news, and good. Whadda ya want first?"

Before they replied, he continued, "Here's the bad. We're not picking the girls up to go to the Bibb concert."

"Huh? Thought they were excited that Bibb was performing at Northwestern," Glen replied, as H. L. nodded in agreement.

"So, no need to air up the tires and get the car running," H. L. expressed, as a smile crossed his face.

"Yup!" Ben stated, "But…"

"That's the good news?" Glen interrupted.

"Nope," Ben responded, "Girls will meet us at Herod Hall. Afterwards, walk 'em to the dorm before the 10:00PM curfew."

H. L. teased with a jingle to his voice and a few dance moves, "Four girls, and three guys, Two for me."

"Dreamin'," Glen shot back in a sarcastic tone.

"And no kissy-face in the bushes," Ben teased with a grin. "Reserved for the Big Guy here!"

"Nope!" retorted H. L., "You and Glen have to save your strength for Langston University Saturday." … "Better buckle your chin-straps. Two black guys against an all-black team."

After the fun evening, photos and a note were prepared for *Northwestern's Ranger Annual: Folk singer, Leon Bibb scored a solid hit with a student audience that filled Herod Hall Auditorium, October 28*[th].

Folk singer Leon Bibb, shown here with his guitarist, Stuart Scharf, and Charles Fischer, who gave technical assistance backstage, scored a solid hit with a student audience filling Herod Hall auditorium October 28.

Leon Bibb performed to a packed house in Northwestern Herod Hall. He was so popular he was booked as the main attraction in the 'Big Show' for Northwestern's next home-coming. Courtesy use from Northwestern.

23.

MIRACLE GAME AT EASTERN
NEW MEXICO UNIVERSITY

November 9, 1963, Roadtrip to Eastern New Mexico University
Northwestern Oklahoma State University

"Any idea why Coach wants to see us?" Receiver Ken Strunk asked running back Ed 'Butch' Amerin.

"None," Butch replied.

"Want to see us?" Strunk asked, as he and Amerin poked their heads into Coach Art Parkhurst's office.

"Uh, yes," Parkhurst replied, after seeing who spoke. "Come in." As they walked inside, he continued, "We're at Eastern New Mexico this weekend, it'll be overnight, and we'll bunk 4 players to a room." Coach closed the file drawer and looked intensely into Strunk's eyes and then Amerin's. "Any problems bunking with Ben and Glen Smith?"

The question startled the two football players, and a pained look crossed their faces. Simultaneously, they glanced at each other with a look of: *Why is he asking this of us? Season's about over, and never had an issue with them!* They replied with a nod, "No."

24.

November 9, 1963, Miracle at Eastern New Mexico
Portales, New Mexico

The beat-up boxer, sprawled on the canvas floor, was barely able to open his eyes, as the referee yelled and signaled a ten-count: "One!" ... "Two!" ... "Three!"

Half the crowd screamed, "Get up! Get up!"

The other half countered with, "Stay down! Stay down!"

"Four!" ... "Five!" The boxer somehow raised his head and upper body. "Six!" ... "Seven!"

"Stay down!" ... "Get up!"

He struggled to his knees. "Eight!" ... "Nine!" Then to his feet, and was saved from "Ten" and a knockout. At least, until the next round.

In the same way, the Northwestern football team staggered into the dressing room at half-time of the Eastern New Mexico University homecoming game trailing 27 to 7. A second-half knockout seemed likely, unless a miracle occurred.

"Get off your feet!" "Rest!" "Get off your feet!" admonished trainers, as they tended to the injuries and passed out drinks to the discouraged players entering the large dressing room.

Coaches tried to hide the anguish from the first-half thumping, but the look on Coach Parkhurst's face seemed to be someone with really bad news for a family—"It's time to unplug the life-support."

Everyone could hear his frustration, "Offensive line, you're not blocking anyone! Nowhere for backs to run. Defense not stopping them either, and on the field too long!"

His anguish seemed to cause a loss for words and slowly he looked around the room again. The silence dominated, except for the heavy breathing from the frustrated players. A whisper in a far corner would've sounded like a train whistle at a crossing.

"Coach," a voice broke the silence. All eyes turned to senior offense lineman, Jack Kippenberger, sprawled on the floor and leaning against a wall. "Coach, ... We're blocking. Just seems like their whole defense knows what play we're going to run and stacks up there."

Others nodded agreement, and all eyes turned to see how Parkhurst would respond, but a referee entered at that moment and said, "Ten minutes before second-half kickoff, Coach."

Parkhurst nodded, turned back to face Kippenberger and asked, "Any suggestions?"

"Let's run that unbalanced formation like we did a few days ago in practice. Same plays. Only needs a couple linemen switch blocking, and backs hit the right hole." When he noticed the puzzled look on Parkhurst's face and his glance at the other coaches for an explanation, he told them, "It was at the end of practice after coaches left early to scout some high schools."

Parkhurst glanced at the other coaches again, then at his watch and replied in a frustrated tone, "Well, what we were running wasn't working. ... Do it, if we can."

End of game: Northwestern 35, Eastern New Mexico 27.

After the hoopla of winning died down and the bus had been loaded, players settled down for the long trip back to Northwestern and Alva, Oklahoma.

"Don't think they enjoyed their homecoming," Roids Garrison quipped to fellow lineman, Bill Mitchell, seated next to him in the bus seat.

Mitchell nodded and added, "Huge crowd, but we had a few fans along with our great cheerleaders." He paused. "Too bad Senate President

Larry Layman wasn't able to arrange that train ride for Northwestern students from Alva out here."

A couple rows back, receiver Glen Smith commented to Butch Amerin, as they relived the game, "Backs had a great second-half today."

"Yeah, it was fun! Line opened holes. Think we had over 300 yards."

"You must've had half of those. That long run was a beauty. You'll probably be on Eastern's All-Opponent Team."

"Don't know about that. At least, we won," Amerin replied. "You had a good game yourself. That catch in the end zone looked higher than the crossbar."

"Thanks. Massey threw it where no one else was gonna catch it."

Amerin chuckled, "Probably really just throwing it away. Great catch anyway. Maybe you should go out for basketball."

"Basketball coach suggested that strongly to Ben and me."

"If you do, you and H. L. Brown will be the first blacks to ever play basketball at Northwestern, right?"

"Guess so, but not the reason Ben or I play," Smith replied. Both of the players tried to snooze after that, but were still wide-awake a couple hours down the road. "Defense played lights-out in the second-half, too," Glen mumbled.

"You're right. They shut Eastern out. Even scored a touchdown themselves on Bobby Steven's interception."

"Yeah," Smith replied with a laugh. "Did you hear what Savoy, who was running just behind Stephens, say to him afterwards? 'Next time if you don't lateral to me when you have 2 guys in front of you to tackle you, I'll tackle you myself!'"

Amerin laughed. "He probably meant it." A few minutes passed, and he added above the clacking sound of the tires hitting the grooves in the pavement, "Glad we don't have to spend another night with a sick Strunk."

"Yeah, least he recovered enough to play in the second-half."

Two more hours down the road, a wide-awake Mitchell poked Garrison in the side and asked, "You awake?"

Garrison slowly grumbled a reply, "I am now."

"Glad your parents could come to the game."

"Yeah, nice. Dalhart's just across the Texas line. Not far from Portales, New Mexico. Parents enjoyed seeing you again." After a pause, he asked, "Your Dad still coming next game?"

"Yes," Mitchell responded gleefully. "Arrives Friday."

*1963 Northwestern players (L-R): Jack Kippenberger, Ed
'Butch' Amerine, Glen Smith, and Bobby Stephens
Courtesy of Northwestern Game Program*

25.

NEWS SPECIAL — PRESIDENT
JOHN F. KENNEDY ASSASSINATED

November 22, 1963,
President John F. Kennedy is assassinated News Specials,
Vinson Hall TV Lounge
Northwestern Oklahoma State University

The sun flooded its warmth across the United States on this November day, much like others in the month. By sundown, though, every adult and many youngsters probably remembered where they were, who with, and what doing when they heard the terrible news.

Not long after those deadly gunshots echoed around Dealey Plaza in Dallas, Texas and the startled pigeons settled back down on top of a seven-story book depository, a student burst onto the floor of the Northwestern fieldhouse gym and exclaimed, "President Kennedy's been shot, maybe killed!" Everyone in the half-court basketball games stopped in their tracks, like they'd been turned into statues; and the large place became funeral-parlor quiet, except for the sound of many basketballs dropping to the floor.

It was Friday, November 22nd. Football season had just ended, and I, Clifton Savoy, was standing at the left-side of the free-throw line on the north court. Big Ben Smith and I were guarding each other. Within seconds and without a sound, the 30-or-so sweaty statues returned to life and left the gym to find a radio or TV for more news. Ben and I hustled across the parking lot to the TV lounge of Vinson Hall and found it packed and overflowing out its two entrance doors into the hallway.

We couldn't hear the TV sound, as we approached, but we could see various Texas scenes fading in and out on the screen: President John F. Kennedy and his wife, Jacqueline, at a luncheon in San Antonio a day earlier; the President's breakfast speech in Ft. Worth that Friday morning; Air Force One rolling to a stop at Love Field in Northwest Dallas and President Kennedy and Jacqueline greeting the hundreds of people along a fence; waving to the thousands from his open convertible as the motorcade moved through downtown Dallas; and the Trade Mart where a Dallas-who's who crowd awaited the President to speak at noon.

President John F. Kennedy and wife, Jacqueline, in Dallas motorcade shortly before being assassinated on November 22, 1963. National Archives.

A student near the front of the TV lounge responded to a question, "Yeah. Just got back from the cafeteria, and caught a bit of *As the World Turns.* 'Bout half-way (12:40 p.m. CST), CBS news interrupted, and a voice that sounded like Walter Cronkite came on to say, "President Kennedy's been badly wounded in downtown Dallas. Three shots were fired." Another student added, "Yeah, heard it, too. Also, that Mrs. Kennedy screamed and grabbed the President." After a pause, he continued, "Sounded like it was fatal!"

"Wow! How'd it happen?"

"Betcha a sniper,," another student blurted his 2-cents worth. "Had to be trained like one to hit a moving target."

As Ben and I maneuvered our way to where we could see the TV—actually, I followed the opening his big body created to some standing room along a wall—a student near the TV yelled, "Sh-h-h! Maybe this is new information!" The lounge became deathly-quiet and every eye was glued to the TV screen.

CBS news special—Dallas: The TV cameras panned over the Trade Mart. The anguished looks told the story. Eddie Barker reported, "... As to the story he (President Kennedy) is dead, this cannot (yet) be confirmed. Another (story) is Governor Connally is in the operating room; this we have not confirmed." In the TV background, the presidential seal was seen being removed from the speaker's podium.

"These are just repeats," grumbled a student, "Kennedy was scheduled to speak at the Trade Mart after the motorcade through downtown Dallas. Nothing new. Check another station."

ABC news special—Dallas (1:33 p.m. CST): The TV picture revealed reporter (Cochran), who said in a solemn tone, "Two priests, who administered the last rites to the President, said, 'He had died from his wounds.'" The camera faded to a photo on the screen of the President with the words "JOHN F. KENNEDY -- 1917–1963."

"That's a repeat, too. Check the other station."

News flash—Dallas: "This just in... at 1:15 p.m. Central Standard Tine, a Dallas police officer was shot dead... Thirteen people witnessed the shooting and a man fleeing the scene. It's not known if this is connected to the shooting of the President."

"Heard that earlier!"

"Oh, pipe down," grumbled a student standing in the doorway, "Some of us been in class, and we haven't heard anything."

Another beside him added, "Turn back to CBS. It may have more."

CBS News Special: Cronkite talked about Kennedy's trip, and in Fort Worth earlier that day. The President flew to his "rendezvous with death, apparently, in Dallas." An employee could be seen handing a sheet of paper to Cronkite, who put on his glasses, took a few seconds to read the message: "From Dallas, apparently official: PRESIDENT KENNEDY DIED AT 1 P.M. Central Standard Time, 2:00 Eastern Standard Time, some 38 minutes ago." Cronkite then removed his glasses, looked at the studio clock, paused briefly with a look of inward reflection—visibly moved by the news—and replaced the glasses. "Vice President Johnson..." He paused to clear his throat, "...has left the hospital in Dallas. Presumably, he will be taking the oath of office shortly and become the 36th President of the United States."

A heavy gloom settled on the Vinson Hall TV lounge, as reality thrust a dagger into our thoughts: *President John F. Kennedy is dead.* The Northwestern campus was noticeably solemn the rest of that weekend and into the short week that followed for the Thanksgiving break. For me, Mom's yummy pumpkin custard pie and turkey and, along with seeing family and friends, thoughts of the Kennedy assassination, and Lee Harvey Oswald's, too, on live TV, would be pushed out of mind. Also, there was pheasant and quail hunting, and even Snipe hunting adventures for 'greenhorns' who needed an introduction to western Oklahoma country life.

For me at that moment, a young guy still wet behind the ears in so many ways — like most everyone else I knew, the loss of a President was, well, just that: the loss of a President. One would replace him. Life, as I knew it, would continue.

Big Ben Smith was affected differently, though, but I didn't realize it for a while. The more we shared personal moments, and put bits and pieces together over the next few years, I looked back in time and realize he probably wondered, *Did the meaningful civil rights—freedom and justice—also die with President Kennedy?*

———

Author Note: As information pieces of the Kennedy assassination have come to be known and released to the public over the years, a recall of the day brings back memories and questions:

Dallas, Texas—A sniper tracked the target in the cross-hairs, as the presidential convertible moved through Dealey Plaza. A shot, fired from the eastern-most 6th floor window of the Texas Schoolbook Depository came moments after 12:30 p.m. CST. Two more quickly followed. A Parkland Hospital surgeon was overheard to sadly say, "Never knew what hit him."

At 12:33 p.m., Lee Harvey Oswald, who'd been on a $1.25 per hour job at the Depository only a few weeks, walked un-noticed out its front door into the spectator chaos of the shooting. He then walked seven blocks to catch a bus part-way to his boarding house. In less than an hour, he'd also kill Police Officer J. D. Tippet and, in just over 48 hours, Oswald would be shot dead on live TV by Jacob Leon Rubenstein, known as Jack Ruby, a local night-club owner.

Questions on many minds: Why is the federal government still withholding some information? Did Oswald act alone or was there also someone on the 'grassy knoll'? If alone, why would a U.S citizen, with little money to his name, travel to Mexico City and visit both the Cuban and Russian Embassies just prior to obtaining his job at the Book Depository? How did he acquire the low-paying job at the Depository and just weeks prior to Kennedy's Dallas trip and open-car motorcade, moving slowly by the Depository? Was there a connection between Ruby and someone else? Among other questions, was there a connection in the assassination of President John F. Kennedy to that of his brother, Robert F. Kennedy, in 1968 in Los Angeles?

26.

TOP NEWS OF 1963: CIVIL RIGHTS,
KENNEDY ASSASSINATION, VIETNAM

December 31ˢᵗ, Top Stories of 1963
National News, TV Lounge of Vinson Hall
Northwestern Oklahoma State University

An icy-tear slid down Old Man Winter's chubby cheek, as the last car-load of joyous Northwestern students drove away for the 1963 Christmas break. A lonely expression covered his face, as he mumbled in a frustrated tone, "This is no fun." He kicked at a snow pile like a child throwing a tantrum, blasted wind gusts across campus, and sent powdery snow off roofs and swirling down sidewalks. "No one here to dump snow on or…" He paused as a mischievous grin appeared, "… Cause to fall on my ice."

He wasn't about to toss in the towel, though, as there always was some type of havoc he could cause. *Any unprotected water faucets I can freeze and break?* "Aha!" he exclaimed with a slight grin as he caught sight of tree-limbs hanging over the campus house of Northwestern President Jesse W. Martin. "My freezing rain'll break 'em."

Before he could do much damage, a warm snap pushed him westward towards the Rockies for a week. He'd barely returned to the campus and unpacked with his blast of freezing cold and sleet when something caught his eye. A lone figure slowly moved from building to building.

Hmm, he mused. *Moves like one of those country rabbits, hopping around in my snow, bush-to-bush looking for food.* "Aw rats! Just a security guard," he grumbled. "They're no fun—too serious about their work."

"Br-r-r," the guard mumbled as a foggy cloud from his breath trailed behind like one of those old smoky, steam-engine trains. The wind-chill increased the numbness in his hands and feet with each step. He quickened his pace. *Vinson Hall just ahead. I'll walk through the building and warm a little.* To his surprise, the door didn't open. *Locked? Why? … Oh, yes. Forgot. New Year's Eve. … Students still away.*

If Vinson had been open, the guard might've paused at the TV lounge to warm up some, and heard reports of the top news stories of 1963 broadcast nationwide.

News Special: The reporter declared, "The top story of 1963 is the assassination of John F. Kennedy, the 35th President of the United States in Dallas, Texas, on Friday November 22, 1963, almost 100 years after the shooting assassination of Abraham Lincoln in 1865. Initial reports of the FBI and other investigators point to a lone gunman. Lee Harvey Oswald carried out the assassination. Reports concluded that Oswald also killed Dallas Police Officer J. D. Tippit shortly afterwards and was himself killed on live TV by Dallas nightclub owner, Jack Ruby, 48 hours later. However, a number of questions about whether Oswald acted alone continue to be asked. Among them: Oswald visited both the Russian and Cuban Embassies in Mexico City just a few weeks prior to the assassination. Certainly, both Russia and Cuba had a continuing opposition to the Kennedy Administration from the 1962-63 Russian-Missile Crisis in Cuba. And there was the bounty Kennedy reportedly placed on the Castro Brothers. Also, the southern and northern segregationists have been mentioned, as President Kennedy had submitted strong civil rights legislation to Congress. Even though Kennedy had backing of the Republicans, with him out of the way, its future is uncertain. Also, internationally, it's rumored there may have been payback to the Kennedy administration as it declined to stop the overthrow of the Diem Regime of South Vietnam and killing the two brothers by the generals in early November. And, there's the questions involving the employment of Oswald just weeks before the shooting, and the technical aspects of the gun's rapid fire. It's unofficial but a special commission to look into these questions and give closure to the public has been mentioned."

———

"Another top story," the reporter continued, "Is the civil rights movement. The August march on Washington, D.C., for freedom and jobs by a quarter of a million, mostly black individuals, led by Dr. Martin Luther King, Jr., and others, made a prominent impact on national TV."

"Also, in August, Air Force veteran, James Meredith made history as the first Negro to graduate at the University of Mississippi at Oxford. His journey started a year earlier with deadly riots and killings to keep and enforce segregation. Hundreds of U.S. Marshalls were needed the whole time to ensure Meredith's safety."

"Still," the reporter sadly continued, "bombings and death continued against desegregation activities. Four young girls were killed in the September bombing during Sunday services of the 16th Street Baptist Church of Birmingham, Alabama. King described it as, 'A holy war for freedom and human dignity.' The bombing was the 3rd to Negro homes and churches in Birmingham in 11 days after a court order mandated schools be desegregated. Bombings also occurred in Mississippi, other states, and cities."

"Now, with the death of Kennedy, passage of meaningful civil rights legislation is uncertain under President Lyndon B. Johnson. In the 1957 and 1960 Democrat-controlled Senate, the 2nd and 3rd Civil Rights Acts were passed, but were reduced by then Senator Johnson and other democrat leaders to acts of mere symbolism by gutting its enforcement provisions."

———

"Vietnam is a top story; specifically, the increasing involvement of the

U.S. Since April, the role no longer was just trainers and advisors in South Vietnam, but now combat troops manned guns. And, just weeks before the Kennedy assassination, the nine-year rule of Ngo Dinh Diem came to a bloody end by their deaths by a revolt of fourteen top military officers. Sources say the Kennedy administration knew about the coup. South Vietnam First Lady, Madam Nu, expressed, "A dirty crime has been committed and the U.S. is responsible." The new rulers affirmed they will fight the spread of communism, but it's uncertain what the U.S. involvement in Vietnam will be under the Johnson administration. The U.S. suffered 122 casualties in Vietnam in 1963, bringing the total since involvement in 1956 to 198."

Old Man Winter grinned, as the guard turned away from Vinson Hall. "Maybe, just maybe," he whispered wishfully, "he won't notice my ice on the sidewalk ahead, and…" he added with delirious laughter as he skipped across campus, "Basketballers and the other students'll be back by weekend. I'll be ready for 'em."

27.

HE'S BLACK AND AWOL!
LOCK HIM UP! MEET L'ZAR

January 1964, He's AWOL So Lock Him Up!
Northwestern Oklahoma State University

A cold January wind greeted Curtis Thompson with a slap on the face, as he stepped slowly off the bus. Nervously, he glanced around, somewhat expecting police to meet him. Seeing no one, he stretched, as it'd been a long ride from Oklahoma City, where he left in the middle of the night instead of being bussed out at 6 a.m. to military training at Ft. Polk, Louisiana.

The noon sunlight, filtered by dull-grey clouds, reflected off his black forehead and cheeks, as he looked around again at the bus stop on the eastern edge of town. *So, this is Alva...*

Not many black people came through these parts, and the folks inside the bus depot and café gave Thompson, a slow country-look-over, as he entered. Curiosity satisfied, they soon resumed eating or about their other business.

The tantalizing smells from the short-order food area punched Thompson hard in the stomach. He put his hand in his jeans pocket, hoping, even though he knew nothing was there, as he'd spent his last $5 for his bus ticket. Waiting his turn, he moseyed-up next to the check-out counter in hopes a free mouth mint might be available. *No such luck!*

When the burly man behind the far-end of the counter wasn't busy with someone else, Thompson moved towards him and quietly asked, "Which way to the Northwestern campus?"

The man glanced up, momentarily from what he was doing, pointed with his, arm and said in the same business-tone he spoke to other customers, "Couple miles west down that road."

"Thanks," Thompson mumbled, and headed out the door. Now walking a few miles was no big deal for him, as in his younger days around small-town Harris, in the southeastern tip of Oklahoma, he and other black kids walked almost everywhere. Time was running out for this day, though, with no money, food, or place to stay tonight

Soon, he'd walked half a mile, with his few belongings tucked under an arm, when the sound of a pick-up, pulling up quickly from behind, startled him. After all, a vehicle pulling up to a black person in deep southeastern Oklahoma, an area called, Little Dixie, historically didn't always turn out well.

The cold wind whipped at Thompson's jacket, and he watched nervously, as the passenger door opened. The driver yelled out, "Heard you're headed to Northwestern."

Thompson nodded and mumbled in a somewhat stunned-tone, "Yes," to a young white girl near his age.

"Well," she replied in a friendly tone, as a smile came on her face. "Hop in. I'm headed that way." She introduced herself, as Thompson climbed into the cab. He did the same.

Another half mile or so, Thompson spotted a Sonic, and sharp food pangs hit him again. The hunger was immediately forgotten, though, as he found himself busy answering the girl's questions about his connection to Northwestern.

"Let me see if I understand what you're saying," she told him in a disbelieving voice, as she glanced frequently at him. "You've never been to Alva or Northwestern? You're not enrolled there? No one there knows you are coming? And, you expect to play on the basketball team?"

"Yes," Thompson answered in a confident voice, which led to more questions. His last response stunned her.

"You mean to tell me, the reason you decided to come to Northwestern is you thought, since Alva was so close to Kansas, there would be lots of black students enrolled?"

She glanced to see his nod, then continued, "Well, you are in for a big surprise. From articles in the paper, there seems to be only three black athletes who play football and basketball. Also, heard there are only three or four black girls. That's it."

As the reality of her comments sunk in, Thompson's lips tightened and his brow furrowed. *Only a few black students?* The disappointment was immediately forgotten, though, as they turned at that moment into the front entrance of the Northwestern campus and parked.

The young girl nodded towards a building, and told him as she stepped out of the pick-up, "Here's where you can talk to the administrators about what you would like to do."

In what seemed like a whirl-wind experience, Thompson talked to several administrators each one higher ranked than the last. As he came out of each office, he noticed the young girl still nearby. Before long, a person came to usher him to the Office of President Jesse W. Martin, and Thompson turned to thank the girl for her kindness, but she had disappeared. *What was her name?* He was disappointed he couldn't remember.

"Curtis..." a seasoned-looking old man—everyone above fifty looks like old people to young college students—in a dark suit greeted Thompson. "Curtis Thompson?"

"Yes sir," Thompson replied, not knowing what to expect.

"Come, sit down," President Martin requested in a quiet voice.

After what seemed to Thompson like hours, Martin spoke. "Staff tells me you want to enroll at Northwestern."

"Yes sir," Thompson answered with a nod.

President Martin looked him squarely in the face. "They also say you have a draft problem. Maybe AWOL."

"Yes," Thompson responded in a subdued, apologetic tone, and then told the whole story of his desire to enroll at Northwestern, play basketball, and major in math. He wanted to teach and coach someday. When he came to the part about the military draft and his last 48-hours, he handed his induction papers to President Martin.

January 1964, Curtis Thompson, "Greetings: You are hereby ordered for induction into the Armed Forces of the United States..." Induction Station, Robinson Ave, Oklahoma City, Oklahoma. Lodging: Huckins Hotel. 6:00 a.m. breakfast and 7:00 a.m. induction physical...

President Martin looked slowly through the papers, and studied them for a while... Then he looked again at Thompson, eye-to-eye. "You say you passed the physical, and then left the hotel in the middle of the night to catch a bus to Alva instead of being shipped out with the other inductees for training?"

"Yes sir," Thompson replied in an almost whisper.

President Martin flipped slowly through the induction papers again. When he finished, he looked at Thompson for a while without saying a word... Before long, he spoke, "Stay here," as he stood and walked from the room.

After a while, President Martin returned to a nervous Thompson, "I'll see what I can do about your military draft problem. We'll put you up overnight in Shockley Hall, and Mr. Noel Taylor, manager of the

Student Union Cafeteria will feed you a couple of meals. My assistant will have someone walk you to those places. Come back in the morning, and we'll see how your problems turn out."

Thompson's face burst into an ear-to-ear grin as he stood quickly and exclaimed, "Yes sir!"

Next morning, Thompson met President Martin, as instructed. "Good news for you, Curtis. The military will postpone your induction, but you'll receive an order to report about every six months. If you are making academic progress, you'll receive another postponement. Bring that notice to me, and I'll send a confirmation if you are a student in good standing. Understand?"

"Yes sir!" Thompson exclaimed in a giddy tone.

"My assistant will walk you down to Academic Affairs, where you'll enroll and obtain a voucher for books and supplies. Mr. Noel Taylor says he has a cafeteria student worker position where you can earn your tuition, books, food and lodging. I've contacted Northwestern's basketball coach, Keith Covey, of your desire to play, and he'll talk to you about that. Says to come to the gymnasium offices. A varsity player named, John Altramura, will walk you around and meet the other players."

Thompson's head was spinning from the great news, and he could barely mumble the words, "Thank you, sir."

"You're most welcome," President Martin replied, as he walked Thompson to the door. Before Thompson walked out of sight, around the corner, he added, "Good luck."

When President Martin's assistant returned, she peered into his office. He sat quietly at his desk, deep into another Northwestern issue. She watched for a moment. *Just another day at the office. But will anyone ever know of the warm reception, treatment, and hope for the future President Martin and Northwestern just gave to young Curtis Thompson…* She sighed sadly, as she returned to her work. *Probably not!*

28.

January 1964, L'Zar
Northwestern Oklahoma State University

Like a wild-fire powered across the prairie by wind gusts up one gorge and down another, a rumor spread rapidly across the Northwestern campus, "There's a gay guy here!" A student added fuel, "Heard his name is L'Zar (Anonymous name)." Another piped in, "He's a foreigner, from…, I think." And the embers spread. "He has dark hair, and a dark-olive complexion." Quickly, the wildfire made its way to Vinson Hall.

Step into a group of guys, and you might've heard a joke or two, even though, few of us had any idea what a gay guy was. Most of us would've had a rural town or farm or ranch background, where the bull-cow and male-female breeding would've been, at the least, a not-so-subtle part of the foundation to our sexual education. Of course, that knowledge would've made its way into group talks with our rural-town friends.

But, with homosexuality, many were in the dark. In fact, when I enrolled as a freshman, I'd never even heard the word, let alone known what it meant. Same with everyone I knew, but that didn't stop the talk, pretending we knew, and teasing. With the rumors, wild stories followed—each larger than the preceding one.

Not long after I experienced a group session of this wild-fire, I was headed to the student center from Vinson Hall, and I panicked at what I saw! *Oh, my gosh! That L'Zar guy is coming down the walk towards me!* All the rumors I'd heard raced through my mind. *What do I do? Think, Savoy, come up with a plan. Aha, I know. I'll ignore him, and pass on by.*

But I unconsciously nodded and said, "Howdy," though. My being raised in the Oklahoma Panhandle where folks nodded or lifted a hand off the steering wheel to say, "Howdy," when meeting another vehicle on the rural roads, controlled my actions. *Oops! Maybe he didn't notice.* Trying not to panic, I walked on by.

Immediately, he called out my name and in a melodic way, "Clif...ton."

I walked on a few more steps. *Did he just say my name?* I stopped, and glanced around to see if anyone noticed. *Didn't see anyone.* I turned slightly towards him.

Before I said anything, he asked, "Would you sign this picture?" He held a newspaper clipping towards me. It was photos and story of the Northwestern footballers who'd been selected to the 1963 Oklahoma Collegiate Conference team: Jack Kippenberger, Billy Foster, Bob Stephens, Bill Massey, and me, Clifton Savoy.

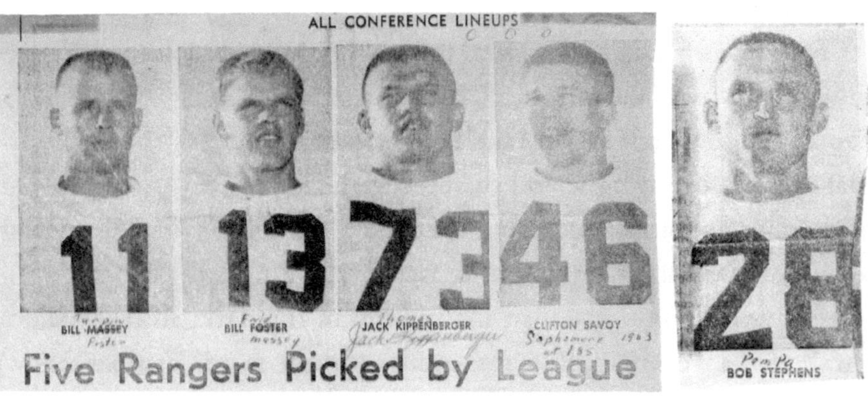

I lost myself in the moment, big head and all, as I'd been asked for an autograph only a couple times before this. Now, frankly, a pleasurable feeling took control of my senses and flushed my face—everyone likes to be recognized for their performances. And, this was my first for college football.

Still, I could hear the tease, "Clifton's got a queer friend. Clifton's got a queer friend."

Just as I started to sign the clipping, he blurted out, "Sign it, 'Donk.'"

Immediately, I jerked backward, as this was a nick-name thrust on me by some of the footballers. With L'Zar, I assumed the worst, and my temper flared.

My eyes probably bulged outwardly, as I raised my voice, "I know what you are, L'Zar!" I felt the heat of anger as it flushed my face. "I'll be friendly, but if you ever touch me or make a move on me, I'll beat the you-know-what out of you!"

I guess L'Zar understood, but I don't recall ever seeing him or hearing his name again at Northwestern... And, yes... I autographed his photo clipping... but with, "Clifton."

29.

1964 NORTHWESTERN BASKETBALL.
"HOW DO YOU GET IT OFF?"

February 1964, "… Get to it!"
Northwestern Oklahoma State University

"Okay, fifty free throws, and a fast lap for each miss! Get to it!" admonished Northwestern basketball Coach Keith Covey to the varsity players. He challenged them, as he momentarily looked away and tossed some practice shirts to team trainer, Joe Hoover, who gathered equipment nearby. "Focus on your form! … Help your team!"

Assistant Coach Chirold Epp had already sent the JV to the locker room. Big Ben Smith was one of the few JV still around when the varsity players started to arrive after their practice. His brother Glen and Curtis Thompson were among the first, and H.L. Brown appeared a few minutes later, exchanging friendly, but aggressive, ribbing with fellow freshman players, Bob Drake and Larry Prochnau. "You guys have 5-6 inches on me, but I probably can outjump you."

"In your dreams," shot back Prochnau, as he looked around for a cold towel or something to throw on H.L.

"Yeah, you twerp!" Drake exclaimed teasingly, and also looked for something to douse H.L.'s taunting. "We'll see!"

Big Ben finished dressing about the time as H. L. and asked him, "We still playing ping pong at the Baptist Union after eating?"

"Yeah," H. L. nodded, "But it's just you and me unless we pick up someone else."

"Whadda ya mean?" Ben asked. Then he noticed both Glen and Thompson had dressed and left without saying anything.

H. L. noticed his inquisitive look. "Your brother is attracted to one of the girls. Said he was going to walk her back to Oklahoma Hall after eating."

"Waste of time," Ben replied as a grimace tightened the corners of his mouth. "If it's who I think, she has a friend back home—a close friend."

"Yeah," H. L. chuckled, "But ya never know 'til ya try."

"What about Thompson?"

"Said he had a better offer." He continued when he noticed another puzzled look. "Said there are two sets of twins, girls, who work with him in the cafeteria. They've invited Thompson to a Christian Church just north of campus. It has a study area and game room in the basement. Beverly and Barbara Biggs name of one set, but don't remember the names of the other twins."

"Yeah, sure," Ben replied in a doubtful tone, as a big grin covered his face. "Going there to study with four girls? ... And games?" He laughed and added, "Thompson'll have to tell us all about his adventure!"

At that moment, the sound of Drake's voice across the room to Jim Schroeder caught their attention. "What about them?" Big Ben asked. "Think I've seen them there, too."

"Nope, forget it! Drake's crazy in the head about Judy Wolgamott. When he sees her at the cafeteria, he won't even know we're around." After a moment of laughter, H. L. added, "Should've seen him in the basketball game. Ball went out of bounds by Wolgamott and the rest of the cheerleaders. Drake just had to be the one standing close to her, and throw in the ball."

"Okay, let's get Schroeder and pick up another. He's usually there."

"Forget him, too!" H. L. replied with a laugh. "There's a pair of short-shorts at the Vinson Hall girls annex that's had his attention lately."

"Him, too?" Ben asked as he rolled his eyes. He didn't wait for a reply, "Aw, let's go and maybe we'll team up with somebody new." … As they passed through the dressing room doors, Ben chuckled. "We can always play singles, and I'll give you another whoopin'."

"Dreamin', Big Man!"

30.

February 1964, Basketball Team Road Trip
Innocence of a Child
Panhandle Oklahoma State University at Goodwill, OK

Deep thoughts, life-changing ones, filled Northwestern basketball player H. L. Brown's mind as he stared out the athletic bus window at the wide-open Oklahoma Panhandle country-side and the brilliant spread of stars above.

Oklahoma Panhandle Starry Night© used with permission by
Arlene Wynfree of Guymon, Oklahoma.

"The heavens declare the glory of God…" (Psalm 19:1).

"I'll never forget this day!" He slowly mouthed, but so low no one heard him above the hum of the tires on the highway. "…Never."

"You alright?" Larry Prochnau asked in a concerned tone, as he looked at his friend and teammate, who sat in the seat beside him. H. L. glanced at him, and Prochnau added, "You've stared out that window since we left Panhandle an hour ago." Prochnau paused and then asked, "You sick or something?"

H. L. glanced at him again, shook his head, "No," and resumed his stare out the window.

"Well, something's up." Prochnau pressed. "Upset 'cause we played poorly? Lost 74 – 81?"

H. L. kept looking out at the star-lite country side, but shook his head as he responded. "No, that's not it… But, we should-da won. Schroeder and Inman played good. We're better!"

A long silence set in, and H. L. continued staring outside. After a while, he mumbled softly, "It's so bright out there… See farm buildings in the distance… Even drive without car lights."

A few minutes later, H. L. turned to face his friend and began to touch on the deep thoughts of his mind. "Proc… remember when we first arrived at the Panhandle gym in our street clothes today?" He continued without Prochnau answering, "How there were about ten small kids shooting baskets? Well, one boy about six, maybe seven came up to me. Took my hand. Rubbed the back side. Looked up at me. Then rubbed and looked up at me again. He looked into my eyes and asked so seriously, 'How do you get it off?'"

The words stunned Prochnau and, for a long time afterwards, neither said anything. … Eventually, H. L. whispered over his shoulder as he continued his gaze at the star-lit countryside, "Guess we're all like that until we're taught something else."

31.

NATIONAL NEWS: ROADBLOCKS TO 1964 CIVIL RIGHTS ACT, VIETNAM

March 29, 1964, National News
TV Lounge of Vinson Hall
Northwestern Oklahoma State University

"Those boys!" Ma Griggs exclaimed in frustration. "What am I going to do with 'em? … TV blaring, no one around, and the lounge left in a mess!" In a way, a subtle response seemed to come from the clatter of a soda bottle hitting the floor, as she moved a chair. Dark juice oozed onto the floor. "Snuff spit!" she blurted hotly and with a repulsive grimmace. As she wiped it up with a rag, she mumbled in an angry tone, "I'd like to get my hands on who did this." She continued to express how she felt. "Lounge is packed for programs like *Bonanza*, *Gunsmoke*, *Combat*, *The Virginian*, *Beverly Hillbillies*, or sports; but where's the cleanup afterwards?"

A couple of her boys stuck their heads into the doorway, and she gave them a stern look. "Uh, oh." one whispered to the other, "Ma's on the war path. Best get outa here."

Not skipping a beat, Ma continued, "No! They wouldn't miss one of those programs. But national news or something no interest, and everyone disappears."

Through with cleaning, she reached to switch off the TV, but stopped, as what appeared next grabbed her interest.

News special — Washington, D.C.: "There's discord in the Capitol with…" a voice sounded in the background, "…President Lyndon B. Johnson's public comment that, 'No memorial oration or eulogy could more eloquently honor President Kennedy's

1964 Civil Rights Act, the 4ᵗʰ one!

memory than the earliest possible passage of the civil rights bill for which he fought so long.'"

A photo appeared of President Kennedy taken a few months prior to his assassination, and the reporter's voice continued, 'Kennedy asked for legislation, "Giving all Americans the right to be served in facilities which are open to the public—hotels, theaters, retail stores, restaurants, and similar places" as well as "protection for the right to vote."'

Hostile opposition and longest filibuster in U.S. Senate history!

As the reporter continued, "There is considerable, sometimes hostile, opposition," the picture faded to a view of the Capitol and then in and out to faces of several senators, including: J. William Fulbright (D-AR), Albert Gore, Sr. (D-TN), Robert Byrd (D-WV), Richard Russell (D-GA), and Strom Thurmond (D-SC)…"

"…Primarily, a block of Democrats in Congress, who've stated, 'There will be no passage.' They give various reasons, including: 'Three Civil Rights Acts have already been passed—1875, 1957, and 1960.' They ask, 'Why do we need another one?'"

The reporter added, "Several wondered off the record, 'What's Johnson up to with his about-face in support of Kennedy's civil Rights legislation?' They pointed out, 'Johnson didn't have a history in support of protecting black people.'" The reporter continued, "Under Johnson's leadership in the senate, the enforcement provisions of the 1957 Civil Rights Act were removed to where it was mere symbolism. And Johnson's

Democrats, after opponents subsequently attempted to restore them in the 1960 Act, again removed the enforcement teeth of the Act. 'So, they wondered, what's his end-game?' Sources said, 'A filibuster is probable, as Johnson's explanation isn't satisfactory, and 18 Democrats and 1 Republican will launch it tomorrow, March 30th, when the legislation comes before the full Senate.'"

Ma Griggs again reached to turn the TV off, but the next issue—lowering the voting age from 21 to 18—was beginning to be mentioned some around Vinson Hall and on campus.

News special — Washington, D.C.: "Another issue beginning to get traction in Congress with the increasing involvement in Vietnam," a reporter expressed, as a front view of the Capitol appeared on the screen, "…

Lowering voting age to eighteen!

is lowering, in behalf of young men, once they turn 18, being drafted into a war that can kill them without a voice in the matter. "If we're old enough to die for our country, we should be old enough to be part of the decision making!" … "And," they add, 'The draft board process is unfair, as a disproportionately higher percentage of poor and those with less influence in the local area are drafted and sent to war.'"

"They have a point," Ma Griggs said softly, as she switched the TV off. "My boys, at least most of them, probably have more maturity and responsibility on their farms and ranches and lives by age twelve to fourteen than most others do in their upper 20s. Not sure, though, many keep up on national politics and government issues that affect their daily lives." She flipped the lounge light off and added, "Guess we'll see."

32.

NORTHWESTERN'S FIRST STREAKER?
PIPESTEM AND 'WHITE EYES' SWIGGOT

April 1964, Northwestern's First Streaker?
Northwestern Oklahoma State University

As Joe Hoover walked to the Northwestern campus and classes, he agonized over his day. *Lots of work to do: final cleaning of basketball uniforms and towels—man, there's always lots of towels, and Coach Parkhurst wants to inventory the football equipment. When am I going to study?* Never crossed his mind, though, that by end of the day, he'd become a streaker.

Wham! The wire cage front above the athletic equipment counter rattled from the football purposely thrown against it. "Wake up!" shouted the Smith brothers, as they laughed at the sleepy-eyed student whose head rested on the stack of freshly folded towels. "Stop sleeping on the job!" exclaimed Big Ben with a deep belly laugh that could be heard in a few of the coaches' offices out the main entrance and down the hallway.

"Uh…" mumbled Hoover, the athletic department's 'do everything guru,' as his head jerked upward and body backward, with such force, he almost tipped over in the chair.

The Smiths bellowed with glee, as Hoover struggled to keep his balance. "Dreaming about some pretty girl?" teased Big Ben. His pearly whites beamed from the ear-to-ear grin.

Glen added, "Dreams like that could land you in jail!"

Players knew Hoover was a full-time student, but seemed he was always in the main men's dressing room, since he, basically, had some responsibility for everything in the athletic department except coaching and teaching. Need equipment? Hoover was the man. Need some physical rehab help? See Hoover. Uniforms and towels cleaned? Check with Hoover. And, if you need a good track time in the mile or two-mile race, Hoover can deliver.

As Hoover yawned and collected his thoughts, Big Ben added, "Come out to the field and throw passes with us."

Hoover shook his head, and replied, "Not my sport."

Glen asked, "Didn't you play high school football?"

Hoover rubbed his eyes as he replied. "Yeah, three years and two state championship teams, but… too much to do and Coach Parkhurst wants extra track work today. Conference Meet soon, and…" he reminded again as he looked them over, "I don't play football now."

"Aw, you're no fun," Big Ben replied in a teasing tone, as he and Glen headed out to the football field. At the same moment they passed through the exit door, Darrel Inman and Bill Massey entered the locker room.

"'Bout time you two turned in your basketball uniforms." Hoover scolded in a stern tone, as he tried to keep a serious face, "Coach Covey was about to send a posse to fetch 'em."

"Yeah! Yeah!" Inman and Massey answered with laughs.

"By the way, congrats," Hoover replied, "In being selected to the 1964 Conference Basketball Team."

"Just honorable mention," Inman replied in a humble tone. Massey nodded in agreement.

"Maybe so, but it's a recognition by the other conference coaches, and…" Hoover inserted a point, "some promote their players for recognition much better than others do. So, I think any conference recognition is an honor."

Inman and Massey smiled and nodded to acknowledge the compliment. They left quickly to work out for baseball or just have some physical fun in the warm sun.

As Hoover finished the last lap of his workout on the quarter track, he passed near the Smith brothers still on the football field. He laughed and taunted them, "Getting anything done, or you just faking it?" He heard a reply from back over his shoulder, but didn't understand them.

He was in the shower when the Smiths returned from their workout. As they walked past the back entrance, he heard Big Ben whisper, "When we shower, let's give 'em a bar soap enema."

"Yeah!" Glen gleefully responded with an ear-to-ear grin.

Friends or not, they sounded serious. So, Hoover darted out the front shower entrance.

"Hey, he's getting away!" Glen yelled. "Head 'im off!"

Hoover grabbed his clothes and shoes, and just as Big Ben reached for him, he burst out the main entrance double-doors and headed down the hallway.

Coach Parkhurst and track vaulter Chip Myers were talking about the new fiberglass pole and heard the ruckus. Parkhurst stepped part way out of his office door in time to see Hoover dripping wet and hobbling to slip on his underwear, and the Smith brothers laughing back at the locker room entrance. "Didn't you forget something?" Parkhurst asked with a laugh, as Hoover streaked by, past anyone working out in the gym, and out the entrance doors of the fieldhouse. No telling how many others saw the streaker, too.

Northwestern distance runners (L-R): Ron Goff, Bob Knoll, and Joe Hoover. Later as trainer, Hoover with all-conference Northwestern fullback, George Chastain. Courtesy Northwestern.

33.

April 1964, Pipestem and "White Eyes" Swiggot
Northwestern Oklahoma State University

The night was late—really late and, normally, the Northwestern Vinson Hall students would've been either sacked out or hitting the books. Something strange, very strange, though, was afoot on the top floor, south wing this night.

The scene could've easily been part of a Hitchcock cinema thriller where the imagination gone wild is powerful. His 1960 *Psycho,* is a classic example, as the famous shower scene probably forever implanted a frightful memory into every viewer only to be dredged up later in some tormenting dream. After all, who could forget the screams of Marion Crane upon seeing the shadow of a person holding a knife and then the blade slashing through the curtain? Certainly, the viewer noticed the uneasieness of Ms. Crane, as Norman Bates confided to her of his mother's mental illness, and the viewer likely was pushed to the edge of the seat, as Bates calmly said, "All of us go a little mad sometimes." Was this Vinson Hall scene any different?

"Ya! Ya! Ya!" … "Ya! Ya! Ya!" … "Ya! Ya! Ya!" The strange sounds, along with what seemed like the flap of bare feet on the floor, repeatedly pulsed from the Vinson Hall room. "Ya! Ya! Ya!" … "Ya! Ya! Ya!" … "Ya! Ya! Ya!"

"Swiggot!" yelled a student in a desperate tone, as he banged on the door. "Wake up!"

Dale Swiggot, a pitcher for Northwestern, was trying to get some shut eye, but tossed and turned from a nightmare dream, like he was in

Hitchcock's *Psycho* shower, fighting for his life. His nightmare, though, was being on the pitcher's mound in a game against Philips University, arguably, one of the top baseball teams in the conference year in and out. He looked over at the runner at first base. *How'd he get there?* There was one out. Catcher gave the signal, and Swiggot looked the runner back to first. As he threw the pitch, someone yelled, *"He's running!"* Swiggot agonized, *Someone make a play!* … Next scene, one runner on base and one scored. Suddenly, Coach Walter Johnson stood in front of him. *"But Coach, he's on by error, and that's an unearned run."* … *"It's not your day,"* Johnson replied. *"It's Not your day."*

"Wake up, Swiggot!" demanded several students, now outside his door.

"Uh…" Swiggot mumbled, as his nightmare rolled through his mind, *"Not your day!"* … *"Not your day!"*

"Swiggot! Come on! Wake up!" another student yelled and banged on the door. "Wake up!"

"Uh…" Swiggot mumbled, as he managed to roll out of bed and staggered to the door half asleep. "Whadda ya want!" he blurted out in an angry tone for their waking him. Before they answered, he heard the strange sounds coming from next door.

"Ya! Ya! Ya!" … "Ya! Ya! Ya!" … "Ya! Ya! Ya!"

A student sarcastically replied to Swiggot, "White Eyes, go tell your friend, Pipestem to knock it off!" White Eyes was the name Browning Pipestem usually called Swiggot.

Still half asleep, Swiggot stumbled around and finally managed to get to Pipestem's door. It wasn't locked. Cautiously, he cracked it slightly and peeked inside. The 6'5" and 285 lbs Pipestem was bare chested, and had a big headdress of feathers on that trailed down his backside to the floor. A tiny hatchet was in one hand, held up like he was about to strike something. Pipestem ignored White Eyes or never noticed him, as he danced around the room, and chanted, "Ya! Ya! Ya!" … "Ya! Ya! Ya!" … "Ya! Ya! Ya!"

White Eyes watched the dance for a few moments. *He must be practicing a pow wow ceremonial dance or something, and… I'm not going to interrupt that.*

Swiggot closed the door, headed back to his room, and shouted over his shoulder to those gathered in the hallway, "If you want Pipestem to knock it off, go tell him yourself!"

White Eyes was soon back in the sack, fighting monsters and nightmares… *"Not your day!"* … *"Not your day!"* And, roomie, Dewayne Brunkin, slept through the whole thing.

Northwestern 1964 Baseball. Pitchers (L-R): Jerry Devore, Dale Swigget, Bill Moore, Glenn Hornung, H. L. Brown, and Dan Stewart. Courtesy use, Northwestern Annual.

34.

NEWS SPECIAL — DR. KING ESCAPES
ASSASSINATION IN FLORIDA

June 1964, TV Lounge of Oklahoma Hall
Northwestern Oklahoma State University

"Warm here," commented a middle-aged man, as he walked with a small group towards Oklahoma Hall, which was a co-ed living quarters for summer classes at Northwestern. He was one of many who'd returned for additional study. "Seems extra hot for early June."

"Glad this place is air conditioned," another in the group responded, as they walked up to the rear entrance of the building.

"Me, too. Vinson and Shockley Halls would be like ovens," stated a male middle-school teacher. After a pause, he added, "Well, maybe not Vinson's basement rooms." A few more steps he teased, "Nice you women are sharing for the summer."

A woman laughed and quipped, "Oh, you guys are just pansies! Better be on your best behavior or we'll get the house Mom to put you on curfew restrictions."

"Oh, yeah?" Another guy jousted back. "Maybe we can arrange a swap next semester. Women in Vinson and Shockley and guys take air-conditioned Oklahoma Hall."

"Fine with me," she laughed and returned the joust. "I won't be here, but I doubt those male students can handle those curfews."

When they entered the lounge-reception area, the TV program, *As the World Turns*, was going off the air. The size of the crowd, though, was much larger than usual for the popular weekday, noon-time, program. "What's up?" a young man in the group asked loudly.

A person perched on a corner of a front sofa gave him a quick look, and expressed, "Shh," with a finger held over the mouth. "A 'Breaking news' announcement appeared a few minutes ago. Something about a gunman kicking in a door and putting a gun to the head of Martin Luther King. Details are coming on now!"

News special — St. Augustine, FL: A photo of the front of a house with the door boarded up appeared on the screen. "Apparently, sometime last night in St. Augustine, Florida, a gunman kicked in the door of the house where Dr. Martin Luther King, Jr. was staying, and put a gun to King's head." … "Seems the gunman, after a time, dropped the gun and quickly disappeared." … "Not sure how long the gunman had the gun at Dr. King's head, or what caused him to not to kill him." … "We're trying to get more information about this scary time from Dr. King or the Southern Christian Leadership Conference, a non-violent protest group that works for civil rights and justice—a group which Dr. King heads."

The screen faded in and out to photos of an old town business area and streets, beaches, and a few public eating and sleeping places. "While the Democrat filibuster, started on March 30th against passing the Kennedy Civil Rights bill in Congress, hotbeds of segregation and injustice continue to occur in the Nation. One of the hottest is St. Augustine, Florida—oldest European settlement in the United States."

"…Segregation has been front and center in its schools, beaches, public eating places and lodging and swimming pools to name a few places. Only a few black students attend the white schools, and homes of some have been burned recently to intimidate them. There have been large Klan crowds that enforce the segregation and Jim Crow laws. Even small groups have shot from cars as they drive through black neighborhoods. Some blacks have been driven into the Alantic waters when they tried to use previously "Whites only" beaches."

"...Local push-back has been lead by Dr. Robert Hayling, an Air Force veteran and dentist. Reports reveal he and three other blacks were arrested and charged with inciting a riot when they encountered some 200 Klansmen and were beat up. Dr. Hayling's hands reportedly were broken at the time..."

"Dr. King was called for help, along with others who shared the dream for equality and justice." "...Apparently, the hostility was so aggressive against King that he was moved to a different house to sleep each night. One house was burned, but the gunman was able to locate King, and kicked in the door to kill him."

"...Dr. King and others vowed to continue their non-violent protests against segregation and civil rights injustice, not only in St. Augustine but across the Nation, until progress is made to solve these issues, and ... All people are free indeed."

The TV screen faded to black, and the lounge emptied quickly. One person asked another, as they headed out the door, "Wonder what King said to get the gunman not to shoot?"

35.

CLASS ASSIGNMENT: PAPER ON 4TH OF JULY AND 4TH CIVIL RIGHTS ACT TO BE ENACTED

July 2, 1964, TV Lounge of Oklahoma Hall
Northwestern Oklahoma State University

"What did I get myself into?" mumbled Pamela James (fictional name), the early-thirties high school teacher, in an agonizing tone. Actually, she could've yelled it, as she was alone in the TV lounge of Oklahoma Hall, waiting for the special news. She'd returned to Northwestern for the summer session for hours towards her Master's, but went home early each Thursday. "Hubby's not going to be happy I'm late." She was following up on an assignment: "President Lyndon Johnson signed Civil Rights legislation today, July 2, 1964. Write a brief paper of this event and incorporate it into your observations of our July 4th holiday."

Why? she wondered, as she waited impatiently for the news to begin. *I didn't need this advanced course for my degree?* She knew why, though. She'd become fascinated in how and why historical facts and people impacted later events and, most important, her family life. It was like a personal treat. Still, she brow-beat herself. *I didn't need this extra pressure; at least, not on my July 4th weekend.* She sighed deeply and glanced at her watch. *Have time to read some of my resource material.*

July 4, 1776, In Congress: "We hold these truths to be self-evident, that all men are created equal, that they are endowed by their Creator with certain unalienable Rights, that among these are Life, Liberty and the pursuit of Happiness."

She studied the words. *This Declaration of Independence to the English Crown was really courageous. Tough on the signers, but guess they knew it was treason. Wow! They recognized a Creator, too! … And everyone is equal and endowed by that Creator!*

The distinctive sound of cowboy boots hitting the floor caused her to look up. Two guys walked within spittoon spittin' distance, but they paid her no mind, though, as they disappeared around the corner and their talk faded away. "You riding the bulls in that big rodeo at…" Neither noticed the news promo that was beginning to fill the TV lounge.

News Special — Washington, D.C.: The screen faded to a view of President Lyndon B. Johnson sitting at a desk, with about thirty standing behind him, as a reporter's voice announced. "President Johnson signed the latest version of a Civil Rights Act this day, July 2, 1964, and among the witnesses was civil rights leader, Dr. Martin Luther King, Jr.."

President Lyndon B. Johnson signed the 1964 Civil Rights Act, July 2ⁿᵈ, with Dr. Martin Luther King, Jr. and many others observing. National Archives. This 1964 Act was the fourth; preceded by one in 1960, 1957, and 1875. "The legislation was introduced over a year ago by then President John F. Kennedy. With his death, President Johnson took up the mantle, but…"

The screen faded to the senate chambers with Senator Robert Byrd at the podium. "…Johnson ran into a long filibuster from March 30th to June 10th by former Senate colleagues of his, primarily Democrats."

Other senators in the chamber appeared on the screen. "Only a bi-partisan effort, led by Democrat Senators Hubert Humphrey and Mike Mansfield and Republican Senators Everett Dirkson and Thomas Kuchel, and a watered-down version of the legislation ended the fili-buster. …During debate, some in opposition were skeptical this passage was just show and stated off the record, 'Why pass another one, since this will be the Fourth Civil Rights Act?'"

"Why the about face now?"

The screen faded to a few years earlier and the senate chambers of then Senator Johnson. "Some Republican opponents of Johnson's were quick to remind anyone who'd listen, 'Not one Democrat in congress voted for the 13th, 14th or 15th Amendments to the Constitution. Same for the Civil Rights Act of 1875. These covered "end of slavery, equal protection of the laws, and "right to vote." Yes, those were almost a hundred years ago, but they're still in the Constitution. They've been applicable ever since. Johnson and his Senate Democrats and some "go-along-Republicans" gutted most of the enforcement parts from both the 1957 and 1960 Civil Rights Acts. So, why the about face now?'"

The scene returned to President Johnson as he signed the 1964 Act, and panned towards Dr. King standing close behind. "Dr. King seemed pleased in the Act was forward action, as opposed to sitting back and waiting, hoping segregation and its injustice will fade away over the next hundred years or so." The voice paused momentarily, then added, "King or someone close by was heard to say, though, 'Voting rights protections are needed now.'"

"Also, overheard," the reporter expressed as various historical scenes scrolled across the screen, "were comments by several witnesses to Johnson's signing: 'How far we've come since the first black slaves in the early 1600s (in North America); black people involved early in the 1770s Revolutionary events; President Abraham Lincoln's 1863 Emancipation Proclamation; all the 'separate but equal' which was only segregation; and the intimidations of the Klan, the lynchings, the bombings, brutality, injustices, and other atrocities. But, we have far, far to go!'"

When the TV news report ended, the young teacher mumbled in a frustrated tone as she stood to walk away, "No 4th of July holiday for me this year."

> "…we have come a long, long way, but have far, far to go."

36.

ASSIGNMENT COMPLETED: "WE LOSE WHEN WE FORGET OR NEVER KNOW HISTORY."

July 6, 1964, Assignment Completed
Northwestern Oklahoma State University

Pamela James kept thinking about the assignment: *"President Lyndon Johnson signed Civil Rights legislation on July 2, 1964. Write a brief paper of this event and incorporate it into your observations of the July 4th holiday."*

By the time she handed the professor her paper, she felt she'd been on an emotional rollercoaster. At the top of the ride: *This is fascinating! Never knew or remembered much of this history! ... Probably the latter!* She concluded with a chuckle. ... At the bottom, she questioned: *Are my findings and observations valid? Did I overlook some important piece of history? Will he be open to understand my reasoning and questions?*

We Lose When We Forget or Never Know History
By Pamela James

The soil atop the grave was still fresh, as the stone, inscribed with a promise, was erected. "Gone, but not forgotten." No day light to waste, Mary, the pioneer widow and her two youngest climbed aboard the wagon. Her two young teenage sons were on horses to drive their cattle westward from Indian Territory to a homestead in No Man's Land, which would be the Oklahoma Panhandle on statehood. "Frank, you and John, have to be the men of the Spangler Family now." As they topped the ridge, Mary glanced tearfully back for a look and promise. "No, John William. We won't ever forget you!" … Sincere intentions, yes, but time, distance, and daily survival took a toll, as returns became fewer and family passed.

This is much the same for any historical event, no matter how important, like the Revolutionary War and 1776 Adoption of the Declaration of Independence. Time and distance move them first, to the daily back burner of future generations. By the mid-1900s, July 4th celebrations often were filled only with family gatherings, fireworks, fun, and relaxation.

In many towns across western Oklahoma as well as other states in the Great Plains, rodeos became popular July 4th celebrations, as ranch and farm country extended throughout the area to the Rockies. Yes, the creed within the Declaration of Independence—Equality, Life, Liberty, and Pursuit of Happiness—undergirded family, community, and freedom; but the talk in cafés was about such things as putting food on the table, raising the children, helping a neighbor and, of course, roping times, eight-second survival on a bull, bronc-riding points, and so on. Over the last 400 years, many important historical events have occurred in the area that became the United States. Staying with Equality, Life, Liberty, and Pursuit of Happiness; we've forgotten much about how slavery came to be in the States and, just as important, who did and did not help it bloom along the way. It's dishonest and lazy to think of it as simply a black versus white issue. It isn't! We've forgotten much of why and how the Revolutionary War started, except for 4th of July celebrations of the signing of the Declaration of Independence. We've forgotten who was the first killed, the loss of life and property of most of those who signed the Declaration, which side individuals aligned, and so on. We've forgotten who championed freedom and equality for all, and even the Amendments that ensure rights to all people. These and many other important things have been pushed to the back burner by our life events and even off the stove altogether in many cases. Over and over we forget—we repeat history and, if fortunate, re-invent the wheel, so to speak. We are either blind-lucky or divinely blessed the embers of history remain and, when fanned, reveal such details and truths.

Are there rotten apples in the barrel? ... Absolutely! They've impacted the culture of generation after generation not only in geographical regions and parts of cities, but also some elected officials up to and including the Congress and White House, as well as the justice system and Supreme Court. Without that cultural and political bias, how did slavery become affirmed in the Supreme Court 1857 Dred Scott decision, or give an "Equal but Separate" decision in its 1896 *Plessy v. Ferguson*, or the legal cover for Jim Crow laws and wink an eye at Sanger's eugenics of "deplorables?" And without that cultural depravity, how does President Woodrow Wilson allow the Klan movie, *Birth of a Nation*, be shown in the White House, let alone be the first? The rest of us, though, are good people, if we don't bend to the rotton culture.

Events like the 4th are opportunities to pause and reflect on our God given freedoms. With respect to and sorrow for all the atrocities leading up to the signing of the 1964 Civil Rights Act, slavery and ethnic injustice—not racial because we are all of the human race—were here before the United States became a country, with the July 4, 1776 signing of the Declaration of Independence. Please note, included here is the slavery between many of the Indian tribes which existed in these lands before any non-Indian arrived. The mindset of slavery was not imported; only another opportunity allowed by the Thrown of England. Black slaves are purported to have been brought by ship to the Virginia settlement as early as 1619. This student (the author), though, did not find documentation that explained how and why slavery inserted this way into the Virginian economy meshed with the established English indentured servant system. Also, unexplained are frequent findings of "free black people" after 1619. Non-Indian slavery in the Colonies did sprout in the mid-1600s, under England rule and its court system. Both white and black men, who committed crimes, while working as indentured servants, were sometimes sentenced to lifetime indentureship. No crime seems to have been committed, though, when Anthony Johnson, a free black man who himself had worked his way out of indentured service, convinced the English court he was entitled to the lifetime services of John Casor, another black man. Casor seems not to have committed a crime. Thus, non-Indian slavery sprouted that did not involve arrival by slave ship. Did it bloom among others in the area, including the other black men and women who had gained their freedom working, like Johnson, their way out of indentured service? With respect to Johnson, what kind of cultural history made it okay to own another person? Were Johnson and Casor from African tribes that were enemies, like some Indian tribes were, and slavery was a cultural reality?

Slavery of black people, no matter how it started, had over 100 years under the English Crown to be entrenched into the new colonies of England before the 1776 adoption of the Declaration of Independence began the long and bloody steps of undoing this mess. Free blacks and white sympathizers joined together to form the Republican Party and elect President Abraham

Lincoln. He was one casualty, followed by 600,000 in the Civil War. Thousands more—black and white—have given all, along the way to 1964.

Hopefully, we won't forget such milestones of history, as we celebrate our July 4th events, although, we probably will for a time. … Now, where are my spurs?

———

Author Note: The person, Pamela James, named above is a fictional character. However, the message in her paper and questions raised are important to review and consider. Moreover, readers may have ones of their own reference list. The following source is provided to initiate the search: Williams, Kevin D. - *Civil Rights. National Review.* May 28, 2012.

37.

1964 PRE-SEASON FOOTBALL, DEATH OF BILL WOLTJE, PIPESTEM AND CAMPBELL WAR!

August 1964, Pre-season Football
Northwestern Oklahoma State University

"Make sure you watch your oil gage," Mom cautioned me, Clifton Savoy, in one of her looks that also conveyed, 'Be careful', which meant all kinds of things, including on the road and at college.

I learned early on it was a look that shouldn't be ignored. I nodded with a respectful grin that I understood, as the V-8 in my two-door hardtop '55 Ford roared to life. Its muscles tensed, as I slipped it into gear—something like the feel of a massive bull preparing to explode the instant the rodeo chute gate swings open and it's one-on-one, cowboy versus beast.

Yip-pe-e! Summer was finally over! I could barely keep from squealing the tires, which wouldn't be wise in front of Mom! In seconds, I was on the 130-mile journey back to Northwestern for the start of preseason football. I was on an exhilarating high, and I expected the team and me to do as well or better than the good season in 1963.

Geographical markers—Dodge City fork, sagebrush hills, Cimarron River, and Red Horse Creek—greeted me as I passed. *How could things be any better?* Before daylight faded into one of those awe-inspiring western Oklahoma sunsets, though, I was hit square in the face with the reality of how brief life can be. It was one of the most shameful moments of my young days.

As I flew down the highway, with windows down and any radio station I could find loud enough to hear, thoughts of scenes and talk to come filled my mind. *It'll be great to see the guys again. ... There'll be some new faces: recruits, transfers, and walk-ons. ...* A flash-back to the year before and being a walk-on brought a painful memory. *Hope they get a fair chance.*

"Oops, I'm late," I mumbled, as I rolled into the parking lot between Vinson Hall and Percefell Field House, and parked between two other beasts: Glen Smith's 2-tone pink, 2-door hard-top '55 Chevy and Mike 'Roids' Garrison's red and black '55 Plymouth. My Ford was still snortin' like a bull that wanted another go at me, as I hurried towards the field house.

It struck me, as I was about to enter the double doors into the dressing rooms, how things were much the same as last year. Practice schedule for 1st day would include the usual upper classmen banter: "Newbies'n walk-ons won't know what hit 'em." ... "How many'll dropout after they meet, Coach Johnson and the iron mule?" ... "Or discover they're 'red meat' for our scrimmages?"

I can imagine, with my adrenaline high, I probably burst through both entrance doors with the commotion of an entourage of a half-a-dozen guys. Immediately, the odors of sweaty-bodies hit my nostrils, even though all we were doing was putting gear and uniforms together for practice. Strange as it may seem, the smell and scene gave me a comforting, 'Welcome back' to the competitive journey I was about to travel.

Players looked up and nodded a quick, "Hello, glad to see ya, Savoy." As I returned the greetings, the closest ones with a forearm bump, I scanned the names in this dressing area: Hiner, Kippenberger, Mitchell, Garrison, Don and Ron Sweat, Massey, Davis, Strunk... Suddenly, it struck me. *Kippenberger and Mitchell? They were seniors last year. What's up?* Then I remembered, they were Graduate Assistant Coaches this year.

Bill "Buster" Mitchell and Jack "Kip" Kippenberger (L-R) were the 1964 Graduate Assistant Coaches for the Northwestern football season. Mitchell is from the Mohawk Reservation in northern New York State, and Kippenberger is from Thomas, Oklahoma. Both were standout offensive linemen in the 1963 season. Northwestern 1965 Annual.

The bark of these two new GAs filled the air, "Savoy! You're late!" . . . And before I could respond with even the slightest greeting, they bellowed while trying to mask their snickers, "You're in the back (dressing room) with the walk-ons!" I pursed my lips and nodded an understanding with a grin, as I headed that way. I knew other good players were there, too. Later on, Kippenberger and Mitchel gave me a warm welcome.

Before I rounded the corner, I heard Big Ben Smith's voice, and laughed as I remembered our country dance do si do first time we met. I'd looked forward to seeing him and brother, Glen, as I'd gained strength and 15 lbs. up to 195. Then I gulped when they came into view. *Ben's even bigger than last year, up to 265 maybe 270 lbs.! And, Glen, why, he's up a little—even more perfectly shaped! ... Just not fair, Lord!* "Ben still looks like he has bird-legs, though," I muttered in some delusional type of consolation.

"Hey, guys," I called out in a joyful tone, while trying to catch sight of my locker. *Awe, there it is—by Big Ben.*

Greetings were immediately sent my direction by those from the year before: Big Ben and Glen, Ira Dale and Larry Campbell, Pipestem, who seemed bigger than his 285 lbs. last year, Amerin, Myers, Stewart, John Estep, who introduced me to his brother, Larry. There were other new faces who looked my way and nodded. Some had an impressive physical look.

Yikes! Any of them play my positions? In any sports competition, especially football, I'd come to realize first impressions may not always prove to hold true. Quickness and instincts of knowing where to be and when to be there usually off-set straight-away speed and over-powering size. But, still, each time I competed against an athlete for the same position on the team who was taller and stronger and faster after a short distance, I had to initially wonder if I'd be riding the bench that season.

Big Ben motioned towards another black footballer and expressed, "Harold Malloy. Plays HB\FB. Junior transfer from Dodge City Juco."

Malloy looked to be about 215 lbs. I nodded a greeting, and he returned it. *Hope you're as good as Glen or Ben.* "Good to meet ya," I told him.

"You, too," he replied, as I headed to my locker.

When I saw the six inches of space left for me when Big Ben sat on the bench, I muttered, "Huh?" ... "Gotta be a joke!"

Friendly jousting, also over bench space, between Ira Dale Campbell and Pipestem, momentarily distracted me, though.

"You Big Indian..." teased Campbell in a gruff voice and muffled laugh.

"When you going to grow up, White Eyes?" Pipestem fired back with a grin.

Back to my own problem. *How can Big Ben and I dress at the same time?* Nobody else seemed to notice, though, as laughter and the buzz of talk filled the room. Then I saw it. *A new helmet! Where's the old, beat up one I had last year? ... And, why this game jersey instead of a practice one?* With that, I headed to check with the equipment manager.

"Savoy!" barked the multi-tasking figure behind the counter. "What's wrong?" he asked, as I held the new helmet up.

"It's new!"

A quizzical look appeared on his face. "I can see that!" he exclaimed sarcastically.

"I'd like the old, beat-up one I had last year."

"Huh?" he replied in a tone of disbelief, and added when he saw I wasn't joking, "Coach sent all those for recycle."

I grimaced, and started to walk away then remembered the game jersey in my hand. "Well, what's up with this?" I asked as I thrust it towards him.

"We're getting new game jerseys, and using the ones from last year for practice."

"Well, the number is 89. I had 85 and 46. Who had 89?"

The manager's face softened, as he replied, "Eighty-nine was the number Bill Woltje had."

"Well," I barked, "give it to Woltje, and..." Suddenly, I noticed the sudden hush over the whole room and felt all eyes on me.

After what seemed like several minutes, he responded in a shocked and disbelieving tone, "Where ya been, Savoy?"

Confusion reigned supreme in my head. "What do you mean?"

"Woltje was killed in a work accident, downtown in Alva, last April! ... Remember?"

Bill Woltje
October 12ᵗʰ 1942 – April 23ʳᵈ 1964
An outstanding Northwestern football athlete!

I was stunned. *Four months ago! How did I not know?*

As I returned to my locker, I heard several players talking about Woltje, and that night, I relived those comments about him in my sleep.

Butch Amerine, "Bill Woltje was selected on the 1959 Kansas All-state Football Team. I knew him well. He graduated from Meade, Kansas in 1960. A man playing against boys. I was a sophomore when he was a Senior. He didn't tackle me. Ran over me! Woltje came to Northwestern, started as a sophomore in 1963, and wore the number 89.

Mike Garrison, "Woltje was a good guy and a good player. Everyone liked him, and his ability. He was married and worked hard to make ends meet so we didn't see a lot of him."

Amerine, "I was very happy that Woltje was blocking for me at Northwestern. In track he threw the Discus and Shotput. I think he placed well in both events in the Oklahoma Collegiate Conference Meet." … "I admired Woltje for going to school, working a job, and playing football and track. He had two small daughters and a wife to support."

Garrison, "Woltje was not at Northwestern long because of the accident that killed him. He was working construction in Alva, and fell off a roof. It was sad he died."

I couldn't sleep that night, as scenes about Woltje replayed in my mind. One was when I first saw him. It was preseason 1963. A well-built person came into the dressing room in dirty, I mean very dirty, work clothes, and dressed for practice. *How can a person put in hours of work and then go through the physical demands of pre-season conditioning, running, hitting, and scrimmage? He had to be super-human!*

How did I not know about his accident and passing? I hoped, some-day, there'll be a chance to give respects to Woltje and family. For the moment, I was honored to wear number eighty-nine in that pre-season, and it seemed to make me a tougher, more determined player.

38.

August 1964, Pipestem and Campbell War
Northwestern Oklahoma State University

About the time a person thinks they've made it through an Oklahoma heatwave, one that hovers above 110, the thermometer red line seems to climb a few degrees. Add a heavy dose of humidity and a drill sergeant-type setting, and explosive reactions are but a spark away.

"Ramp the pressure up again!" Northwestern football coach Art Parkhurst instructed his staff five days into the 1964 preseason practices. "Let's find our strongest players!"

Right on schedule for the afternoon session, a group of football players suddenly came out of Vinson Hall and headed to the dressing rooms. "Look!" one exclaimed, as he lifted his foot up and down on the drive way asphalt. "It's sticking to my shoe. It's so hot, the tar's melting!" Although everyone glanced momentarily, no one lingered to reply.

The players checked the daily schedule posted outside the entrance before heading into the dressing rooms. "Huh? What's this? Ben, lists you with the backs on offense."

Another asked, as the other players shot a quizzical look at Ben, "What's a 265 lb. guy doing with them?"

Glen Smith laughed and stepped out of reach by his brother, Ben, who anticipated what Glen was about to say. "Thought that was a trick by Coach Parkhurst to get Ben to work out over the summer and come back in shape." Glen's facial expression then softened now that he'd seen the schedule. "It may be for real," he expressed over his shoulder, as they passed through the doors. "Gonna try 'em at running the ball on short distances."

Savoy commented to Ben as they neared their lockers, "Glad I don't have to tackle you."

Ben at running back was immediately forgotten, as friendly jousting between Ira Dale Campbell and Browning Pipestem took center stage. "You Big Indian," Ira chided, with his disarming laugh. "You don't need all the bench to dress."

The Campbell and Pipestem jawing war had steadily increased with each day of practice. Pipestem would just smile and continue on his way. After all, he had nearly a 100-pound size advantage on the talented back. Same with Ira's brother, Larry. This day, though, their war would carry out to the practice field and boil over back into the dressing room.

A full scrimmage, with first teams against each other, including a few ball carries by Big Ben, was part of Coach Parkhurst's pressure ramp up. So, it was no surprise that offensive tackle Pipestem had a few blocking plays at Ira Dale and other defensive backs. "Missed me!" taunted the backs to the big tackle quietly, as they sidestepped him to help defend the play.

But, when Big Ben carried the ball, all defensive eyes were on him charging, like a wild horse, through a break in the corral, and it only took once for Pipestem to lay a blow. "Take that!" he quipped, as he piled Ira Dale or anyone else to the ground. Fortunately, coaches substituted others into the "Take no prisoners" smashing before every temper reached the boiling point and all-out war erupted.

Players were soon separated into position groups. As defensive backs trotted to their drill area, they passed the linemen. One mouthed off, "Hey, Pipestem, heard you're a pow wow dancer. Why don't you do a rain dance, and give us a break from this heat?" Browning looked up and, of course, noticed Ira Dale.

Coach Parkhurst saw the players struggling from the heat, and sent word for each group to hit the showers once their joyous time with Coach Johnson and the Iron Mule was completed. The linemen finished first and, as they trotted past the defensive backs, Pipestem tossed a verbal poke at Ira Dale, "If you hadn't missed so many tackles, you'd get to go in, too."

When the defensive backs finally entered the dressing room—totally exhausted and the last group of the day, Pipestem was already in the shower. Ira Dale, with only his helmet off, noticed a two-gallon ice-water bucket by the trainer table. It was there to treat the swelling of any player sprains. He grabbed it, walked into the large shower area, and threw the icy water on Pipestem, who let out a blood-curdling yell and gave immediate chase.

Ira Dale still had on his cleats, pads, and uniform, and couldn't move very fast because of sliding on the tile floor. Pipestem caught him in a corner of the large dressing room, lifted him up, and hooked him by his shoulder pads backwards on a clothing hook above the bench. Ira's feet couldn't touch, and he dangled on the hook. He was at the mercy of someone else to get down. Larry, Ira's brother, wisely chose not to interfere in this one-on-one war and local standout lineman, Ed Stewart, dressing nearby motioned, don't look at me!.

Pipestem, laughed as he dried off and took his time to dress. As he stood to leave, he turned toward Ira Dale dangling on the hook, and said with a deep laugh, "See ya, White Eyes!"

———

Author Note: F. Browning Pipestem, after graduating from Northwestern and a brief time with the Kansas City Chiefs football team, obtained a law degree, and dedicated his professional career in behalf of Native Americans. He was an attorney, judge, and lecturer; and served as chief justice for the supreme court of the Iowa Tribe of Oklahoma, as well as a justice for the Citizens Band Potawatomi Tribe of Oklahoma and the Kaw Nation. Pipestem passed away in 1999 but, over the years, he received numerous awards for his passion on defending tribal sovereignty and contributions to the legal profession. He was honored with the Spirit of Excellence Award from the American Bar Association. He and wife, Sharon, who passed in 2012, are survived by three children and two grandchildren. In 2015, Pipestem was further honored by Northwestern OSU as an Outstanding Graduate in the Humanitarian area.

Ed Stewart was one of a long line of standout athletes from the local area of Alva, Oklahoma, who played for the Northwestern Rangers. Of this writing, he resides there today in retirement.

Upper L to R: Browning Pipestem, Larry Campbell, Ed Stewart; Lower: Ira Dale and Kay Campbell. Courtesy Northwestern 1963 Football Program and Ranger Annual.

Ira Dale Campbell and brother, Larry, starred on the 1959 and 1960 football state championship teams of Beaver, Oklahoma prior to Northwestern. Ira Dale was quarterback and Larry was halfback\ linebacker. At Northwestern, they were key players from 1963-1966. Larry married hometown sweetheart, Erma Fowler. After Northwestern, they returned to a ranching career west of Beaver. They were blessed with three sons. Larry passed in 2011 and Erma 2021.

Ira Dale married Kay Coffman of Alva. Kay and her twin sister, Vicki, were outstanding sports figures at Northwestern in the 1960s; and blazed a trail for other women prior to Title IX by competing in swimming, gymnastics, trampoline, and tennis. Ira Dale also loved horses and ranch life, and he and Kay combined that rural life on a spread near the Salt Fork River, just northeast of Alva, with a long career in education, coaching, and mentoring Alva area youth. Ira Dale became known as "Coach" to the numerous individuals under his guidance, and Kay not only was a mother, but also a life-long educator and mentor of 32 years, including four as an adjunct professor in the Physical Ed Department of Northwestern. In 2012, they moved to a ranch east of Bartlesville, where they now raise red angus cattle. They've been blessed with two children and four grandchildren.

39.

SCIENCE CLASS CADAVERS, AND VINSON HALL SPIES

September 1964, Cadavers and More
Northwestern Oklahoma State University

"Savoy!" … "You here?" Big Ben yelled, as he stuck his head into my Vinson Hall basement room. A pungent odor, almost intolerable, hit him square in the face. He asked with a sour face and wrinkled nose, "What's that smell?"

I stepped out of the small shower-rest room, towel wrapped around my waist, and replied, "It's formaldehyde." Ben's brow wrinkled, as a puzzled look flashed onto his face.

I couldn't let the opportunity pass for a tongue-in-cheek moment, but I had to look away for a second to hide my delight. Straight-faced, I stated, "My comparative anatomy class. Dissecting cadavers." I noticed him step backward, so I continued, "You know, human bodies."

Ben's eyes opened wider and wider, as I set the hook in the joke. "Science professors get 'em from the local morgue. Hear tell they're hobos and others who die and no one claims them." I had to look away again, and coughed to hide the laugh I choked back. "Giving them to the science department saves them embalming and burial money." … "We store 'em in formaldehyde tanks, and a cadaver arm splashed it all over my lab coat when we put the body back." … "That's the smell and reason for my shower." I turned just in time to suppress another laugh. "Guess I better soak these clothes in water, too."

He didn't seem to process what he'd heard. He just stood there, with mouth gaped wide open. Seconds seemed like minutes. Soon, I regained my composure. "So, what's up?"

Ben blinked, and tried to speak, but only muttered. He raised an envelope in his hand, but only managed a whisper, "Photographer left this with us."

Dormitory council this year consisted of, *seated*, Terry Chase, John Estep, Dale Swiggett, Clifton Savoy, Ken Strunk, Leland McNabb, Jim Schroeder. *Standing:* Doug Winston, Doug Plank, Don Hiner and Dean Campbell.

"It's from Mr. Wayne Lane," I gleefully replied. "Northwestern's photographer." The moment prodded me onward—to step up the 'tongue-in-cheek' affect. "It's a photo of Ma Grigg's Vinson Hall security squad." I glanced at Ben quickly out of the corners of my eyes to see if there was a reaction. It did.

"Huh?" he asked, as his ebony-colored forehead and eyebrows wrinkled again and a puzzled look flashed across his face. I imagined his mental wheels spinning, trying to process things.

Got him! I decided to continue this ruse. "Ma Griggs has this secret squad that spies on unruly students in Vinson Hall." *This is good.* It was all I could do to keep from laughing, so I added, "She must've not been upstairs in the office."

Ben looked at the photo. "You, Strunk, Schroeder, Hiner, and others I recognize." He paused and asked in a serious tone, "You guys really do that?"

"Yeah," I replied while doing everything to hold back my laugh. "Why do you think three of us live across the hall?" I paused to let the idea sink in. "To keep an eye on ya!"

Strunk bopped into the room at that moment, and noticed the photo. Before I could give him a sign to play along with the joke, he blurted out, "Our Student Council photo. Turned out good."

Ben wagged a finger in warning in my direction, and fired a look of, *I'm on to ya, Savoy,* as Strunk reacted to the pungent odor. "Playing in the formaldehyde again, I see."

I grinned, but kept the focus on the photo before Ben could pin me down about the cadavers. "Students are selected from each wing of Vinson Hall. We work with Ma Griggs to do innovative things. For the 1964-65 year, we've come up with a way to pay for several projects. The new color 23-inch TV in the lounge is one of them. Remember, Ben, the old 19 inch black & white screen we had last year? We also have three other major projects."

"Yeah," Strunk inserted. "My favorite is the Christmas Party we give to the Orphanage at Enid, Oklahoma. Vinson guys pair up with a date to be the host for one orphan that day. Some are just 4 years old. Buy each one a present and set up a tree in the lounge. Try to make the day really special. My girlfriend, Dian, and I had a blast last year. Doing it this year, too."

"Yeah," I affirmed. "It's a fun day and a really great cause."

"We're also sole sponsors of a campus dance that'll have the popular Roadrunner Band from Amarillo, Texas. Date not set yet." I grinned, and added, "Heard Glen, H.L., and you sometimes show a few dance moves in the student union. Ben's response was an ear-to-ear grin that fully exposed his 'pearly whites,' when he learned others had noticed.

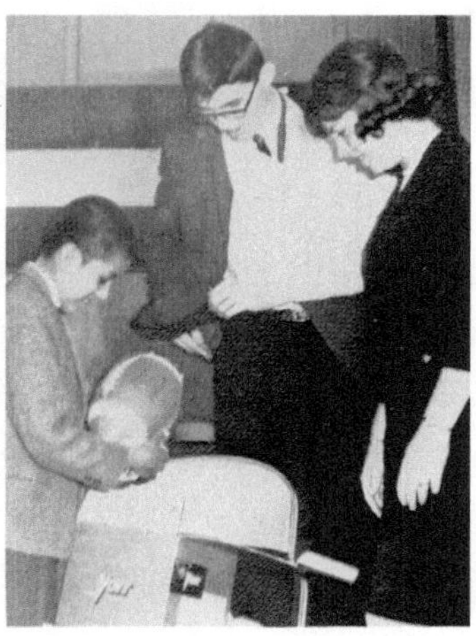

Ken Strunk and future wife, Dian Henninger, assisting as hosts for the Vinson Hall student's annual Christmas party for an orphan house. Strunk is in a sling and recovering from a football injury. Courtesy use from Northwestern.

"Top that off, we're co-sponsors again for the big Homecoming Event. Leon Bibb, the nationally-known singer, is the main attraction. He was here last year, remember?"

Big Ben nodded and replied with another grin. "Yeah. Saw him. Met up with the four black girls at Herod Hall. Great evening," he added, as a warm smile covered his face.

"Well, you guys can go to the homecoming and Bibb show in the fieldhouse."

Ben parsed his lips and slowly moved his head back and forth but, before he could speak, I added, "If money's a problem, the organizers need extra staff and ushers to help folks."

"No," Ben expressed sadly. "That's not it. None of those girls came back this semester to Northwestern. H. L. has a girl back home, and Glen's mind seems to be in Tulsa right now." ... "Probably have a big pinnacle card game that lasts the weekend."

"You mean, the four here last year? None returned?"

A discouraged look appeared on Ben's face, as he nodded yes.

"Any reason, why?"

Ben just shrugged his shoulders and lifted his arms.

"Well, I'll be. What about other girls? I noticed you guys talking to some in the union. Even saw the cute cheerleaders giving you a hug after a ball game."

"Yeah, got some hugs," Ben replied with a slight grin and in a tone, like he was recognized as a 'Lady's Man.' "But they also gave 'em to other players." Ben paused, as he thought about the issue. "Think some girl's at Northwestern are comfortable around guys like me, but they seem to be the ones from towns and high schools that had blacks there." A serious look crossed his face as he added, "Not sure Northwestern is ready for any mixed color dating."

"But," I asked, "what about those two Indians, Benny Smith, a Cherokee, and Wayne Postoak, a Choctaw? They graduated just before we arrived at Northwestern. They played sports. Both dated and married palefaces—one from here in Alva, and the other from Beaver, my hometown."

"It's a shade difference. Not sure folks are comfortable with blacks, yet. Most haven't been around us, and..." Ben laughed as he added, "Besides, can you imagine, say one of those 5'2" with a 6'5" guy, one who outweighs her by 170 pounds trying to do some dance moves?"

"Yeah," I laughed, "That'd be entertaining, but..." I couldn't resist, "We could sell some tickets! Why, we wouldn't even need the band. Just have you whirl the girls around to the sounds of the old juke box and music of Johnny Horton's, *I'm a Honky Tonk Man, and I know how to dance... and when my money's all gone, I'm on the telephone saying Hey, Hey Baby...*"

Big Ben's stern look conveyed the message, *Move on Savoy!*

"Not talking about marriage! Makes for lonesome times here, don't ya think?"

"Savoy!" Ben replied in a tone like he'd lost patience with me. "Like

I said, H. L. has a girl back home, and Glen has the hots for one in Tulsa." He paused, took a deep sigh, and added, "And as for me, my times back in my stomping grounds get me by." A few seconds passed again and, as a warm grin filled his face, our give and take opened to another level. "Savoy, if you were a black boy just one Saturday night, you'd never want to be a white boy again!"

Strunk poked his head back into the room and yelled, "We're late for practice!"

As we entered the dressing room double doors, I came clean and whispered to Ben, "It's dogfish sharks, not cadavers." With that, my conscious was clear. Still, I kept an eye out in practice if Big Ben was running my direction with the ball.

40.

FOOTBALL ROAD TRIP ROOMMATES

October 10, 1964, Pipestem and Basset
Southeastern Oklahoma State University

The Northwestern athletic bus was a late 1940s or early 1950s model and, as it slowly rolled up the road by Vinson Hall to the fieldhouse where players loaded their football gear, it creaked like an old man's joints in the first few steps after struggling to rise from a recliner.

The old bus always reminded me of a similar one in that 1955 movie, *Picnic,* where actor, William Holden, stepped down, and slowly gazed around at a rural, prairie town, located not far from the Northwestern campus. Could be wrong, but I think that was the scene. Others in the movie were Kim Novak and Rosalind Russell.

The Northwestern bus had seen its best days in the rearview mirror long ago. The tight budget, though, for travel and lodging necessitated 'Getting by for one more trip and, if possible, the season.' Didn't matter the bus was slow, overly crowded on football trips, or air conditioning was an open window. Finishing each trip was cause to breathe a sigh of relief and celebrate.

Seats were hard and narrow, and not conducive for anyone's comfort, let alone large bodies. Once rolling, it didn't take long to hear: "Oh, man! My bottom hurts!" … "Scoot over. You're taking too much room!" … "Hey it's hot. Open a window up there, and let a little air in here!" … "Aren't we there yet?"

No, cushy rides were not a reality for those on road trips in the mid-1960s. Players not on the travel list, though, would've gladly traded places with anyone who was. Campus life was similar, as few classrooms and men's lodging had air conditioning either.

To help, coaches often matched a large and small player in the same seat and bunked them together when stopping overnight. "Pipestem, you're bunking with Bassett…"

"Oh, no-o-o-o-o-o-o!" exclaimed promising freshman defensive/ offensive back Milt Bassett under his breath, as Graduate Assistant Coach Jack Kippenberger announced the bunk pairings for the trip to play Southeastern Oklahoma State University, known as the Savages.

Bassett moaned as his lips mumbled the words, "That big tackle outweighs me by 120 lbs. He'll crush me if he rolls over in bed."

As players headed off to find their rooms, Bassett's friend and wide receiver, Chip Myers, laughed and yelled to him in a teasing tone, "See ya in the morn'un … Mil-tee!"

Early the next morning, sleepy-eyed Bassett realized he was alone. *Where is that big guy?* As he rolled out of bed, he noticed a pillow and a couple of blankets on the floor. *Huh? He slept down there?*

Bassett's buddies snickered and teased, "There's Mil-tee!" when he arrived for breakfast. "'Bout time!" The laughter grew, as one asked in an inquiring tone, "How was your night?"

Bassett replied as he rubbed eyes, yawned, and sat at the table, "Pipestem been here?"

"Yeah. Came and gone." Then they joked, "Said something about you tossing and turning and mumbling, 'Oh, Mary Jane.' Final straw was when you planted a juicy kiss on Pipestem's cheek. He jumped out of bed and slept on the floor!" Everyone nearby laughed loudly, and another player added, "Think I heard, 'Didn't get much sleep 'cause I was leery of what Bassett would do next!'"

While dressing for the game, Myers quietly confessed to his friend, "Pipestem only mentioned something about you tossing so much he finally moved to the floor to sleep." Myers laughed as he added, "The other version's funnier, though."

After the game, a tough loss, 23 to 14, and as players pulled off sweat-soaked gear, Bassett heard a voice from behind, "Nice catch and TD run." When he looked, Pipestem was walking away, and added bacl over his shoulder, "Needed more of them."

Northwestern 1964 footballers (L-R): Milt Bassett, L. Browning Pipestem, Chip Myers, and Bassett catching a pass out of halfback position. Courtesy Northwestern.

41.

1964 LANGSTON UNIVERSITY HOMECOMING, CHEERLEADERS AT GAME

November 7, 1964, Homecoming Day at Langston University
Originally known as the Oklahoma Colored Agricultural
& Normal University

A cloud of dust hung in the air well after the Northwestern player intercepted the Langston University pass, and was tackled near mid-field. The huge overflow Langston homecoming crowd had no worry, though. Its team was ahead 14 to zip, and people were gyrating joyously to the rockin' sounds and shakin' moves of its band. Besides, "It's the 4th quarter! Enjoy!"

On the opposite side, the one facing the intense November sun as it moved lower towards mid-afternoon, Northwestern's team, cheerleaders, and followers squinted into the sunlight and dust. The Langston crowd must've seemed like a heat mirage rising from the Oklahoma plains.

"Here's our chance!" Northwestern Head Coach Art Parkhurst exclaimed, as he glanced at the other coaches, who were anxiously pacing, like he was, along the sideline. The defense created another ball turn-over from Langston, but time was running out.

"Feed Ben the ball," Parkhurst instructed quarterback, Bill Massey. "He's pumped from the taunts they (Ben and Glen Smith, and Harold Malloy) have been getting from the Langston crowd and some players."

Seven carries and 40⁺ yards of *plow-horse work,'* as the paper later described, and Big Ben scored. Unfortunately, the game ended at 14 to 7, a loss, and Northwestern's players and coaches congratulated the Langston team.

Northwestern at Langston 1964 (L-R): Head Coach Art Parkhurst, QB Bill Massey, and RB Ben Smith. Courtesy of Northwestern.

In the quiet of the long bus ride back to Northwestern, Parkhurst reflected on the game and the season. ... *Didn't score enough. And their forced fumble and TD return didn't help—another disastrous single play! ... Just like the season! ... Hope those two cheerleaders are okay after that big pile-up on the sideline—Sharon Boruff and... Who was the other one?*

Started the season with a bang—44 to 13 over Colorado State College— like I thought we would with the talent returning from last year: all-conference players plus Amerine's running back speed. He had 228 yards and a TD, and Savoy had a defensive interception TD.

Then, snake-bit from the second game. Season ending injury to Amerine. Others along the way: Strunk, Davis (Jim), Garrison, Savoy twice, Massey, and...

Freak turnovers and scores, like the Langston game today. Not clicking together at key times. When we pulled out the Central game 20-13, thought maybe we'd finish strong with some of those injuries healed and we'd have a win over Langston. ... Parkhurst sighed deeply. Two games to go. ... Have to win them.

Back in the athletic bus, a player nudged and congratulated an exhausted Ben Smith, "Good game big guy."

"Ooo, careful. Little tender there," Ben replied, and added, "Thanks."

"If we'd handed you the ball like that early in the game, you'd worn 'em down."

"Don't think I'd lasted. Langston was hittin' me pretty hard."

"Yeah, saw that. Seemed like there was some piling on, too."

Ben grinned as he replied, "Refs were lettin' everyone play. … Rough in the pile." A bigger gren filled his face as he continued, "Glen and I and Malloy gave a little payback, too."

"What was that jawing about? Also, heard some from the crowd."

"You mean, the 'Uncle Tom and traitor' stuff?"

"Yeah."

"Glen had several offers out of high school to play at the next level. We chose Northwestern, and were the first black athletes to play a sport. He started as a freshman. I played a lot, but came more into my own this year." Ben paused a moment to catch his breath, "Didn't sit well that two guys, who started out at little Booker T. Washington near the town of Dover, Oklahoma, chose an all-white university, 'cept for a couple Indians and a few black girls, over an all-colored one."

Glen, sitting near by, nodded his head as his brother spoke. "People at other schools don't know us or our relationships at Northwestern." Ben paused again to catch his breath, "We couldn't be treated better by anyone on campus or downtown in Alva."

"Yeah," Glen agreed. "I've been hit in some games that I thought were extra rough and might've been racial. A ref had to grab me once from going after another player, who hit me dirty in the back, but the ref just warned me. Didn't penalize the other guy, though. Wondered why not. Others, nothing consistent, like the two games against Langston. Especially, the one today. It was rougher than any others, and the taunts were only from a few."

"Yeah," Big Ben grinned as he added, "its not all love'n peace among blacks. The eleven kids in our Smith family had a few heated 'tugs of war' on our eighty acre farm. … Also, have a black friend in Stillwater, who went to stay with relatives in Atlanta for a month. He was back in three days. Said, 'Treated worse by the blacks there then the whites in Oklahoma.'"

"Today, I just wanted to beat 'em, and they wanted to beat us. When I ran, didn't think what color guy blocked for me or tackled. Wanted to run over 'em and score." An ear-to ear grin spread across Big Ben's face, as he added, "An' I did!"

———

Author Note: Langston University was originally the Oklahoma colored Agricultural and Normal University. It was founded in 1897, a year after the Supreme Court decision in its, *Plessy v. Ferguson, 163 U.S. 537 (1896)* decision that upheld the constitutionality of racial segregation laws for public facilities that were equal in quality—known as 'Separate but equal.' Truth is, a supreme court ruling is only as fair and equal as the mindset of the political party and president that appoints and approves individual judges, so "Separate but equal" became law of the nation.

Oklahoma statehood was still ten years to the future (1907). Langston was established in a rural area, northeast of Oklahoma City, as a result of the 2nd Morrill Act of 1890 {26 Stat. 417, U.S.C. 321 et seq}. This law required states\territories with land-grant colleges that were established under the 1862 Morrill Act {7 U.S.C. 301 et seq}, such as Oklahoma A&M (Oklahoma State University) located in Stillwater, Oklahoma Territory, to either admit blacks and others of color, or provide an alternative school for them, as a condition of receiving federal funds.

The school was renamed Langston University, after John Mercer Langston, born free and of mixed race in Virginia (one fourth black, one fourth Indian and half white). His white father provided for an excellent education (B.S. and M.S.) in slave-free Ohio but, after Langston was denied admission to law school in both New York and Ohio, he was provided the opportunity to read and study the law, as an apprentice to attorney and Republican U.S. Congressman, Philemon Bliss.

Langston's life was renowned for numerous causes in behalf of people of color; especially, blacks—all exceptionally noteworthy. Among them: he assisted numerous slaves in the underground railroad to escape to freedom; education; and he assisted Republican Senator Charles Sumner of Massachusetts in drafting the bill that was enacted as the Civil Rights Act of 1875. In 1888, he was elected as a Republican to the U.S. congress, as the first person of color from Virginia. He passed away in 1897, the same year Langston University was established.

With John Mercer Langston's involvement in political and government circles in Ohio Washington, D.C., and Virginia, it's easy to speculate of his influence on the fledgling Republican Party; deliberations of Republican President Abraham Lincoln (1860-1865), the U.S. Congress, and others in Civil War matters; how to overcome the 'separate but equal' allowance of the 1862 Morrill Act, and President Lincoln's 1863 Emancipation Proclamation. Surely, Langston, like many others, were devastated by the news of Lincoln's assasination April 14, 1865, just a month before the end of the Civil War May 13, 1865. But one can speculate Langston's influence continued with drafting the texts to the End of Slavery Amendment or 13th, and the 14th and 15th Amendments to the U.S. Constitution adopted on July 9, 1868 and Februrary 3, 1870, respectively. Afterall, these occurred during the time Langston assisted Republican Senator Charles Sumner of Massachusetts in drafting the bill that was enacted as the Civil Rights Act of 1875. None of these activities would've been carried out in a vacuum.

Numerous references for John Mercer Langston are easily available in an internet search. Those few that follow should be considered only a starting point of discovery: 1) Roundtree, Helen C. Pocahontas's People: The Powhatan Indians of Virginia Through Four Centuries. Vol. 196. U. of Oklahoma Press, 1990; 2) Litwack, Leon F., and August Meier, eds, *Black Leaders of the Nineteenth Century*, U. of IL, 1991; 3) *Turkel,*

Stanley (2009). Heroes of the American Reconstruction: Profiles of Sixteen Educators. Politicians and Activists. ISBN 978-0-7864-4250-8; and 4) Cheek, William and Aimee Lee, *John Mercer Langston and the Fight for Black Freedom, 1829-65.* Urbana and Chicago, U. of IL Press, 1989.

42.

---

*November 7, 1964, Northwestern Cheerleaders at
Langston University Homecoming*

"Love you, Mom, Sis," Pam Armstead whispered, as they group hugged. "Glad you could come to the ballgame." She tossed a tease over her shoulder to them, as she started towards the other Northwestern cheerleaders, who were slowly walking away through the joyous Langston homecoming crowd exiting the stadium, "Don't let Peggy drive. Might wind up north in Topeka instead of Oklahoma City!"

Her mom laughed and replied, "Drive safe," and Sis exclaimed, "I owe you!"

In minutes, Judy Wolgamott, Sharon Boruff, Gloria Metcalf, and Pam Armstead were headed back to Northwestern and Alva. In their chatter, one asked, "And what were the reasons Mary Ann Roepke and Larisa Allen couldn't come?" No one could remember. Soon, all but the driver snuggled down for the long ride.

Boruff noticed how dirty her white tennis shoes and bobby socks were, and memories of the day flooded her mind. *That was a huge crowd! … And that band—just outstanding! Had a style of their own. Very entertaining. Everyone rockin' and shakin', even the Langston players.* "I'll always remember this day," she mumbled.

For a moment, visions of Northwestern's band and director, Oscar Stover, filled Boruff's mind. *They are really good, too. He does a great job, and has so much pep and school spirit. Cheerleaders always enjoyed being part of the halftime formations.* She pondered the question, *Wonder what Mr. Stover would think of the high-steppin' and shakin' Langston band?*

1964-65 Northwestern Cheerleaders (L-R): Judy Wolgamott, Mary Anne Roepke, Sharon Boruff, Larissa Allen, Gloria Metcalf, and Pam Armstead. Courtesy Northwestern.

The Langston game returned to Boruff's mind. *Cheerleaders were lucky we didn't get hurt when players made a tackle and rolled into us on the sidelines.* "All we could see of you, Sharon, was your tennis shoes and socks sticking out of the pile!" Boruff looked at her legs again. *No wonder they're so dirty! They mentioned another cheerleader. Wonder who it was?*

Further thoughts of the game brought on a look of sadness—a *14 to 7 Northwestern loss. Except one play, that fumble for a TD, we'd at least tied!*

A few hours into the ride, a sleepy voice broke the silence, "How much longer?"

"Be there soon. Thirty minutes or so."

As they pulled into the parking lot of Oklahoma Hall, Boruff shared a thought she had from the day. "Remember those four black girls who attended Northwestern last year, 1963-64: Dorothy Dodson, Vera Dodson, Wanda Randle, and Rosa Thompson?"

The other cheerleaders sleepily nodded, as they gathered their belongings and started towards the entrance.

"Think about it," Boruff expressed. "They were the only black students in an all-white school." She paused, as they entered the door, and corrected herself. "Well, except for the four black athletes and a few others of color. … How'd they feel? … Today, at Langston, the four of us—white cheerleaders mingled among people at an all-black school. We even joined their cheerleaders in front of their huge crowd and band! Once we started cheering, didn't notice anything different. … Did any of those four girls, a couple of whom lived down the hall from Wolgamott's room and mine, feel any different while at Northwestern?"

The group stopped at the front desk to sign back in from their trip to Langston, and Boruff quietly quipped to the others, "We don't want to get into trouble with Mrs. Lasley!"

"Remember how those four girls," Boruff asked, as they struggled up the stairs, "Would come to our rooms where we talked and laughed? We got along really well."

"Yes," Judy Wolgamott added with a sigh of relief, as they reached their floor. "Good singers, too. I remember Wanda had a guinea pig a boyfriend had given her. On the last day of school, it bit me on a finger when I tried to pet it. Mom took me to a doctor for a tetanus shot. The doctor wanted to monitor it to make sure it didn't have rabies. So, Wanda gave the pet to me. I remember she wrinkled her nose, as she said, "I didn't want the fuzzy little thing anyway."

When the door to Wolgamott's room closed behind her, she glanced at the small scar on her finger. *What ever happened to that guinea pig? … Why didn't any of those four girls return to Northwestern the next year?*

———

Author Note: An objective of this writing project included interviews with these four black female students who attended Northwestern in the 1963-64 academic year. The author and others who provided assistance, however, were unable to locate any of them. Reference to any of the four in the text is from information provided from either the Northwestern administration or comments made by others during their individual interviews.

43.

HOME FOR THANKSGIVING: AN INDIAN, COWBOY, AND CUSTER & THE 7TH CALVARY

November 1964, an Indian, Cowboy, Custer and the 7th Calvary
Northwest Oklahoma and Texas

"Do I need to get a pair of those?" Bill Mitchell teased with a laugh, as his friend, Mike 'Roids' Garrison, walked out the basement stairs of Vinson Hall and placed a dress pair of cowboy boots into the trunk of his '55 Plymouth. Mitchell noticed he was purposely ignored, so he pressed further with a joyous belly laugh, "And, one of those ten-gallon hats, too?"

Garrison rolled his eyes and shot a, *You're kidding me* look at 'em for a moment, then hitched up his jeans. Soon, the two were headed West on Highway 64 through much of the Oklahoma Panhandle. Their destination? Dalhart in northwest Texas for Thanksgiving.

"Sure kind of your Mom and Dad, to invite me."

"Look forward to seeing you again."

A few miles later, Mitchell asked in a teasing cowboy drawl, "How far did ya say it was?" He quipped before an answer, "Sure this car'll make it?"

"Come on! … She's a jewel. … Listen to 'er purr."

Thirty-five, forty miles down the road Mitchell mumbled another question, as he gazed out the window at the hill and gulley terrain,

"Ever wonder how these creeks we've crossed, like White Horse, Red Horse, and Moccosin, get their names?"

Garrison's forehead and eyebrows wrinkled and a puzzled look crossed his face, as he glanced momentarily in Mitchell's direction. "Never gave 'em a moments thought," he replied in a slow Texan tone.

"What about Cimarron River?"

Garrison glanced several times at his friend, and asked with a curious look on his face, "How's it you're so interested in all these things?"

Unfazed, Mitchell responded. "While playing ball at Dodge City— there for two years—learned a little about the Great Plains. It's so wide open and different than northern New York and the Mohawk Reservation. History out here is interesting to me."

"And, why is that?"

With a look of deep reflection, Mitchell replied slowly. "Well, lots of it involves Indians." ... "And I'm an Indian." ... Neither said more for a while.

Garrison broke the silence about a mile before the town of Buffalo. A road forked to the North, and he pointed that direction. "See those tall hills couple miles down that way?" ... "Understand fossilized oyster shells are on top of some!"

Mitchell glanced at his friend with a disbelieving look, but Garrison continued before he could ask. "Clifton Savoy has family, a sister I think, who lives there and whose farm includes some of those hills. Heard they found the shells on them." Mitchell looked towards the hills, and was about to speak, but Garrison continued. "They say long ago this area was part of a sea bed. Can you believe that? This far inland?"

"Well, I'm glad you explained," Mitchell laughed in a tongue-in-cheek tone. "I thought you were going to tell me the Indians had an oyster-shucking party on top of those hills while scouting wagon trains and watching calvary."

Garrison's expression said it all, *You kidding me?*

"That reminds me," Mitchell added. "Some of the guys knew I was going with you for Thanksgiving. Said, 'Mitchell, since you love seafood, make sure Roids gets you some sweetbread and mountain oysters while you're so close to the Rockies.'"

Garrison burst into laughter, even though he was trying to hold back, and the car momentarily headed toward the ditch. "Sounds like the Sweat twins (Don and Ron)!" ... "We'll make sure to do that!" he expressed with an ear-to-ear grin. ... "Sure will!"

As they headed West out of Buffalo, Mitchell noticed a sign on the road leading South: Fort Supply. The name of the town, coupled to what he'd learned about Fort Dodge when he was playing ball at Dodge Juco, reminded him of George Custer and the 7th Calvary in this area and Indian Territory (Oklahoma) in the 1860s U.S. military campaign against the Plains Indians.

A few miles down the road, Garrison pointed out the window. "Look at the sage brush. Just think, Zane Grey wrote all those western books like, *Riders of the Purple Sage.*"

After about 18 miles West, Highway 64 forked again. The North road was to Dodge City. "Had some good experiences there," Mitchell expressed warmly. "Wonder if old Lady Merridith is still boarding and feeding those junior college footballers?"

"Ever go to Boot Hill and check its history?"

"Yeah," Mitchell responded excitedly, "Can even see a body uncovered partially in a grave with the boots still on the guy."

"Was that real?"

"Looked like it to me. ... Guess that's what matters. ... Could buy stuff in a saloon, too. There were other things you could buy and, of course, food."

"Think Matt Dillon and Kitty of TV *Gunsmoke* fame ever set foot in Dodge City?"

"Doubt it!" Mitchell responded emphatically.

Within a mile or so, they came to the large roadside markers of the eastern boundary of the Oklahoma Panhandle, 'No Man's Land.

Mitchell mumbled, as he gazed around, "Do you know Custer and the 7ᵗʰ Calvary and 250 wagons with supplies, about 1,100 men in total, crossed this highway headed south about here?"

"Huh?" Garrison replied in a puzzled tone.

"Yeah. Traveled from Fort Dodge to set up what would become Fort Supply. November 1868. Custer and the 7ᵗʰ were on a mission to find and wipe out Black Kettle and the Southern Cheyenne with him. Indian scouts, guess enemies of the Cheyenne, were with Custer." Garrison looked at him in a curious way, and Mitchell added, "We don't all get along." … He continued, "Large military group traveled to the Beaver River, somewhere South of Gate, the town ahead."

General Custer and the 7ᵗʰ Calvary escorted a military supply train of 250 wagons from Ft. Dodge, Kansas, to (then) Camp Supply in Indian Territory

Oklahoma. From Supply, Custer and the 7ᵗʰ marched south to ambush Black Kettle and the Cheyenne winter camp along the Washita River. Photos from the National Archives.

Mitchell continued, "…had to be about a mile and half or more long, and nearly a thousand horses. … Can you imagine the logistics in feeding and watering that many people and animals? Also, learned a cold northerner blew in the first part of their journey and snowed."

The comments caught Garrison off guard at the serious tone of his friend, and he wondered, *Where you going with this?*

Mitchell added more before Garrison had a say. "Custer and the 7ᵗʰ then rode southeast from Supply and killed Black Kettle and many Cheyenne at their winter village on the Washita River in Southwest Oklahoma. Returned on the same trail with prisoners—mostly, women."

Garrison asked with a puzzled look and tone, "How do you know these things?"

"Learned a lot of the history when I was at Dodge City. *Harper's Weekly Magazine, January 1869*—I think—reported on the trip of Custer and the 7ᵗʰ and the 250-wagon supply train from Fort Dodge to Supply a few months earlier. Other history is out there." Mitchell paused before continuing, "He got his due at The Little Big Horn. … Besides. … Indians know these things … And I'm an Indian."

Over the next twenty miles towards the town of Forgan, the terrain turned to rolling pasture hills, with flat farmland in between. "I'll never get over how few trees are out here!" Mitchell exclaimed. "Notice when you see a clump of them, it's an old homestead. … Sometimes a creek bottom with cottonwoods."

"Yeah," Garrison acknowledged. "Ever hear 'em sing?"

"Huh?"

"The cottonwoods when the wind blows through the leaves. … By-the-way, see that split in the road up there? One heads south to the town of Beaver. It's where Savoy is from."

"Really? … Hope the surgery successful in repairing those football injuries." He paused for a moment then added, "But you know with your knee how some injuries stay around."

Garrison nodded, "Sure do. Had to tape it all the time." After a moment, he asked, "Rember Northwestern star high jumper, Blue?"

"You mean, Ken Blue?"

"Yeah. He's from here, town of Forgan. Said, he learned to high jump by betting others he could clear barbed-wire fences."

"That'd take a lot of courage," Mitchell said with a laugh.

"Yeah," Garrison responded with a chuckle.

The terrain became flatter and flatter as they traveled west. Another twenty miles or so they passed through the town of Turpin, and Garrison said, "Billy Foster's from here." He added after a moment, "Actually, think he grew up on a farm somewhere here abouts."

"That right?" Mitchell asked in a surprised tone, then added, "He was a good athlete—started every sport. Recognized as Northwestern's best halfback his last year, 1963. Think went on to vetinary school."

"Seems you're right. ... I remember your roomie, Kip (Jack Kippenberger), got the best lineman that year—you were up there, too."

"Thanks. Been fun to rent a house with Kip. Keep reminding him, though," Mitchell said with a laugh, "he got it because he's taller. People couldn't see me low in the trenches."

"Hear ya'."

Neither said much after that, until Mitchel mumbled, as he gazed out the window at the land as it unfolded before them. "It's so wide open. You can see for miles—almost forever."

"Yeah! That's why they call it the Great Plains!"

*Oklahoma Panhandle Landscape© Permission of
Arlene Winfry of Guymon, OK*

Mitchell asked in an unbelieving tone, "Can you imagine what the place looked like with those huge herds of buffalo grazing out here?"

"Lots of 'em. Supposedly, millions in their prime days. Actually, along our entire drive from Northwestern in Alva across the plains to Dalhart and to the Rockies. There's lots of buffalo wallows around."

"What's a buffalo wallow?"

"Buffalo'd create a low spot by kicking up the dirt onto their back to help keep off biting flies. Sometimes, they'd lay down in the dirt and roll around—wallow—on their backs to coat themselves with the dirt. Cattle'll do this, too. ... Sometimes collect rain runoff."

Mindful of his Mohawk history and reservation in Northern New York, Mitchell asked a question he didn't expect an answer. "The Plains Indians lived off of the buffalo. There were so many. Would the

Indian lifestyle have survived if they could've kept from being placed on reservations and kept the buffalo alive? I mean, it wasn't until buffalo hunters and settlers flooded the plains in the mid 1800s did all that happen. That's less than 100 years ago."

Garrison glanced at his friend and asked, "Why do you think about all this?" But before Mitchell responded, Garrison answered in a tongue-in-cheek tone, "Yeah, I know. You're an Indian. ... And, did you know pure genetic lines of buffalo herds still exist?"

Mitchell glanced at him with an inquisitive look.

"Yeah. One of the herds is on the Wichita Mountains Wildlife Refuge (WMWR), headquartered at Indiahoma, Oklahoma. ... Need to go there someday."

Buffalo herd on range and two bulls fighting by D. Hirshman (R). Courtesy of Wichita Mountains Wildlife Refuge (WMWR), Indianhoma, Oklahoma

Soon, Garrison and Mitchell drove by the towns of Hooker and Guymon and, as they approached Goodwell, Mitchell expressed, "So, this is where Panhandle Oklahoma State University is located! No wonder it seemed so far out here from Northwestern to play a game." ... "Guess about there."

"No. Dalhart's another sixty miles, but," Garrison responded in an excited tone and added, "We'll soon be in Northwest Texas!"

"That far still?" Mitchell responded. Then he had a little fun with his friend. "Texas? What's so special about Texas?"

Garrison stared at Mitchell in a disbelief look that only those from Texas and the west would understand, as he replied, "You haven't lived until you've been a cowboy in Texas. Things are bigger out here. ... We even have one of the largest ranches, maybe the biggest ever called the XIT Ranch. It was so big, several million acres, it covered 10 counties in Texas. Just think: a section of land is 640 acres and 1 mile square. Can you imagine a ranch about 4,000 square miles in size? Heard it had over 100,000 cattle. ... There were other cattle spreads, too. How difficult and dangerous being a cowboy on them and on those cattle drives to market."

"How do you know these things?" Mitchell asked with an astonished face and voice.

Garrison looked at him, and exclaimed, gleefully, "I'm a cowboy—a Texas cowboy!"

Vintage photos of a cattle drive on the western plains (upper) and a cowboy gathering. Courtesy use from the Panhandle Oklahoma State University Museum, Goodwell, Oklahoma.

They soon crossed into Texas, and Garrison excitedly added, "Be home soon!" Over the next few miles, they were silent until Garrison spoke. His tone now was one of sadness as he inquired of the near-future departure of his friend. "Guess you'll be leaving Northwestern end of the semester."

"Yeah," Mitchell answered quietly, almost in a mumble. "Time to step out into the world."

"One of those teaching and coaching positions you've been offered?"

"None near Northwestern or out in these parts."

"Huh? ... Thought you were gun-ho about taking..."

Mitchel cut him off, "I really like this wide-open country, but..." He paused and looked around at the beauty of the Plains, "I've decided to follow the lead of Benny Smith, Cherokee."

"What do you mean?"

"Remember Benny saying how he felt called to teach and mentor other Indians at Indian Nations University in Lawrence, Kansas? I, too, need to go back to my Mohawk Reservation in Northern New York and help other young Mohawks learn they can have a future." ... "One besides just working on the river and in the mills out of high school—if they even finished." ... "Yes, I know, the Mohawk steel workers are known for their fearlessness, like high on New York's Empire Building, but..." His voice softened, as he added, "Maybe someday I can send some super stars to Northwestern. Being a Ranger has been a highlight of my life—a great ride!"

———

Author Note: Bill 'Buster' Mitchell was true to his word, and held several teaching, coaching, administrative positions in the school system of his beloved Mohawk Reservation in Northern New York. In all his positions, he was a life-long mentor of young Mohawks. 'Buster,' the Mohawk student-athlete who didn't have the money to travel home in his four years playing football at Dodge City Junior College and at Northwestern Oklahoma State University, sent one of his student athletes, Brian Sochia, from the Mohawk Reservation to Northwestern. Socha became a football All-American, and played pro ball.

Soon after returning to the reservation, Buster married another Mohawk, Marie, and they were blessed with a daughter, Allison. Unfortunately, Buster passed away in 2003, but his wonderful wife, Marie, assisted with Garrison's recollection to draft this true story. ... And, yes, Buster, the Mohawk Indian, and Roids Garrison, the Texas cowboy, remained life-long friends, along with others on their North-western football teams.

———

Brian Sochia was an outstanding defensive lineman for Northwestern from 1979-82. He earned first-team All-Oklahoma Intercollegiate Conference as well as all-district honors for his junior and senior seasons. And, in 1982, he was an honorable mention to the NAIA All-American team. ... After graduation in 1983, Sochia began a ten-year profession-al career, playing for the Houston Oilers, Miami Dolphins where he gained all-pro honors in 1988, and the Denver Broncos. In 10 seasons, the Brasher Falls, N.Y., native played in 112 games and was credited with 243 tackles and 23.5 sacks. Certainly, Sochia lived up to the faith and expectations of mentor, Bill 'Buster' Mitchell.

———

As for Jack 'Kip' Kippenberger, both Mitchell's and Garrison's fellow Northwestern football lineman and friend, whom Mitchell served with as a football graduate assistant coach, his life journey took him to challenging positions as well in the military, the U.S. Secret Service where he had tours of protecting the President and Congress as well as many other national and international assignments in almost every nation. Later, he would do the same for the Billy Gram (and Franklin) world ministries. He would think each time stepping off an airplane, "the country kid from little old Thomas, Oklahoma, you've come a long way." Kip never forgot Northwestern. He, Buster, and Roids have all passed away as of April 2021, but they all expressed fond memories of Northwestern, and often exclaimed, "Ride Rangers, Ride!"

44.

TOP NEWS OF 1964: CIVIL RIGHTS ACT,
LONGEST FILIBUSTER IN SENATE
HISTORY, LBJ'S GREAT SOCIETY
MOVEMENT, VIETNAM,
THE BEATLES

December 31, 1964, TV Studio, New York City

Student dormitories, and the few TV lounges in them, on the Northwestern campus normally were closed for the Christmas and New Year's break. Still, local and national top stories of the year could be seen in other TV outlets and homes.

New York—"The top news stories of 1964," a reporter expressed, "revolved around President Lyndon B. Johnson." A scene of the Oval Office appeared, with Johnson sitting at a desk, with a number of others around. "The first was the July 2, 1964, signing of the latest version of a Civil Rights Act. Civil rights leader, Dr. Martin Luther King, Jr. was among the witnesses." … "Johnson heralded the legislation as a memorial to former President John F. Kennedy, since Kennedy had pushed it in Congress before his assassination last November 1963."

Another watered-down Civil Rights Act?

The Senate chambers appeared on the screen and Democrat Senator Robert Byrd at the podium. "Johnson spoke to support for Kennedy's bill, but ran into a long fillabuster by former Senate colleagues of Johnson's, primarily Democrats." Others in the chamber appeared. "Only a bi-partisan effort and a weaker version of the legislation ended the fillabuster." … "During debate, some Republican opponents were skeptical the legislation would be just for show. 'Why pass another Act, since this is the 4th Civil Rights Act and the 3rd in eight years?'"

"Some Republican Senate opponents of Johnson's were quick to remind anyone who'd listen, 'Not one Democrat in congress voted for either the 14th or 15th Amendments to the Constitution. Same for the 1st Civil Rights Act, the one of 1875. These covered equal protection of the laws and the right **"Why not just enforce the 13th, 14th, and 15th Amendments to the Constitution?"** to vote. Yes, these were almost a hundred years ago, but they're still in the Constitution! Why not just enforce them? … Since Johnson and his Senate Democrats gutted most of the enforcement parts from both the 1957 and 1960 Civil Rights Acts, why's he now pushing the 1964 one?'" The reporter pause, then continued, "This also seems to be on the minds of a few of Johnson's fellow Democrats."

The screen filled again with President Johnson as he signed the 1964 Act, and panned towards Dr. King standing close behind. "Johnson used momentum from passage of this Civil Rights Act, to introduce the Great Society and several programs purported to be anti-poverty. Incumbent Johnson went on to defeat Senator Barry Goldwater, a conservative; who espoused low-taxes, maller government, and opposed passage of yet, another Civil Rights Act." … "Also, he failed to receive support of the GOP Northeastern wing led by Governor's Nelson Rockefeller and William Scranton. Many conservative Republican congressmen also lost, and left almost a totally free hand to Johnson and the Democrats, and the liberal Republicans."

* * *

"Another top story of 1964 is Vietnam," the reporter expressed, as a scene of the Asian country appeared. "It's uncertain at this time how deep the Johnson Administration will involve the United States and its military. Fatalities have increased each year, though, since involvement in 1956 through 1964, with 414 total. These have doubled each year since 1960.

Vietnam, and increasing U.S. involvement and deaths!

With 216 in 1964, will they double again in 1965, and will the increasing unpopularity of the draft system boil over from the simmer now being detected?"

———

"On the lighter side, the top songs of 1964 included The Beatles, "I Want To Hold Your Hand," and "Hello Dolly!" by the immortal Louis Armstrong, whose been producing popular songs since the '20s."

45.

"HE CAN'T EAT HERE!" NORTHWESTERN 1965 BASKETBALL ROAD TRIP

January 1965, "He can't eat here!"
Northwestern OSU Basketball Roadtrip

"Ritzy place," Larry Prochnau expressed to teammate, H. L. Brown, as they left the restroom and approached the maître d'. "Hope the chow's as good as the place looks."

"Yeah," H. L. replied in a weary tone. "I'm starvin'."

After waiting a while, Prochnau grumbled, "Where are the other players?"

"They're down the hall in our dining room," the maître d' replied, as he sized the two over. "But," he added in a chilling tone, as he nodded towards H. L., "he can't eat here!"

The two players stopped abruptly in their tracks and, after a moment, Prochnau responded in stunned disbelief, "Huh?"

In a cold monotone, the maître d' replied, "Owner policy: blacks are not allowed here."

At that moment, Northwestern basketball coach, Keith Covey, walked up, looking for his team. Immediately, he noticed the anguish and frustration all over the faces of H. L. and Prochnau. "What's going on?" he asked.

"They won't let H. L. eat here!" Prochnau blurted out angrily. "Says blacks not allowed!"

The maître d' nodded a confirmation, as Covey looked his way.

"We'll go some place else!" Covey responded sharply. "Plenty of other restaurants in Oklahoma City, who'd want our business! I'll get the other players."

Prochnau exclaimed loudly over his shoulder, as the Northwestern basketball team walked out passed the maître d', "Ain't right! Just ain't right!"

46.

"THEY'RE GONNA MAKE ME FAT" TO ALVA CHURCH AND CHARLES LINDBERG

A smile crossed Curtis Thompson's face, as he closed the parsonage door to another church member who'd brought some food. "They're gonna make me fat," he chuckled on his way to the refrigerator. "Glad Northwestern's basketball season is over!" He paused momentarily, as he wondered, *who'd guess a kid from Harris, a small all-black town in Little Dixie Oklahoma—the southeast tip of the state, would become a student in basically an all-white university, located in an all-white town—Alva, and welcomed with open arms by an all-white church?*

Why is my treatment here, so opposite to what black people have received across the South and in Washington D.C., and in big cities of the North?

He'd seen TV coverage, just a few days earlier, March 1965, of Dr. Martin Luther King, Jr., and others as they marched along the hostile road from Selma to the Alabama State Capital in Montgomery. Thompson recalled a few of Dr. King's comments as he led this and many other non-violent protests:

"Across the South, homes are bombed and churches burned down. In just the

Sunday morning bombing of the 16th Street Baptist Church in Birmingham September 1963 four innocent girls were killed. ... Civil rights workers are brutally murdered, and few are convicted. Ghettos in the North are being intensified, and northern school segregation is increasing. ... Long way to go for equal justice."

"...equal justice?" "And," Thompson mumbled, "who can forget King in D.C.?"

"I have a dream that one day this nation will rise up and live out the true meaning of its creed: "We hold these truths to be self-evident, that all men are created equal." ... Martin Luther King, Jr., 28 August 1963, Washington, D.C.

A knock on the door interrupted Thompson's thoughts. *More food!* ... "Thank you very much. Yes, the Lindberghs are supposed to be back for Sunday services. No, there's nothing else I need. ... Thanks again." *The Lindberghs were pretty trusting,* Thompson thought, as he remembered how he came to be in their home.

"Curtis Thompson!" Minister Charles Lindbergh called out across the Sunday morning congregation. "Curtis Thompson!" he joyously expressed, as Thompson raised slowly from his seat among his college friends. "Come down to the front please!"

"For the two weeks my family and I will be out of town, I've asked Curtis to house sit for us and watch over the church building and grounds." He laughed as he added, "Not sure he can cook, so you might bring him a little food to get him through."

As Thompson closed the refrigerator door one more time, his thoughts turned to what's happened since he arrived at Northwestern a little over a year ago, January 1964. *A lot of people here have opened doors for me. I had no money, was AWOL, and knew no one when I stepped off that bus!*

The girl who gave me, a stranger, a ride to Northwestern. President Martin going to bat for me in so many ways. Coach Covey and the basketball team and John Altramura showing me around. Dr. Arthors and my other professors. The cafeteria job, and Mr. Taylor and Patty, his daughter, so positive and complimentary. "If we can ever help, let us know."

The kindness of those twins, Beverly and Barbara Biggs and another pair, who also worked in the cafeteria, they invited me to go with them to the Christian Church. When I wasn't working, in class, or at basketball, I was with friends at the church in its study or rec room. Felt like a king. Never out of place.

Suddenly, the chill of other words by Dr. King came to Thompson's mind. "…lynchings of Negros have about ceased today…"

Thompson pondered the words, "…lynchings have about ceased." He wondered, *Why am I treated so differently here?*

47.

SCARY NIGHT AT THE MORGUE

Spring 1965, Scary Night at the Morgue
Alva, Oklahoma

The evening began as a study session of some Northwestern science students in a small, back room of a mortuary where Jerry Hoover and Les Jacobs, both of Beaver, Oklahoma, bunked and worked part time. Before the night ended, it was filled with fun and fright!

"You're telling us," I asked in a nervous tone, as we stopped for a break in our study, "the bodies are prepped in the next room?"

"Yep, Savoy," replied Hoover with a raspy country laugh, which no one would mistake for anyone else, as he opened a door to a restroom and pointed to a door on the other side. "This is also used by people in the body prep-room." He was excited, seeing the place made us uneasy.

"Yeah," Jacobs gleefully added, as he purposely stroked the fire to our nerves. "We bring the bodies in from the hearse through these back doors. And…" Suddenly, Hoover startled us, like he and Jacobs had rehearsed for this very moment, by noisily opening the nearby double doors to the prep room. "And," Jacobs continued in a giddy tone, as he pointed to an object located just a few feet inside, "we place them on that embalming table."

All of us immediately crowded into the doorway to scan the scene.

… A walkway extended along the left wall, down to double doors at the end. … The far walls to the front and right were covered by glass door cabinets with bottles of fluid and supplies on the shelves. … Underneath were drawers, which later we learned had tools and prep materials. … The wall to our right had a deep sink and the door to the restroom. … My imagination might've been playing tricks, but it seemed the lights cast an unusual, eerie effect around the room.

The embalming table, which Jacobs mentioned earlier, was the elephant in the room, though. It was kitchen counter high, and seemed so close to the back entrance. A person would almost touch it going in or out if not careful. The white sheet covering it created a sense of mystery. I noticed its extra length and width. *Must be to accommodate all body sizes.*

A tour of the building was suggested, and all exclaimed, "Yes!"

"Okay," Hoover replied, and started walking towards the double doors at the far end. Over his shoulder, he added, "We'll start at the front. No viewings or funerals are scheduled. The place is empty."

An hour passed, but seemed like only minutes when we returned to the prep-room where we began. Our hearts were pounding and the study session was far in the rearview mirror of our thoughts, as excited comments rolled out.

"Wow! This gives me chills up and down my spine!"

"Yeah, me too! What if we had to spend a hands-on learning week here as part of our human anatomy class?"

"I'd like it, but bet some students would drop the class."

Another person hustled up to the group. He was breathless and acted spooked. "Y'all walked off and left me standing next to one of those caskets in the sales room. Lights went off, and then the chamber music sounded. Freaked me out!" … Looking around at the place like it had dawned on him for the first time, he asked, "Hoover and Jacobs really sleep back here?"

The joyous fright had us on an adrenaline high, and a mischievous comment was made. "Hey, let's bring some of our Northwestern class-mates out here, and scare 'em!"

It was a short distance to campus and Vinson Hall, and it didn't take long to drive and return. Three guys were with me: football starters, Ben and Glen Smith, and basketball starter, Jim Schroeder. Greetings were exchanged with Hoover and Jacobs at the rear entrance door of the mortuary. "Hi, guys, glad to meet you."

"Savoy," Hoover said, but with a wink where no one else could see, "Unless someone pulls up right away, we need to go ahead with the tour."

"Okay," but I had no idea what was up. Didn't have long to think about it, though, as Jacobs opened the double doors to the prep room at that moment. When I saw the embalming table, I understood. ... *They've spiced up the tour! ... Unless, ... I gulped. ... Unless that's not a student prankster under that white sheet!*

Ben, Glen, and Schroeder abruptly stepped backwards like they were about to head out the back door, but Hoover quickly called out in a sharp tone like a military drill sergeant, "Follow me." He started walking along the wall past the table towards the far end of the room.

I brought up the rear, but had to turn away a couple of times because I couldn't hold my laugh. These three big college athletes kept their eyes on the table, as they cautiously moved sideways along the wall next to it. They pressed their bodies so tightly to the wall, they looked like they were creeping along an outside ledge, 6 inches wide and 20 stories up!

Suddenly, an "Uhh…" ghoulish sound came from under the white sheet and, simultaneously, an arm—elbow and hand—dropped down into sight along the table. It was inches away from the three Northwestern athletes, and all froze in place, as they yelled out in surprise, "Ahh ugh."

Before they could stampede out of the building or notice the heart pulse in the wrist of the dangling arm, Hoover casually walked over, lifted it back under the white cloth, and said, "Happens sometimes. Body temp's dropping, and muscles are constricting. Causes parts to move and the diaphragm to squeeze the lungs."

The sound and arm movement shocked me too, but the looks on Ben's, Glen's, and Schroeder's faces was so funny I had to step quickly back into the other room to keep from blowing the fun.

A subtle grin appeared on Hoover's face, as he stoked their imagination, "Sometimes the temperature drop causes the stomach muscles to constrict so much the body will sit up and even make sounds like you heard." … He paused to let the concept sink in and to turn away to hide his laugh, which he choked back. He added over his shoulder, as he headed down the walkway, "Then those preparing it have to use force to weigh the body down to straighten it out. If that doesn't work, then the stomach muscles are cut." His performance was priceless.

Ben, Glen, and Schroeder quickly followed Hoover—almost pushing him along, but they glanced back several times at the table until they left the room. The sight of their faces, big eyes, and nervous steps kept me choking back the laughs.

Emotions calmed some once we left the prep room, but the lights and chamber music in the front area kept nerves on edge, and it wouldn't take much for them to stampede out the building.

"Made up your mind which one you want?" Hoover asked with a

slight ribbing tone, as we toured the casket sales room. He looked at the guys and added, "See one that catches your attention, I could help you get in and try it on. See if it fits."

Everyone laughed. Big Ben responded with more uneasy laughter. "No thanks. Not me!" He followed with, "Schroeder might, though."

"I'll pass, too," Schroeder replied as he took a step back.

Glen nodded and said emphatically so everyone understood, "Not me!"

One of the viewing rooms was next. In the earlier tour, it was empty. This time, they'd added another bit of spice—a closed casket. *Is there another student prankster inside? ... No, they'd never find one with guts to do it. ... But, did they?*

Hoover somehow, though, manipulated us to the casket side. He turned away for a moment to exchange his ear-to-ear grin for a serious look, and whispered, "I can open it if you'd like to see how a body looks after..." At that point, the three athletes bolted out the door, almost running me over. Hoover and I caught up with them just inside the prep room, where they stopped upon sight of the embalming table with the sheet-covered body, down by the exit door.

Hoover managed to direct their attention to the glass cabinets in the opposite corner and walls, but the three guys kept an eye on that embalming table.

I caught sight of Hoover's eyes, and we both choked back laughter. To make things worse, I thought I heard Jacobs laughing in the back room. *What's he and Hoover up to?*

Ben, Glen, and Schroeder were breathing heavily and they were so tense it reminded me of when runners are in the blocks to sprint down a track. Bodies are wound so tight, almost anything—a twitch or flinch—and they'll explode away!

Hoover was a great actor, and in a serious tone, "Like I explained earlier, the fluids in these bottles are used in the prep process." He paused. "Yes, some for embalming." Quickly, he opened several drawers before pulling a huge knife from one. "This is what they use to cut those stomach muscles I mentioned." ... He stepped to hand it to Big Ben, but pulled it back quickly. ... "Hmm," he said examining it closely. ... "Think it still has blood on it." ... Hoover had our total attention, and all of us stepped towards him to look.

I guess that was the cue for Jacobs and whoever was under the white sheet to do their things as, simultaneously, a loud "bang," sounded from the restroom and a ghoulish moan, "Uhh...", came from the embalming table.

All of us jumped and stared at the sight. The body under the white sheet was half-way sitting up, and that ghoulish sound, "Uhh..." filled the air.

Ben and Glen exploded out of that room, like wild cattle charging from a pen. In a flash, they were out of the building. Schroeder froze, but was coughing, like me, in trying to catch his breath. His was fright, though, and mine from laughter.

"Did you see how fast they shot out of here?" Jacobs asked in a joyous but concerned tone.

Hoover replied, "I think one of them actually jumped over the end of that table!" He laughed and coughed to catch his breath. "Just not room for both to go by it at the same time!"

Neither of them was outside, so Schroeder and I drove directly to Vinson Hall, and knocked on their door. "Ben? Glen?" They wouldn't answer but, after a couple of weeks, we were friends again. ... And, I have no memory of how we did on the science test.

———

Author Note: Both Jerry Hoover and Les Jacobs went on to become highly successful and well respected business entrepreneurs. They seemed to delight, though, in retelling and reliving their 'Scary night at the morgue,' even fifty years later. It would be difficult to guess how many times between.

Unfortunately, Jerry Hoover passed before the final draft of this chapter, but it was approved by his wife, Sue as well as by Lester Jacobs, Glen Smith, and Jim Schroeder. During his recorded interview, Hoover did share the disappointment of not being able to participate in athletics at the university level because of a major knee injury; especially, after what I personally know to have been a fantastic high school athletic career in football and track as a halfback and sprinter with two state football championships. Northwestern's loss. I am sure, however, the joyous spirit of Hoover and Jacobs, as well as the others involved, will live on forever.

48.

1965 NEWS SPECIAL:
VIETNAM DECLARED AN 'OFFICIAL WAR'

August 1965, Vietnam declared "Official War"
Northwestern Oklahoma State University

The 1965 summer was over, and I (Clifton Savoy) was driving back to Northwestern to begin practice for the football season. I didn't realize it at the time, but I'd become a different person, as my thoughts of life had been forever changed in those few months.

Normally, I would've felt sky high in anticipation of seeing teammates and friends again, meeting new faces, and studies towards my degree. Instead, thoughts of the Vietnam news reports and death numbers I'd heard over tv and radio the last few weeks filled my mind. They troubled me greatly, and I soon learned, also troubled most other single, able-bodied guys my age—eighteen to about twenty-six.

The visual part of my trip was a blur. The United States military involvement in Vietnam had escalated rapidly from twenty-three thousand troops the start of 1965 to more than one hundred eighty thousand, and President Lyndon B. Johnson's administration now described it as an Official War. To help build up the military, the draft was implemented, and Johnson declared, "…raise the Draft Call…"

I glanced at my wallet lying in the seat beside me with my Selective Service card in it and my draft classification stamped on it—1-A. *How do I fit into this draft business?* Another disturbing comment by President Johnson popped into my head. "War in Vietnam will get worse before it gets better. … More troops will be sent."

I was naive, probably like most other guys my age, and didn't know many of the details about the U.S. military involvement in Vietnam, but thought I understood that Draft calls were selective and I'd at least be given time to finish my college studies. Still, the words of President Johnson to the nation were not comforting, "Involvement in Vietnam is a national horror." … And, I saw on the tv screen reports of guys like me were being killed daily.

As my car topped the last hill about six miles west of campus, my mind was filled with news scenes of flag-draped coffins being loaded for the long ride to family and a final resting place. A life cut short of any potential and a personal story likely never to be known—just a hyphen between two dates on a cemetery stone. … *Is that what will become of me?*

Guys in my circle and others I interacted with after the summer of 1965 at Northwestern, especially, those with a 1-A Draft classification, didn't talk much about Vietnam, but I'm sure, like me, it was ever-present on their minds. And, when we'd pass tv lounges, like the one in Vinson Hall, we'd slow our walks to give a listen when any Vietnam news was reported. Unfortunately, the scenes didn't change of flag-draped coffins, and Johnson's words kept rolling through my mind, "Involvement in Vietnam is a national horror… and, more men are needed."

49.

1965 NORTHWESTERN SEASON: NEW FOOTBALL COACH, NEW HOPE

August 1965, New Football Coach, New Hope
Northwestern Oklahoma State University

The sun was barely up the morning of our first preseason practice. Already it was a couple degrees warmer, and heatwaves would soon be rising from the parking lot pavement.

Big Ben Smith and I jawed at each other in a friendly, but aggressive way, as we walked towards the dressing rooms in Percival Fieldhouse from the Vinson Hall basement. Ben's brother, Glen, and Leon Stewart, another standout player from Crescent, Oklahoma, laughed and purposely avoided the banter.

"Ben," I teased with a gentle forearm poke at the big bear of a guy. "Better hope coach doesn't let the defense have a crack at you carrying the ball in practice. Put a hurt on you!"

"Yeah, yeah, Savoy!" He snickered with a skeptical tone, as my forearm bounced off his body. "I'd run ya over with such force, it'd tear that muscle from the arm bone like ya got last year! You'd hafta nurse it along, have surgery again, and I'd be in coach's doghouse."

Soon we were walking through the large court area and heard the cheerleaders working out at the far end. Someone in the group expressed, "Looks like Dr. Carmichael has the new squad—several new ones."

"Yeah," Big Ben commented with a chuckle. "Wonder how many footballers will linger around today?"

"Probably, most," another snickered.

Northwestern 1965-66 Cheerleaders (L-R): Gloria Metcalf, Lois Sears, Mary Drake, Gloria Huslig, Claudia Nichols, and Jan Clark.

Before long we were headed down the hall to the dressing rooms. New head coach, Bill Schnebel, greeted players, as they passed by his office. "Expect big things from you four this year," he told us with a hand tap on Ben's shoulder.

Coach Schnebel was upbeat, as Northwestern had received lots of preseason publicity. *New Coach, New Hope* were the headlines in the Oklahoma City and Tulsa papers, and across western Oklahoma, northwest Texas, and southwest Kansas. Optimism was stoked by return of some proven performers.

A few steps inside, the season excitement was apparent. Players were busy finding lockers, assessing equipment, talking and friendly jousting with others, whom they'd not seen since start of summer break. Ben, Glen, Stewart, and I soon were deep into the moment. A graduate assistant reminded everyone, "Offense in the front room and defense in back. If you play both or don't know, look for your name."

Stewart peeled off and said over a shoulder, "See you."

Rangers Get New Coach, New Hope

Northwestern State College averaged 8.7 points a game in Oklahoma Collegiate Conference action last year. Its loop opponents averaged 16.0 points a contest. And that was just about the season-long story. The Rangers always seem to be finishing one touchdown short of their foes.

The result was a 3-7-0 overall reading and a 1-6-0 conference standing, thus returning the Rangers to the league's cellar after a year's elevation to fifth place.

Northwestern's returning performers may be used to the dampness of the league's basement (the Rangers have finished there three of the last four campaigns) but their new coach is not.

Bill Schnebel arrives at Alva this fall to become the only new coaching face in the OCC. With him he brings a 62-23-1 overall record from nine years of bossing the College of Emporia, Kan. He was actually at the school 10 years, one as an assistant before taking over the head coor job. In that time, his teams won three Kansas Colleg-

THE ROSTER

End — Chip Myers (176) Stillwater, jr.; Clifton Savoy (185) Beaver, sr.; Glen Smith (200) Cresent, jr.; Ken Strunk (175) Del City, sr.

Tackle — Lee Crowdis (199) Thomas, soph.; Jim Davis (240) Carmen, sr.; Glen Roberson (206) Dalhart, Tex., soph; Jim Speaks (191) Woodward, sr.; Ed Stewart (205) Alva, sr.; Leon Stewart (212) Crescent, jr.

Guard — Larry Estep (188) Calumet, soph.; Bruce Foster (182) Turpin, jr.; Rober Herold (202) Patchogue, N.Y., jr.; Phil Reinking (180) Arkansas City, jr.

Center — John Estep (206) Calumet, jr.; Dick Tatro (190) Alva, soph.

Quarterback — Jim Elliott (165) Wakita, soph.; Larry Atkinson (169) Beaver, soph.

Halfback — Ed Amerin (185) Plains, Kan., jr.; Melton Bassett (175) Woodward, soph.; Jeff Coburn (170) Geary, soph.; Ed Herchock (157) Waynoka, soph.; Don Newman (150) Enid, soph; Ron Pryor (174) Louisville, Ky. sr.; Paul Whitman (175) Alva, soph.

BILL SCHNEBEL
New Coach

GLEN SMITH
Big Receiver

I glanced at Ben and Glen with a quizzical look, as we headed on to the back room. Ben played lots of offense last year, and Glen started every game on offense his first two years. His second-year performance had been recognized by being named to the Oklahoma Collegiate Conference Team.

Ben read my thoughts and replied, "We asked to play some defense this season."

"Yeah," Glen added in a giddy tone. "Want to give out hits instead of getting them, but will still play some on offense."

A teasing question struck me, as I looked their way, and I couldn't resist blurting out, "A little payback to white guys?"

"Whoever comes our way," Ben responded with a slight grin. "Whoever comes our way."

Our lockers were side-by-side, and Ben gave a shout out to Harold Maloy, as we entered the room. He was the third black player on the team the year before. "Hey, Maloy!" Ben laughed loudly, as he teased, "Didn't think you'd find your way back from Slickville, Pennsylvania!"

Maloy flashed his pearly-whites in an ear-to-ear grin, and hustled over to give us a welcome. After a minute, he added, "Wan'cha meet some brothers, new on the team: Johnny Davis of Ft. Worth, Texas, and Dave Billups of Niagara Falls, New York." Another walked around the corner, as Maloy finished, "And this this is Ron Washington."

After greetings, I sized them up: *Backs and a lineman. Not my positions.* "Six, now," I teased. "Gonna take over the team?"

They laughed, as Big Ben quipped, "Yep!"

The 1965 season had begun.

50.

A COMANCHE, COWBOY, AND MA GRIGGS. "BEST GET THAT STUFF OFF . . ."

September 1965, a Comanche and Cowboy
Northwestern Oklahoma State University

"Don't get comfy!" Richard 'Dick' Robinson exclaimed from a sprawled position on his bed to Lance Rollins, who staggered, exhausted, into their third floor Vinson Hall room after a grueling, hot afternoon of football practice. He handed Rollins a note, but didn't wait for him to read it.

"Ma Griggs (dormitory manager and Ma to every resident guy) wants to see us, pronto!" As they headed down the stairs, Robinson asked, "You do anything?"

"Nah," Rollins mumbled. "At least, nothing I recall. You?"

"Nope!"

The office\apartment door suddenly opened as they started to knock. It was almost like Ma Griggs saw them through it. Before they could ask, she swished passed them, with an arm and hand in the air and a finger motion of, 'follow me.' It was the equivalent of the strict pioneer schoolmarm towing a disruptive student by the ear to stand in the corner!

A few steps and Ma Griggs was out the East entrance of Vinson Hall. Rollins and Robinson had to hustle to keep up!

On the front porch, she turned, pointed upwards, and asked, in a you-best-be-truthful tone, "What is that dark stuff running three-four feet down the bricks from your window?"

Both guys glanced at each other and stammered, "Uh, … ah," as they searched for a way to explain how a near-full soft drink bottle had tipped over in their window and the contents slowly dripped through the loose cap and down the outside of the building. It turned dark and gooey as it dried.

Ma Griggs didn't wait for an answer. "Best be gone by this Saturday." She looked sternly at Rollins, and added, "Or you'll not be playing in the Northwestern football game!" Then at Robinson, "And you'll lose a major privilege, too! … Understand?"

Rollins' Comanche ancestors of Rollins might've understood the connection of a descendent with a cowboy, but they'd surely wondered how this petite white woman had him so restrained. And, the cowboys, who Robinson had worked with on those ranches the prior summers, likely would've been puzzled to how easily his rawhide, western toughness had been hogtied!

"Yes, ma'am," they blurted in unison. And sure enough, the only thing left of the black stuff was a slightly visible stain and their memory.

51.

NORTHWESTERN ROAD TRIP:
"WE DON'T SERVE COLOREDS HERE!"

September 1965, Football Roadtrip to Northeastern OSU
Tahlequah, Oklahoma[FN]

"We don't serve Coloreds here!" Ben and Glen Smith had experienced those words before. They'd also heard the follow-up insult whispered, "Come to the back door. We'll serve you there." Never expected this, though, after a Northwestern game at Northeastern OSU, the Redmen, in Tahlequah, OK, where the capital of the Cherokee Nation is located.

Northwestern lost, and the team had stopped for the after-game-meal before the long bus ride back to Alva. The mood was solemn, and sounds were mostly from the shuffle of feet. Anger and frustration raged within Glen Smith, as he and brother, Ben, watched the other players file slowly by into the rear door of the restaurant. *Where's the coaches?* *… Why aren't my teammates refusing to eat without us?*

"What's the problem here?" exhausted head coach, Bill Schnebel asked in a puzzled look as he walked up to the end of the line, and noticed Ben and Glen not entering with the others.

"Restaurant won't feed 'em inside," a grad assistant responded. "Said they weren't allowed in. But," he added with a nod towards a nearby picnic table, "they'll feed them here in back."

"That won't do!" shot back Schnebel in an angry voice. "We'll go somewhere else."

"Where?" the grad assistant replied in a frustrated tone. "Remember? We checked before the trip. Few places near here that'll sit this many."

Big Ben stepped toward them at that moment. "Coach." Schnebel and the grad assistant looked up at the big, 6'5," 275 lbs athlete. He spoke in a voice of controlled anguish. "Coach, Glen and I've been down this road before." Ben glanced momentarily at his brother, and continued. "We'll make do. We'll eat out here," he added as Glen nodded his head.

Schnebel rejected the idea, but Ben pressed the suggestion. "No!" Schnebel exclaimed. Ben pressed further and more emphatically. "Well, okay," Schnebel agreed reluctantly. "I'd rather not, though."

Before long, three meals were delivered to the Smith brothers, who'd been biding time sitting on top of the table. "Who's the extra one for?" Ben asked.

The waiter shrugged and replied over his shoulder, as he walked away, "Dunno. Told only to bring out to this table."

Glen and Ben looked at each other for a moment, and then Glen concluded, "Must be for Milt Bassett. Injured a knee in the game, and I think he's still on the bus."

"Maybe right. Let's go eat with him."

"This was against me as a black person!"

"Why didn't my teammates stand up for us?"

"My worst time at Northwestern!"

Author Note: Fifty years later, in 2015, Clifton Savoy interviewed Glen Smith for this Northwestern story. Big Ben had passed away. Glen's voice quivered, with an anguished, sometimes bitter tone, as he spoke. "Savoy, I remember that moment, just like it was only a few minutes ago. My thoughts of that time have haunted me all these years. I agonized, 'This is Tahlequah, capital of the Cherokee Nation! This wasn't about people of color. It was against me as a black person. ... And, why didn't the 1964 Civil Rights Act prevent how we were treated? It was passed the year before. ... And, worst of all, why didn't my Northwestern teammates stay outside with us? My stomach cramped, as I watched them walk past us! That was the worst experience of my time at Northwestern! ... For all of it, I wanted to double over, and cry out, 'Why?' It made Ben and me feel like a half man! God didn't make any junk!"

I was stunned, and paused to collect my composure and anger at what I'd just heard. "Glen I was one of those who walked by you and Ben. I remember you two standing there, outside the restaurant, with a couple of others on the team. I was exhausted from the game, and my mind was to get off my feet. I had no idea why you were there until this interview. No thought of you and Ben eating outside. ... I'm deeply sorry it happened, and hope had I known, others, too, we would've stayed outside with you guys."

"Savoy, you really didn't know?"

"No!"

"You have no idea how good I feel about what you just said."

Over several weeks that followed, I kept thinking about the interview I had with Glen, and what was shared. *That had to be a gut-wrenching time for them. ... And they'd had them before! ... Wished I had the opportunity to talk about this with Big Ben. ... I still do!*

52.

BEN AND GLEN'S ROUND THREE
VERSUS LANGSTON UNIVERSITY

Fall 1965, Round Three vs Langston University
Northwestern Oklahoma State University

No knockouts occurred in rounds one and two against Langston University for Big Ben Smith or brother, Glen; but it did seem they experienced multiple players blocking or tackling them on each snap of the ball, excessively rough hits, and plenty of 'Uncle Tom' taunts, any of which normally result in a penalty flag. None were thrown, though. Coach Art Parkhurst cautioned, "Protect yourselves, but don't get ejected from the game."

"Round three!" Big Ben declared in a 'let's do it' tone, as he finished dressing for the 1965 game against visiting Langston University. His thoughts were on previous games. *Will this one be as rough as the first two?* He was about to find out, as kick-off was an hour away.

Glen, dressing nearby, glanced at Ben, as the muscles in his jaw tightened. He nodded agreement there'd be battles the brothers would face, and instructed, as he reached for his helmet, "Strap 'em on tight, 'cause you're gonna need it if they come at us like before."

"Yeah," Ben replied. "But we play mostly defense this year, and," he paused as a grin slid across his face and a sparkle filled his eyes, "We get to do some tackling and hitting!"

"Yeah," Glen responded in a giddy tone. "Fun's a comin'."

Sidney Smiley, senior defensive line starter, listened from his nearby locker. *What're they talking about?* Once the referee blew his whistle to start the game, he began to understand. Seemed Ben and Glen had some type of contact with a Langston player or players on every play, even if they weren't near the ball. And, it wasn't touch football!

Midway through the second quarter, when the heat of competition was heavy, uniforms were dirty and soaked with sweat, and faces flushed with rivers of sweat, too, Smiley asked the Smiths, as players on defense made their way off the field, "What's the extra rough house stuff all about?"

"No different than first two games," Glen replied, as he plopped down on a sideline bench for a much-deserved breather.

Ben added, "Carried the ball in last year's game, and hit me pretty hard. ... Piled on, too. ... Refs let us play. ... Rough in the piles." An ear-to-ear grin filled Ben's face, as he added, "Glen and I gave a little payback, too. ... Some 'Uncle Tom and traitor' stuff thrown our way. ... Glen had other offers, but we chose Northwestern. ... Didn't go over well we chose an all-white school, over an all-colored one like Langston."

Glen nodded his head in agreement as Ben further explained.

"Not all love'n peace among black folks."

Mid-way through the third quarter, when Northwestern was on defense, a large pile-up occurred away from the ball and Big Ben was near the bottom of it. Long after the whistle, excessive roughness still occurred, and Ben was getting the worst of it. At least, in the eyes of Smiley.

"Get off him! Get off him!" Smiley yelled, and started pulling legs and jerking bodies of Langston players and dragging them off Ben. Referee flags flew. Smiley and three Langston players were ejected from the game.

Later, when the defense made it to the sideline, Ben plopped down beside Smiley and asked, "Why'd you do that?" Before Smiley could respond, Ben added in a somewhat thankful tone, "Best not get involved in our black-on-black fights!"

A few minutes later, as Ben chugged a drink, wiped sweat from his face, and strapped his helmet back on for more defensive battle, Smiley expressed, "I'd do it again!"

53.

BIG BEN, "THOUGHT WE WERE FRIENDS."
"NICE TUSH, BEN!"

November 1965, "Thought we were friends."
Overnight to Beaver, Oklahoma

The engine roared to life, and I waved a goodbye to Mom, who stood on the front porch of our house. My younger brother, Floyd, peered curiously out a second-floor window, as he watched every move of the big black guy with me. I tossed him a head nod. Mom, called out, as she waved, "Ben, come visit again."

In minutes, Ben Smith and I were whizzing along, back to Northwestern after our last-minute decision for the one-night trip to my home town, Beaver, Oklahoma, to see its 1965 state playoff football game against Carnegie.

I felt rejuvenated from the visit with friends, Mom's cooking and, of course, clean clothes. "Great trip," I said to Ben in an exhilarating tone, "Glad you could come with me."

He gave no indication he heard me, but I knew he did. *Why so silent? … Ben's always been an out-going, glad-hearted, happy guy. … Not like him. … What's up?*

Didn't wonder long. A few miles down the road, Ben mumbled something, as he stared out at the lands passing by. I wasn't sure, but it sounded like, "Thought we were friends."

I gave him a glance, but before I could inquire, he turned and looked intently into my eyes and asked, in an anguished, most serious tone I'd ever heard pass from his lips, "Savoy, … am I your Nigger?"

The words hit me, like a heavy body blow! I was stunned and, momentarily, my mind went blank until the rough bounce brought me back to my senses, as I'd driven part way off the highway. Back on the road, I glanced at Ben sitting rigidly in the shotgun seat. The perspiration specs on his dark forehead glistened in the sunlight, and made the big guy look sort of angelic. That wasn't reality, though, as his jaw muscles were clamped so tight they bulged outwardly. Must've been thousands of pounds of pressure on his teeth.

Did I hear what I think I just heard? … His question reverberated through my mind, as the last twenty-four hours flashed through it as well.

"Only conditioning drills today," a Northwestern football graduate assistant coach announced, as players arrived for the Friday practice. "Coaches not here. Will be looking at some high school players this evening. Also, no Saturday practice because they'll be scouting our next opponents."

Practice over, a wild idea hit me, as I stepped from the showers and noticed the time. *Five o'clock. Two hours before kickoff.* "Hey, Ben," I expressed to the big guy dressing beside me. "Let's drive to Beaver and see the high school play-off game. … They're playing Carnegie. … Think both are undefeated. … If we hurry, we can barely make it."

"Well, uh," Ben stammered as his hands felt the pockets of his jeans. … "I'd like, … but…"

"Won't need any dough," I added. "Probably get there after ticket sales close. Stay at my house, and drive back tomorrow."

"Well, if you think…"

"Good!" I exclaimed over my shoulder. "I have to grab my dirty clothes back at Vinson Hall. See you at my car!"

As we entered the city limits of Beaver, it dawned on me we'd walk into the house without Mom having any idea we were coming. *Oops! She won't be happy being surprised.* When Big Ben and I walked through the door, she and my brother, Floyd, had just cleared the table and cleaned the kitchen. "Hi, Mom, Floyd," I blurted out.

"Oh, Clifton!" Mom expressed in a startled, 'glad to see you, but don't let it happen again' tone and facial expression to match. She followed with a warm hug and kiss.

Floyd nodded his head, as I turned sideways to Ben and added, "Remember Ben?" … "Ben Smith. Plays on Northwestern's team with me? You've met him when you came to see me play."

"Sure do," Mom replied and, while drying her hands on a dishtowel and after a few moments of silence to let the reality sink in of the big guy standing a few feet away, added slowly, "Welcome," … "Ben."

Floyd wave and nodded from across the kitchen, as he said, "Good seeing you again."

"Hello, Mam." Ben responded to Mom in a hesitant tone and body language to match. As he nodded back to Floyd, he faced Mom, and said, "Thanks for havin' me."

"Northwestern doesn't play this week," I explained. "So, decided at the last minute to drive out to the Beaver game. Going back tomorrow afternoon," I added over my shoulder, as I set my large bag of dirty clothes by the laundry room door.

Ben and I soon were headed to the game, gobbling down some of Mom's leftovers along the way. Next morning, she fixed a great breakfast, and he and I were driving back to Northwestern by early afternoon.

It was only minutes, but seemed we sat silently for hours after Ben's question.

Until we were ready to talk, thet radio music fading in-and-out, the winds rushing by the open windows, and the whine of the tires on the pavement kept us company.

Our eyes finally locked onto each other. "Ben!" I exclaimed in a puzzled tone. "I don't have the foggiest idea what you're talking about! … I don't know what that word means, and… I've never said it before!"

Ben responded immediately and in a defiant tone, with body language to match. "Savoy, you know what I'm talking about!"

I pleaded for some understanding, "Honestly! I don't."

"Well, what was that reaction from your mom and brother when we walked into your house? … And, that big crowd at the ball game? Did ya notice how quiet they became when they saw me, a black guy, with you? … And last night through the bedroom wall, heard your brother and you laughing and talking, something about 'how startled your mom was and big her eyes became when she saw me as we walked into her house?' … And, your mom shaking her finger at you on the porch as we packed up to leave?

"Easy to read her lips, 'Clifton, don't let this happen again!' … I thought we were friends, and you paraded me, a black guy, around your mom and brother and hometown like I was some type of prized show horse!"

I grasped for some sanity. *How could a couple of people become close, like I thought Ben and I were, and then, in reality, our relationship was so fragile? …* Suddenly, it dawned on me. *Most of this was a huge misunderstanding of each other's life and experiences.*

"Ben," I pleaded for some understanding. "Yes, you're right. Mom and Floyd were shocked when you walked into the house. They weren't expecting even me, let alone you. … And, yes, the large crowd at the ballgame went silent when they first saw you. … Except for a few black people at Liberal, Kansas, don't think there's any in this area of Northwest Oklahoma or its Panhandle. Neither Mom nor the crowd were used to seeing any black people."

"Seemed pretty hostile," Ben responded in a subdued tone that still had a tinge of skepticism. "And why aren't there any blacks around?"

"No jobs, and think the crowd was just shocked. … Did hear towns in this area once had an understanding, 'Don't let the sun go down with you here,' but I've never heard anyone in Beaver or these parts express anything like that. Also, never seen or heard of any 'No

Coloreds Allowed' signs. … Might've been a long time ago. I do not know. … Think folks're like me—no experience around black people."

"Why, the first time I ever saw a black person was when I was about eight years old in Oklahoma City in the Black Hotel—a bellhop running the elevator. … Actually, Ben, you, your brother, Glen, and H. L. Brown are my first black friend experiences."

"Think of it, Ben: wouldn't you expect my Mom to be surprised to suddenly have a big black guy walk into her house? Same with that crowd if it was something unusual?"

"Well, uh, yes," Ben replied slowly, as the tenseness eased some in his face and voice.

"And what you heard of my brother and me through the wall last night. Well, we were laughing so hard from Floyd's description of how shocked Mom looked when she saw you and how her eyes bulged out. We laughed and laughed and, of course, our imagination grew with each laugh. … Ben, his comments and expressions were so funny, you'd probably laughed if you'd been there, too."

Ben nodded his head, as he processed what I'd just said. "Well," he replied, "what about that stern look your mom gave to you from the porch as we left? Her shaking her finger at you, and saying, 'Clifton, don't let this happen again!'"

"That wasn't about you!" I blurted out with laughter. "Mom threatened me 'Don't ever bring a bag of dirty clothes home again and expect them to be washed in one night!' I should've realized she had planned to go to the game, and I walked in with a big bag of dirty clothes."

Ben's pearly whites were beginning to show. "No wonder she was put out," Ben replied with the first fully relaxed face I'd seen since we'd left my house.

I glanced in his direction, "Friends again?"

"Yup," he replied, as we flew down the highway with windows down and a country song of Johnny Horton blaring, *I'm a Honky-Tonk man, and I know how to dance...*

"So, I'm still on your intramural basketball team?"

"Yeah, but," Ben mumbled, "We gotta do something 'bout your music."

1965–66 Northwestern Intramural Basketball Champs. Front (L–R): Johnny Davis, Glen Smith, and Clifton Savoy. Back: Mike Weber, John Streich, and Ben Smith. Davis also was on the Northwestern football team with the Smith brothers, and Savoy. Courtesy of Northwestern.

54.

November 1965, "Nice Tush, Ben!"
Return trip from Beaver, Oklahoma

Ben and I soon crossed the Cimarron River—about fifty miles out from Northwestern. The beauty of the western plains was on full display, as the shadows from the November afternoon sun highlighted the colorful foliage of the hills and creeks along its banks. Up ahead, what looked like a couple of prairie chickens sailed across the road. We talked like friends again.

"Ben…" I said slowly, searching for the right words.

He looked my way, and heard only silence. A puzzled look filled his face, as he asked in a curious tone, "Huh?"

Another moment or two passed before I responded. It stunned both of us. "Let's face it: you're black and I'm white."

Ben shot me a quizzical look of, 'Where you going with this?' After a pause, he added, "And, … that's new?"

"You always seem to be a happy guy. … Tell me, what does it really feel like being a black guy on an all-white campus? … No, that's not it! … What I'm really asking: are you lonely at Northwestern? Do you have any female relationships?"

"Well, yeah. I'm a man!" He answered in an emphasized manner. "At those church group functions and in the student center; especially, when that juke box gets ta steppin' out, we mingle all the time with any females around."

"But do you guys date or meet up one-on-one?"

"Nope. … Not sure how Northwestern or the town folk would react to that. … But a black man would get bad treatment for being with a white woman in places a day's drive or more from here. … Don't get me wrong. We couldn't be treated any better at Northwestern or in town here, but our parents always reminded us to be on best behavior when we went out. Might not be a problem at Northwestern, but not worth chancing it."

"So, that's why I see you and the others on weekend nights back at Vinson Hall?"

"Yes," Ben replied. "That, and need gas money and for other things." Then an ear-to-ear grin appeared on his face, as he added, "Excitement comes sometimes, even then!"

"What do you mean?"

"Well, couple weeks ago, on a late Friday night, I had some excitement that lots of guys wished they could've had."

I had to know more. "What was that?"

"I was in the basement restroom of Vinson Hall. The one in the southwest corner, next to the exterior door and stairs to the road and parking lot. I'd showered and had only one of those small towels like in football wrapped around my waist. Side of my hip and leg were uncovered. I just finished washing my clothes in the sink, and looked at my face up close in the mirror when I heard someone enter. Glanced, but only caught a glimpse of a person, as the door closed to one of the stalls. I did a double take. *Huh? That a girl? Nah! Wouldn't come in here!*

"What?" I blurted out with a quick chuckle. "You mean, a girl came in from outside with you half naked and standing there and went to the restroom?"

"Well, I thought so," Ben replied, "But shrugged it off, and returned to looking in the mirror and trimming my hair. Before long," Ben had to pause for one of his signature belly laughs, "heard the person doing some business, and then the stool flushed."

"Savoy," Ben expressed with another laugh, "My curiosity was going strong, and I forgot about having only the small towel around my waist.

… I even pressed my face so close to the mirror, I could see smears on it later. … When I heard the stall door open, I turned my head slightly, and snuck a peek in the mirror to see who came out."

My laughter joined Ben's. "That had to be a funny scene!"

"Sure was," Ben replied. "Person walked towards me. Guess I didn't want to let on this was something unusual, that anything bothered me. Didn't dare move my head, though, and my eyes hurt from forcing them to look to the side. … I was shocked! It was a female!"

"You mean?" I asked choking with laughter. "It really was a female?"

Ben nodded and kept on with his story. "Well, she acted like being there was no big deal—like she owned the place. She walked up to the sink next to me and, you might've guessed, she was on the same side where my hip and leg were uncovered."

He noticed my laughter was getting the best of me, and blurted out, "Hey, Savoy, watch the road!"

"Uh, Okay," I replied, and tried to focus on driving.

Ben continued, "I never let on like, 'What are you doing in here?' No! Just kept my face inches from the mirror. … I heard her wash her hands, and turn off the faucet. She turned her head looking for something to dry with. I heard her say, 'Nothing!' in an aggravated tone. I sensed she then leaned towards me, and reached out."

"My mind went wild, *No! She's not going to do that!* … I felt a tug on the towel around my waist. I froze, but inside I panicked! *She's drying her hands on it!* … She grasped the lower part, and it felt like she was purposely jerking hard, trying to make the towel come unwrapped from my waist!"

"You mean," I asked but couldn't finish my question, as I laughed so much, tears blurred my vision, and I had to pull the car off the road and stop to keep from wrecking. "You mean, she was drying her hands on that skimpy towel?"

"Yes," Ben replied, we were both roaring with laughter at the thought. No telling what we looked like—a big black guy and a white guy sitting on the side of the road with the car motor running and laughing ourselves silly. Anyone driving by might've thought a couple of drunks stopped to party along the road.

Ben's laughter finally decreased enough to resume. "I even felt her hit my dong, as she dried. … She seemed to do all that on purpose and, when she started to walk away, she paused for a moment and tapped me on the behind and said, 'Nice Tush, Ben!'"

"You're kidding me, right?"

"No! … All true, and I didn't move a muscle until I heard the outside stairway door shut behind her."

"Any idea who she was?"

"No, but I sneak a peek at the females I meet on campus now to see if they giggle and give the secret away."

Soon, we were walking down the steps to the Vinson Hall basement, and paused momentarily as we passed the restroom door. The sinks and mirrors at the far end would always be reminders of Ben's wild story. We chuckled, as we headed on to our rooms around the corner, but I couldn't resist saying to the big guy, "Nice Tush, Ben."

55.

TOP NEWS OF 1965: VIETNAM WAR, DRAFT, DEATHS, PROTESTS, KKK, VOTING RIGHTS, CIVIL RIGHTS HISTORY

December 31, 1965, Top News Stories
National TV Studios, New York

Washington, D.C. — "The top news story of 1965," a reporter's voice sounded, as scenes of Vietnam faded in and out on the TV screen, "was the expanded involvement of the United States military in Vietnam, and its rapid buildup as the year passed.

Vietnam and LBJ

"President Lyndon B. Johnson's administration," the reporter continued, as a scene of the White House Oval Office filled the screen with Hubert Humphrey, Robert McNamara, and others gathered around Johnson, "has been pressed in how best to keep communism from sweeping across Asia from North Vietnam and its allies. ... In short, how to undergird the South Vietnam government—one, where a number of coups have occurred since the last days of President John

F. Kennedy's 1963 administration and where instability seems to increase daily?"

Prisoners of War!

Implement the Draft!

"It wasn't until after American prisoners of war were revealed, midway through 1965, Vietnam was declared an 'Official War.' ... President Johnson spoke of troubling times ahead: 'Vietnam will get worse before it gets better. ... More troops will be sent. ... Implement the Draft.'"

Scenes appeared of soldiers in training at Fort Bragg, North Carolina. "The U.S. military involvement in Vietnam escalated through 1965, from 23,000 to more than 180,000 troops, and this number is expected to increase significantly. To provide the soldiers needed, President Johnson expressed, 'Raise the Draft Call!'"

More soldiers, more deaths!

Saigon, South Vietnam — The reporter paused, as the TV scene filled with flag-covered coffins being loaded onto an airplane, and then continued in a solemn tone, "Soldier buildup in Vietnam—a large percentage from the Draft, carried with it, of course, the tragedy of more soldiers being killed. ... Fatalities have doubled each year from 1960 through 1964 to 414 total. ... The number increased dramatically in 1965, more than five times, to 2,342 total."

"Almost one fifth of the fatalities occurred in one large battle in the Ia Drang Valley in November. After two days and nights of fierce fighting, followed by action a day later, both the U.S. and North Vietnamese had heavy losses—the U.S. 250 soldiers killed and about 1,000 North Vietnamese bodies counted on the battlefield plus more by U.S. air strikes and artillery."

The reporter paused for a moment to let the flag-draped coffins fully impact viewer thoughts. "Sadly, the number of deaths is projected to increase, as the Johnson administration has given no indication to a change of policies and the further military buildup over the year ahead."

Pictures of several world leaders scrolled across the screen. "Other countries have objected and reacted to the U.S. military buildup in Vietnam. China and Russia, the most vocal, have pledged support for Ho Chi Minh and North Vietnam, and have threatened to enter the war unless the U.S. withdraws. Demonstrators have protested there, too, as well as in London and other international locations."

Veterans Memorial Field Courtesy of Kathlyn Carter Smith
Broken Arrow, Oklahoma

Washington, D.C. — "At home, the United States has not been united behind military involvement in Vietnam." As the reporter's voice filled the air, the TV screen faded in and out to scenes within Washington, D.C. and on streets across the country.

National Disunity and Protests

"Reasons include: conscientious objection to war, disagreement in stopping communism or socialism any where, objection to the Draft either to serving in the military or to the 'unfairness of the Draft process' and, of course, political opposition to policies. … Unfortunately, the Johnson administration has been, so far, unable to unite us, and opposition has grown, as the number of soldiers and deaths increased."

"Protestors, some in the tens of thousands, demonstrated at the

White House and Pentagon, on New York streets and the U. N., and also on university campuses. Hostility to the war and Draft has grown, as the year progressed, and they've become known as the 'anti-Vietnam' or 'anti-Draft movement.'"

Anti-war! "Some set selves on fire." "In the last few months of the year," the reporter expressed, "even as military fighting in Vietnam was the highest yet and after the Johnson administration proclaimed further buildup in Vietnam, the anti-draft movement openly advised how to avoid the Draft. ... Even Public Radio in New York got into the action, 'Fake an illness, declare oneself as homosexual...' Anti-draft youth were encouraged to 'Speak Out!'"

"Some objectors were so committed to an anti-war belief," the reporter said sadly, "they sacrificed themselves in suicidal actions. In Washington, D.C., a man set himself on fire. North Vietnam leaders called him, 'A hero.' ... Another man did the same thing at the United Nations during an anti-war rally."

"Major backlashes occurred, though, from draftees, soldiers, families of those and of many who'd been killed, as well as some politicians, and veteran support groups. 'For God and Country,' as one returning soldier put it. By these, the anti-war and anti-draft movement was looked on as 'anti-country.'"

KKK support for Johnson *Texas* — The screen faded to a scene of figures dressed in white hoods and sheets. "Johnson even received support for his Vietnam war policy in Texas from the Ku Klux Klan. ... Some political opponents were overheard to say, 'Probably payback for his Democrat leadership when he was in the Senate to water down both the 1957 and 1960 Civil Rights Acts.'"

Washington, D.C. — "Opposing the sweep of communism across Vietnam is a goal held by many, including Republican congressional leaders, Senators Everett Dirksen and Barry Goldwater, and Congressman

Gerald Ford. But, they express, 'There is failure of Johnson's Vietnam policies and goals.' Debate born out by the crisis and failure in Vietnam."

"Even recent remarks of Robert F. Kennedy on 'giving blood to North Vietnam' do not seem supportive of Johnson's Vietnam war policies. It's an interesting position, being in the same political party as Johnson and being the brother and Attorney General to the late President John F. Kennedy, who snowballed the U.S. military involvement in Vietnam."

The reporter paused momentarily, as the screen faded back to the Oval Office, with President Johnson and others gathered around, "Although no indication has been given by the Johnson administration to a change of policies and further military buildup in Vietnam, Johnson speaks of, 'Peace.' But North Vietnam leader, Ho Chi Minh says, '… will fight five to ten years to drive U.S. out of our country.'" … The reporter added in a solemn tone, as the screen turned black, "Peace in Vietnam seems uncertain."

––––––

Washington, D.C. — "The other top story of the year," a reporter expressed, "was enactment of the Voting Rights Act into law by President Lyndon B. Johnson on August 6, 1965."

Voting Rights Act of 1965

The purpose of this Act was to enforce the voting rights guaranteed about a century ago by the adoption, shortly after the Civil War, of the Fourteenth and Fifteenth Amendments to the United States Constitution—1868 and 1870, respectively." The reporter paused momentarily, then added, "Why did it take so long? … Who stood in the way?"

"To understand why and who, a person almost must take a meaningful course in U.S. civil rights and voting history." As the screen slowly dimmed, the reporter pointed out, "Quickly, one will find the roads to the 1965 Act were not

End of slavery, due process, and voting rights history!

easy—often dangerous and deadly and fraught with political roadblock after roadblock."

English Colonial Days: 1619 slavery, the Indentured System, and 'free' black people.

Scenes of colonial days scrolled across the screen. "Dr. Martin Luther King, Jr, reminds us that "in the year 1619, the first Negro slaves landed on the shores of this nation." … However, in those days of the Colonies and English rule, hundreds of black people also came into the Nation and became 'free' through the English indentured servant system. The roots of slavery also took off in this indentured system when it was permitted by English courts apparently first to a black land owner of another black person, in the mid-1600s."

Slavery entrenched under British crown for over 120-150 years prior to 1776.

"Slavery had more than a hundred and twenty years to push its roots deep into the Colony soils before the United States became a country with its 1776 Declaration of Independence and war victory over England. … Not every black person was a slave, though. There were 'free' black men and women, and not every state was a slave state. Interestingly, one of, if not the first person killed in the Revolutionary War, as it exploded in Massachusetts, was a 'free' black man!"

Emancipation Proclamation and Civil War

The reporter's voice continued, as a rough map of the thirteen colony areas appeared on the TV screen and then quickly faded to a scene of the Declaration of Independence being signed, "Up to 1776, each colony state had been somewhat independent and, thus, the United States Constitution, as initially adopted, provided complete discretion to each state to determine voter qualifications for its residents. Fortunately, the Founders wisely included a process to amend the Constitution in order to address any flaws."

"Indeed," the reporter added, "the slavery mindset entrenched over two-centuries, coupled to state-by-state voting discretion for nearly a century were such flaws." The reporter paused to let this point sink in with viewers before continuing, "but instituting changes to a national way of life and to the Constitution, even if the national consciousness was ready, would be difficult and cost the lives of hundreds of thousands."

Farm-life scenes with black workers, men and women, toiling in the fields scrolled across the TV screen and then faded to mid-1800s scenes of a tall figure in a black stove-top hat, as the reporter continued. "These slavery atrocities over the next eight decades paved the way for a new political party, Republican—one without any historical ties to slavery, being formed by 'free' blacks and sympathetic whites, and then the election of Abraham Lincoln, a Republican, as President on November 1860. ... Soon, the Civil War began on April 15, 1861, followed by Lincoln's Emancipation Proclamation on January 1, 1863."

"War over and Union victory, the state-by-state discretion of voter qualifications was limited soon by adoption of the Thirteenth, Fourteenth, and Fifteenth Amendments to the Constitution. The Thirteenth prohibited slavery in the United States. The Fourteenth granted citizenship to anyone 'born or naturalized in the United States,' and guarantees every person due process and equal protection rights. The Fifteenth provides 'The right of citizens of the United States to vote shall not be denied or abridged by the United States or by any State on account of race, color, or previous condition of servitude.' ... And, to affirm the issues of these Amendments, the Civil Rights Act of 1875 was passed by Congress and enacted into law."

"Sadly, though," the reporter expressed in a solemn tone, as scenes of persecution and killings of minorities as well as white sympathizers—some of bodies on the ground and a rope still dangling from a tree branch—scrolled across the TV screen, "civil rights atrocities still occurred for decades across the country. ... Yes, white sympathizers, as more than a thousand reportedly were killed by the Ku Klux Klan.

Atrocities and killing to minorities and white sympathizers

A new day, however, seems to have dawned with the 1950s."

"The political winds began to shift," the reporter added, as scenes of Washington, D.C. scrolled across the TV screen and then of the White House. "General Dwight D. Eisenhower, a Republican, was elected President in 1952. 'Separate but Equal' was overturned by the Supreme Court in 1954 in *Brown v Topeka Board of Education*, and then Eisenhower signed into law in 1957 the second Civil Rights Act. Its intent was in behalf of persons whose Fifteenth Amendment rights were abridged. Didn't help much, though, and three years later in 1960, Eisenhower signed into law the third Civil Rights Act. It contained further protections for racial minorities in places that engaged in voter discrimination. Although these two Acts were

General Eisenhower elected.

'Separate but Unequal' was ended.

Chief System returned to Indian tribes.

intended to also remedy minority voter discrimination, strict legalities written into them made enforcement difficult."

The reporter continued, "Democrat President John F. Kennedy introduced legislation to address many of the civil rights ills, prior to his being assassinated November 1963. Subsequently, President Lyndon B. Johnson, did an about face to his actions with other Southern Democrats while he was in Congress, and supported the Civil Rights Act of 1964. Unfortunately, little was in it to prohibit minority voting discrimination. Did Johnson leveraged further legislation in exchange for support from civil rights leaders for election to his own four-year term as President in November 1964? Few will know the truth, but newly elected Johnson did live up to his commitment to draft voting rights legislation, but a 'tell-tell' sign might be revealed in the Johnson did not push the voting rights legislation publically or submit it to Congress."

"Consequently," the reporter expressed, as the TV screen faded to scenes of minority leaders and groups demonstrating for civil rights, "organizations, such as the Southern Christian Leadership Conference, and leaders like Martin Luther King, Jr., pressed the Johnson administration with their non-violent protests. They targeted states and cities known to be hostile to minority civil and voting rights. With news and TV coverage, they hoped their plight would be more exposed to the public and cause the Johnson administration to intervene if hostile retaliation occurred."

"Selma, Alabama was one hotbed," the reporter pointed out. "It's in a state where Democrat-controlled government, both local and state level, wasn't tolerant of any protests. Demonstrations did lead to violent clashes with police, and received national media coverage and attention to the issue of voting rights. The pressure worked, and President Johnson sent a proposal to Congress. He did not reveal its content, though, or indicate when it would be considered."

"Civil rights leaders kept the pressure on with more demonstrations. State troopers violently broke one up in Marion, Alabama, and a young protester was killed. Civil rights leaders reacted with a huge march of thousands from Selma to Montgomery, Alabama's Capital, to highlight voting rights issues and present grievances to the Governor."

Civil rights non-violent marches for voting rights, equality, and freedom get violence and death!

"Singing, *'We shall overcome,'* demonstrators were stopped at the Edmund Pettus Bridge near Selma by state and county police on horseback," a reporter's voice sounded, as a scene appeared on the TV screen of Martin Luther King leading a large group across the bridge. "Tear gas into the crowd could be seen in TV footage. Protesters were trampled, and bricks were thrown as well. "The bloody scene generated outrage across the country."

"Back in Washington, D.C.," the reporter added, "President Johnson

1964 Civil Rights legislation finally passed, but only with bipartisan support! soon called on Congress on March 15 to pass the voting rights legislation. Most in Congress, Democrats and Republicans, applauded, but many, mostly Southern Democrats, did not."

"During debate of the legislation, some political opponents of Johnson's were overheard to point out, 'Not one Democrat in Congress voted for either the Fourteenth or Fifteenth Amendments to the Constitution. Same for the 1875 Civil Rights Act. These covered 'Equal protection of the laws' and 'Right to vote.' These rights are still in the Constitution! Why doesn't the Johnson Administration just enforce them?'"

Influence of 'political winds?' The reporter paused with a noticeable sigh, then added in a deep, sarcastic tone, as the TV screen faded to black, "Perhaps this crash course on civil rights and voting history should be expanded to include the influence of political winds!"

56.

SPRING 1966: DOUGLAS HS SENIORS VISIT MOSTLY ALL-WHITE NORTHWESTERN

February 1966, Invite to Visit Northwestern
Northwestern Oklahoma State University

At the tap on the door, Northwestern President J. D. Martin looked up from the paperwork on his desk. "Yes," he replied slowly in his usual soft voice. ... The door opened slightly, and his executive assistant stepped partway into the room. Her frown and body language sent the message, *Something's amiss, and can't wait!*

"Dr. Martin," she expressed in an apologetic tone, "There's a man on the phone who assures me, 'Jesse'll always take a call from an old friend. ... Especially, when he wants a favor.'"

A puzzled look quickly crossed Dr. Martin's face, but before he could speak, the assistant continued, "He said something about both of you once teaching at Nowata, Oklahoma."

A big grin immediately replaced the puzzled look, and Dr. Martin replied, as he reached for the phone, "I'll take it. ... It's Floyd Alexander, Principal of Oklahoma City Moon Junior High. Thank you."

"Hello, Floyd," Dr. Martin expressed in a warm tone and soft chuckle to his friend and long-ago teaching colleague.

A few minutes passed, as they caught up with each other's lives and professional activities. Then they moved to the basic reason of the call.

"Yes, I'd still like for you," Dr. Martin confirmed, "to bring some of those seniors from Oklahoma City Douglas High School for a visit of our Northwestern campus."

Dr. Martin sat quietly, and listened to his friend. A warm smile filled his face again, as he replied. "You think, at least a car load? ... That's excellent!" He paused again and then repeated what he heard. "Some are your former students at Moon, and you've kept in touch. ... One is Mary Williams, and your wife and you were mentors. ... I look forward to meeting her."

As the call drew to a close, he added, "I'll send some information about Northwestern and campus life so you can share this in advance. Some best dates, too. ... Yes, I'm looking forward to seeing you again and meeting these Douglas seniors."

Dr. Martin probably pondered the call for a time. It's unlikely, though, he would've ever imagined it was a springboard of sorts to his beloved Northwestern soon being involved, in a positive way, in a civil rights event of national historical significance.

57.

March 1966, Douglas Seniors Visit Campus
Northwestern Oklahoma State University

"I haven't seen this many cows since the trip with Mom to her childhood home in North Texas a few years ago," mumbled Mary Elaine Williams, after miles of country scenes of farms and small towns had passed along the highway. In a tone of, *What have we gotten ourselves into?* she added, "Sure isn't anything like the busy life of Oklahoma City."

Mr. Floyd Alexander, who was driving the car load of Douglas High School seniors to visit Northwestern in Alva, must have noticed their quizzical looks, and said, "Not far now."

Mary glanced at him and then slowly at the others. *Are they as curious as me about our trip to Northwestern and Alva, an all-white university and town except for a couple of Indians and blacks?* Her thoughts turned to them. *Will we meet any? … How will others treat us?*

About an hour after they turned West off I-35, a road sign caught her eye: Salt Plains Lake and Wildlife Refuge. *How big is it? Like Salt Lake in Utah? What does it mean: salt plains? What kind of wildlife? Northwestern students go there?*

Minutes later, the travelers came to a junction in the road. South to Cherokee and West to Alva and Northwestern. Mary's curiosity was working overtime. *Was Cherokee named after the Cherokee Indian Nation? … Probably, since many towns in Oklahoma have Indian names.*

As the car increased speed, her thoughts turned to what they'd find on their visit. *Won't be long now!* She glanced at the university information in her hand. *It has an art program and strong in education. These will be good for me.* She looked out the car window for a moment. *But, will it be safe for us? Can we mingle? What about Alva? Map shows it's along the Salt Fork River and a railroad runs through it. Does a passenger train stop?*

The thoughts of Alva reminded her of a sour racial experience her Grandfather Jackson Henry Hodge had there once. She could still remember him describe the event.

"Back in the 1930s, my two sons built a Model-T car out of parts, and the three of us decided to drive to California. Our trip was through Alva and on West through the Oklahoma Panhandle. ... Well, the Model-T broke down in Alva. Sons were good mechanics and, if we had the part, they'd fix it quickly."

"Lots of towns at that time had an understanding or an actual ordinance that colored people couldn't spend the night in town. Guess Alva had something like those, too, because, soon, a group of white men pulled up to where we were working on the Model-T and conveyed a message in a rough voice, 'You can't be in this town after dark.'"

A warm smile crossed Mary's face, as she recalled what her Grandfather said happened next. *"I noticed one of the men was wearing a Mason pen. Signaled to him I was one, too, and the men helped repair our car, so we could be on our way before dark."*

Mary wondered, as she stared out the car window and reflected on her visit, *Has Alva changed in these thirty years?*

Five hours later, the car-load of excited, but tired Douglas High School seniors started back on their way to Oklahoma City. As they passed the City of Alva sign, Mary snuggled down for the ride home. Eyes closed, she reflected on their day. *Not a hint of discrimination anywhere!*

A faint smile filled her face, as she thought of how they would fit into campus life. *One cafeteria, so all eat together. ... And, girls on campus lived in one of two dorms. Every place seemed open to all, unless restricted by gender and teacher and administrative offices. And, I like President Martin's comment, "My door's always open." ... And we're not the first dark-skin students. Four black girls were there Spring-Fall 1963, and there were some*

Indian athletes who'd just graduated. Four black guys, who played sports, will still be around next Fall 1966.

Mary rehearsed what she'd say to her mother. *Loved what I saw of Northwestern, and Alva was a beautiful town. I have those scholarship offers from other universities, but think I'll go to Northwestern if any work-study assistance is available.*

Mary Elaine Williams and a few others from Douglas High School—Marlene Fields, Velma Ponds, Ruby Hill, Linda Foster, Gertrude 'Trudie' Lounds, Jo Ann Jordan, and Ardell Smith—attended Northwestern that Fall 1966.

———

Author Note: Ardell Smith went on to play four years of football at Northwestern. Along the way, he was honored by teammates, selected as a captain, and receive 1968 all-conference recognition. … Other Douglas students attended Northwestern in later years. George Graham was one and played football as well. … Tommy Griffin was another, but enrolled as a junior in fall 1968. Griffin's athletic and basketball performances would be recognized with all-conference honors and, later in life, induction into Northwestern's Sports Hall of Fame.

It's unlikely, however, any of these Douglas students ever imagined that in the fall of 1968—one of the most divisive and violent years in the U.S. history—they would be forever linked to Northwestern in an unique national historic event important to civil rights. Some of these experiences are delineated in subsequent chapters of this Northwestern story.

58.

1966: "THAT FOOL IS GOING TO GET SHOT . . ."

March 18, 1966, "That fool is going to get shot…"
Northwestern Oklahoma State University

The old radio squawked with each move of the dial, and Ben Smith's frustration to tune in an early spring game of one of his favorite professional baseball teams came through loud and clear. The noise carried through his open door and to much of the basement of Vinson Hall. I stepped from my room into his doorway directly across the hall to see who was being murdered.

After watching for a few moments from Ben's doorway, his grumpy antics caused me to chuckle. Memories flooded my mind of when I first met Ben and his brother, Glen, nearly three years back—August 1963 in preseason football. I wondered at the time; *How could the Big Guy above be so unfair to bless one human physically so much over another?*

Now, don't get me wrong. This had nothing to do with Ben and Glen being black and I was some shade of white. Not at all! You see, it was my first interaction with them. I rounded a corner in the dressing room and was face-to-face with this big guy towering over me—my forehead to his chin. From the security of my locker, I peered back at him. Out from behind, another guy appeared. It was Glen. He stood naked, in only his glory, except for a jockstrap. Looked about 6'2" and 225 lbs. He had muscles galore! And their contours were even more impressive, with what seemed to be a 30" waist! It was like looking at Jim Thorpe, Jesse Owens, and Jim Brown all mixed together in one body! *Michelangelo couldn't have chiseled it any better!* I looked down over my own body, gulped a sigh of exasperation, tugged my T-shirt down, and mumbled, "Not fair, dear Lord! Just not fair! I could never develop muscles like those no matter how much or long I trained!"

My senses returned me to standing in Big Ben's doorway when he shocked me again with a loud repeat of the comment, "That fool's going to get shot one of these days!"

I knew, after my two and half years of one-on-one experiences with Ben, Glen and, their roomy, H. L. Brown, Ben didn't mean something derogatory by using "fool" in his description of Dr. Martin Luther King, Jr. Absolutely not! Rather, Ben knew Dr. King's actions placed him in the cross-hairs of danger, even death, each time he led a march for civil rights, justice, and freedom. No matter who it was, though, Ben still didn't like his baseball bumped off the radio.

"What's up with King?" I hollered from the doorway.

Ben never turned or looked up, as he replied, "Comments he made at Southern Methodist University. Think, yesterday. Stirring the beehive, and gonna get shot one of these days."

"Well, it's late Friday anyway. Time to go out."

"No black girls around! You know that, Savoy!"

"Yeah, I remember. … But maybe the future will improve. I noticed you guys talking to those visiting campus this week. … Where were they from? … Any enrolling next Fall?"

"Douglas High School. OKC. Maybe some will, but that's not today," Ben mumbled, as he slapped the side of the old radio.

I chuckled again at his determination, but all I heard was mostly King's voice:

"Skin may differ, but affection dwells in black and white the same. … We have come a long, long way but we still have a long, long way to go. … Lynchings have about ceased, but in the last four or five years,

"We have come a long way."

"Lynchings have about ceased…

but murder and bombings still occur…"

some twenty-six Negro and white civil rights workers have been brutally murdered in Alabama. In most cases, nobody has been convicted."

"People are walking scot-free in the streets of our communities who have murdered persons who were simply seeking to gain their basic rights as citizens. The same thing in Mississippi. … We still see homes bombed, and churches burned down. Over the last eighteen months, more than fifty-two Negro churches in Mississippi alone. … How tragic! It reveals have a long, long way to go if equal administration of justice is to be a reality. … The ghetto in the North is being intensified rather than being dispersed. … Segregation in schools in the North is increasing."

"…some things are so precious, some things so eternally true, some things so right that they are worth dying for. If a man has not discovered something that he would die for, he isn't fit to live…"

"Some things so right, they are worth dying for!"

Excerpts: Dr. Martin Luther King, Jr. guest address at Southern Methodist University, Dallas, Texas, on March 17, 1966.

59.

SPRING 1966: MILITARY TO
NORTHWESTERN STUDENT-ATHLETE,
"WE'RE COMING FOR YOU!"

April 1966, "We're coming for you!"
Office of the President
Northwestern Oklahoma State University

Dr. Jesse W. Martin peered over the top rim of his glasses, as his executive assistant stepped just inside the open door and announced, "Curtis Thompson is here."

"Show him in, please."

As Thompson entered the office, Dr. Martin greeted him, "Come in. Have a seat." Both knew the reason for this visit: it was to discuss Thompson's military deferment, ongoing since January 1964 and which Dr. Martin had facilitated, to attend Northwestern and finish his undergraduate degree. This time, though, the outcome would not be what Thompson desired.

Dr. Martin spoke slowly as he picked up some papers from his desk. "An update of your military induction orders came." ... "It's what you concluded in my office the first time. Problem now, two years later, there is no more deferment." He paused to hand them to Thompson and continued, "You either report for service as instructed or they'll come and get you."

Thompson glanced through the papers as Dr. Martin continued. "The good part you'll notice is they allow you to finish this semester."

After another pause, Dr. Martin added in a stern tone, "Make sure you follow the instructions and report on time!"

"Yes, Sir."

"Your academic record, major in mathematics, and overall time at Northwestern are good. Once you complete your basic training, consider applying to the Officer Training School. I think you'll perform well."

"I'll do that, sir. Appreciate your advice."

"Seems you need a few hours after this semester to complete your degree. Is this correct?"

"Yes, sir."

"Well, you have some good news. After serving in the military, you'll be eligible to draw college financial assistance on the G.I. Program. You've been a good student. Come back to Northwestern and finish your degree."

"Sounds good," Thompson replied with a nod.

Dr. Martin started to walked Thompson to the door, but stopped abruptly. "Hold on," he commented with joy in his voice, as he retrieved a letter from his desk. "I have more good news for you. … You and Jim Schroeder, both were selected to the Oklahoma Collegiate Conference 1965-1966 Basketball Team for your outstanding performances. Congratulations!"

Thompson beamed as he walked down the stairs from President Martin's office and out of Herod Hall. *Who'd guess a kid from Harris, a small all-black town in Little Dixie in southeast Oklahoma would become a student in basically an all-white university, located in an all-white town— Alva, make the basketball team and be selected for All-Conference honors?*

———

Author Note: Thompson was accepted, after basic training, August 1966 into Officer Training School at Ft. Benning, Georgia. Afterwards,

Northwestern basketball coach, Keith Covey, and 1965–66 Oklahoma Conference basketball selections, Curtis Thompson and Jim Schroeder. Courtesy use from Northwestern.

he was stationed at Ft. Sill, Oklahoma, for a short time. From there, he had duty in Washington D.C. and other locations in the U.S. for security control in response to Vietnam and civil rights marches and demonstrations.

Eventually he served in Korea and Vietnam and retired with rank of Lt. Colonel. And, yes, he returned to Northwestern to complete his degree and became a highly successful teacher, administrator, mentor, and coach in Oklahoma with several teams winning state basketball championships.

Jim Schroeder had a brief time in high school education, but soon moved into the commercial loan banking profession, with considerable accomplishments and management responsibilities. He is still going strong in the profession. Along the way, he was inducted into the Northwestern Sports Hall of Fame. ... In this writing creation of Northwestern, Schroeder has been a key participant and consultant.

60.

TRAGEDY STRIKES AGAIN, NORTHWESTERN STUDENT-ATHLETE, JIM SPEAKS, IS KILLED

August 1966, Tragedy Struck Again
Northwestern Oklahoma State University

The humid, strength-zapping hot days of August in Oklahoma normally would be on the mind of the Northwestern athletes reporting for preseason football. Not so much this year, 1966. Instead, it was the elephant in the room—the Vietnam War and the military draft.

Upper classmen, especially, like all the others on campus, wondered, *How will it affect me?* And, the heavy burdens seemed to increase with the daily barrage of negative news:

Vietnam War   Highest U.S. casualties in Vietnam in a week: 920 killed, wounded\missing. … U.S. university students protest. … North Vietnam will not seek peace. … U.S. expands war into North Vietnam. … Protestors set selves on fire. … Analysis of President Johnson's frustration with Vietnam War. … 287,000 U.S. troops in Vietnam expected to increase!

Nonetheless, these upper classmen had high expectations of a good football season, and a serious mood filled the air as we convened from the summer break for our first practice.

"About time, Savoy!" a voice I knew quite well bellowed from a group of players, mostly seniors, coming out of Vinson Hall, as my car rolled past them to a stop in the parking lot.

Nope! Couldn't miss that voice anywhere. "What's up, Ben (Smith)? Guys?" I greeted them in a glad-to-see-y'all tone, as I opened the car door, slid out, and stretched. After a few one-on-one greetings, I fell in step towards the field house and football dressing rooms.

Didn't take long to notice Big Ben and brother, Glen, had added a few pounds. Our fourth year, and we'd all increased some. A few steps into the dressing room I sensed something was amiss. *Players are everywhere, but where's the usual laughter and friendly jousting?* Big Ben, Glen, and roomies Leon Stewart and Steve Russell noticed, too. I asked them, "Hey, what's up?"

Ben gazed around and, with a shrug of the shoulders, replied, "No idea."

Puzzled looks filled the three friends faces, as they answered, "Don't know either."

Our thoughts were immediately diverted by a graduate assistant coach directing players.

"Your lockers are in the first room," he motioned with a wave towards the lockers. "Equipment and uniforms are there, too. And, don't forget: pictures in an hour, so be dressed and up on the field. ... Ben, Glen, Chip Myers, John Estep, and Clifton Savoy, photographer wants a pic as this is your fourth-year."

I sat down in front of my locker, and slowly looked around. Mostly seniors: Ben and Glen, Stewart, Chip Myers, Reinking, Mac Branscum, Roger Smith, Zadorozny, *Chastain, Rollins, Steve Russell, Leo Myers, Kilbourne, Richard Smith, and more. ... Great* bunch.

A rush of sadness hit, as the thought of this season being the end of our playing days. I suppose it happens to other seniors. For a few moments, I reflected on the scene from my first year: *far corner of the back room, locker without a door, broken chair, and sharing the space-for-one with two others. The beat-up, old helmet, pieced-together pads, and my first face-to-face with a black person, Big Ben Smith.* I glanced over at Ben, dressing for the pictures, and grinned.

Northwestern 1966 season and the five players who would be with the team all four years. Front (L-R): Chip Myers, Ben Smith, and Clifton Savoy. Back: Glen Smith and John Estep. Year-end, each received all-conference honors. Over the four years, the five garnered ten such honors. The Smith brothers, the first black athletes to play a sport at Northwestern, would receive four—Glen three. Savoy, same. He and Glen started every game—sometimes, both ways. Myers was honored as an all-American for his 1965 performance. Other individual and team accomplishments and awards were received. Even more athletic recognition came from competitors and, soon after the season, Myers and Ben Smith experienced professional ball.

He suddenly gave a shout out to Dave Billups coming into the room with Johnny Davis and several other black players. Billups and Davis returned from last season. "Hey, Billups!" Ben teased loudly, as he approached the group. "Niagara Falls, NY folks run you out of town again?"

A big body laugh hit Billups, and he hustled Ben's way. After hugs and greeting the rest of us nearby, he turned towards the others with him. "Meet these new guys out for the team: Sammy Lee and Ardell Smith of Oklahoma City, Ken and Clyde Jones of Greensburgh, Pennsylvania, and James Cheeley of my stomping grounds, Niagara Falls, NY."

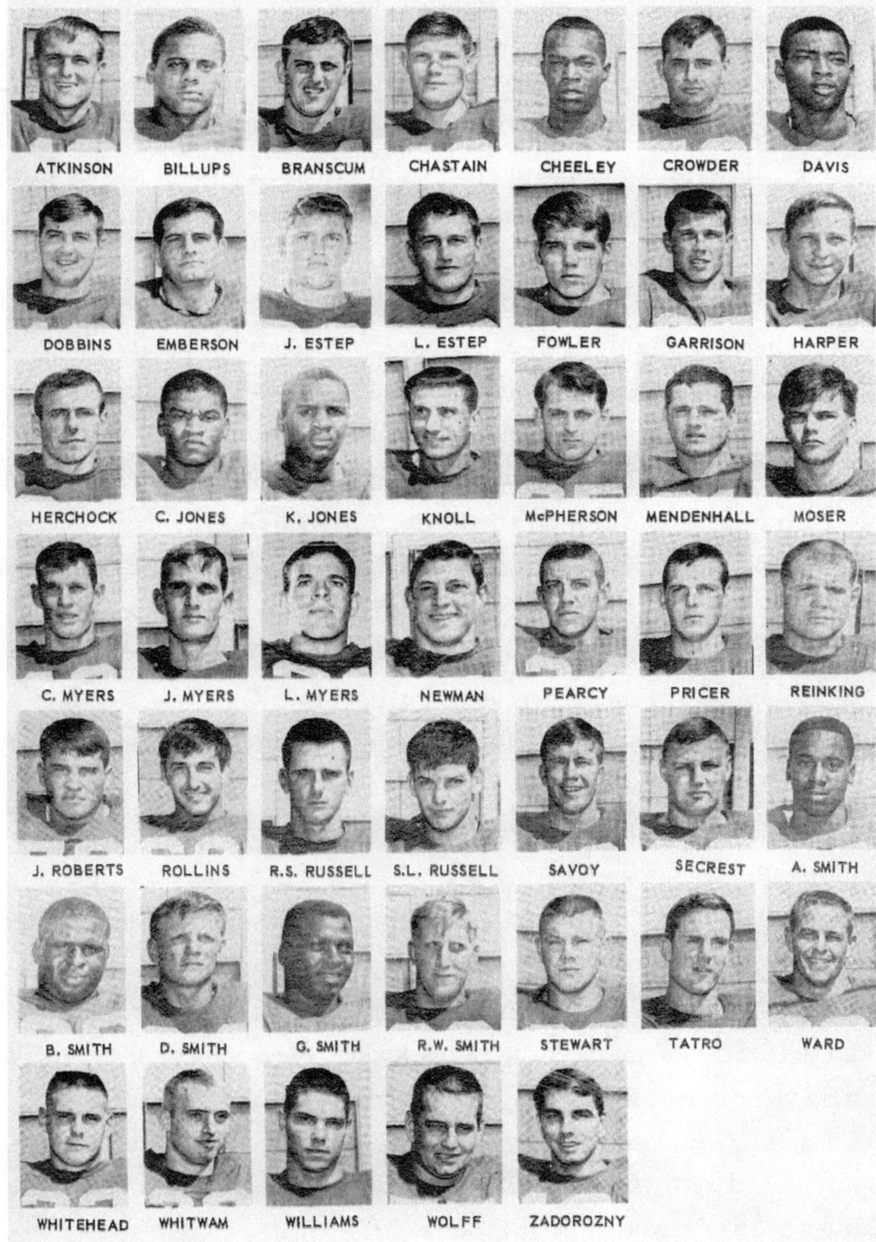

We exchanged greetings and, as they headed to their lockers, I sized them up. *All backs, maybe a linebacker. Hope they can help the team.*

Big Ben beat me to it, and teased with an ear-to-ear grin, "Nine of us, now, Savoy. Gonna take over the team!" The players within hearing distance and who understood, laughed.

One slide of the players on the 1966-67 Northwestern football team. A second slide of player photographs was not located, but included: Darrel Caldwell, Bruce Foster, Jim Elliot, Bruce Davis, Maurice Hill, Jan Kilbourne, Richard Smith, Don Kuenzi, Ronnie Roberts, and Don Kilmer. Northwestern archives.

The unusual quietness, though, quickly fell over the dressing rooms again, and I soon noticed an extra name, written with a marker pen on tape, on several lockers. It was returning standout starter, Jim Speaks, who would anchor the offensive line with Leon Stewart. I wondered, *What's up with that?* Moments later, I was stunned with what I overheard.

"Jim Speaks was from Woodward, my home town," Milt Bassett explained. "He was a very good football player—Oklahoma All-State, and started last year, here at Northwestern. He was killed in a vehicle accident a few weeks ago in July."

"No, way!" another player exclaimed. "How?"

"Heading home for the day from work. Hit a truck on the highway east of Woodward. With another guy, and both were killed."

"What about his family? I think, he was married, right? Any children?"

Someone said, "Married and a son. ... You know his family would be torn up."

"That's terrible!" a player nearby exclaimed, as he pressed a strip of tape with Speaks' name on it to his locker. He added sadly, "Speaks would've been one of our top players again!"

I agonized; *Another young life snuffed out! Bill Woltje and now Jim Speaks.* As I returned to finish dressing, I noticed other players also taping Speaks' name to their lockers.

Jim Speaks, an outstanding starter from Woodward, OK. No. 73, RT, 1964 Northwestern Team (L) and 2nd from left, next to Ed Stewart, on the 1965 team. "Jim, We'll miss you!"

61.

DOUGLAS GRADUATE SETTLES IN
AT NORTHWESTERN

1966, Mary Williams settles in…
Northwestern Oklahoma State University

The Northwestern campus, between classes, with students suddenly appearing everywhere, looked to first year student, Mary Elaine Williams, much like a disturbed ant den with hundreds storming out in all directions.

She was now two months into the 1966 fall semester, and was settling into her classes, library work, and many extra activities on campus and in town. It was homecoming week, and the queen would be crowned with a kiss at halftime, as Northwestern, with a record of four wins and one tie, battled on the gridiron to retain its lead for the conference championship.

Mary quickly entered one end of the student union to vote for the 1966 Homecoming Queen. An adrenaline rush hit her as she absorbed the sight and buzz of all the students scurrying in and out of the book store, buying a snack at the soda fountain, or just hanging out at one of the tables until the next class.

She glanced over her ballot one more time, satisfied with her choice. *Linda Patterson, pretty girl. Hope she wins. That Larry Dobbins is a lucky guy!* As she stuffed her ballot into the box, her eyes fell on the attendant, representing the Student Senate. Mary smiled and commented, "Didn't realize there'd be so many choices."

"Oh, that's normal. You see, every organization, club and residence hall can nominate a candidate. Fifteen is not unusual, and the one who has the most votes wins."

Mary nodded she understood, and soon was out the building and hurrying to art class. She had no idea her life and the legacy of North-western would be forever changed in a homecoming queen election two years later in 1968—one of the most divisive and violent years in the history of the United States.

"Mary, slow down!" exclaimed Gertrude 'Trudie' Lounds, another freshman student from Douglas High School in Oklahoma City. She shifted the art materials in her arms. "Why the peppy step and smiles?"

"Not sure," Mary replied slowly, as they hurried to Oklahoma Hall, the largest women's dorm on campus, to change clothes before Mary reported for work duties in the library.

A thoughtful look crossed Mary's face. "A beautiful day, maybe? … Might be because Northwestern and Alva are turning out to be like I experienced on our Douglas senior visit last spring. Remember? A mostly all-white place, but I didn't notice a hint of discrimination anywhere. And, we wouldn't be the only students of color on campus—the new ones, of course, and the few black guys from last year. I've not been disappointed." She paused as they greeted some students passing by, then cheerfully added, "It's all I hoped college would be!"

"Yes, I remember, and meeting some black students."

"I've not been treated badly," Mary continued, "in any way on campus or downtown in Alva. Nowhere. I love music, and enjoy Fred Newman's music store." She smiled and added, "He's also the music director at the Methodist Church. I joined its choir when he asked."

"Now, that's a picture!" … "Your black face in an all-white choir and congregation!"

"I know you're teasing, Trudie, but, yes, it seems unusual. Don't forget, though, I also interacted with Mr. Newman because of my piano playing. Same with Pastor Leroy Sewell, and I've met several people at the church from Northwestern—Aurice Hugley, University Registrar; Bess Chapple, Art Department Director; and others.

"Okay! Okay! I know you're outgoing. … Never met a stranger, but what about dating, a social life? Few black guys around."

Mary gently rolled her eyes, "Oh, Trudie, you know we don't have to date to have a social life. We often see guys at the campus cafeteria. And, some come to the Wesley Methodist Student Union. Matter of fact, I heard a group is meeting there after the homecoming football game. Out on the town in football players, Ben and Glen Smith's car. First in the car gets to go."

"Maybe, but what about the homecoming big show after the football game? The headliners: The New Orleans Preservation Hall Jazz Band is terrific, and the Four Freshman are good. Even Debbie Bryant, Miss America, is supposed to be there."

"I'd love to go and hear their music, but not sure yet," Mary responded, as they reached Oklahoma Hall. She stopped before entering, hugged her friend warmly, and added, "Trudie, you're such a talented artist," … "and see the big picture of our lives so well."

Neither had any idea one of the worst racial moments Mary would experience in life was brewing on another floor of Oklahoma Hall, and would hit her head-on before the year ended.

62.

PRE-SEASON 1966 NORTHWESTERN BASKETBALL

October 1966, Preseason Basketball
Northwestern Oklahoma State University

Sounds of the Northwestern football team echoed across the campus. "Work hard, fellas!" a coach bellowed in a deep raspy voice. "Have to win this homecoming game to stay in the lead for the conference championship!"

"Glad I left those football scrimmages back in high school," expressed senior Larry Prochnau in a slow, somewhat agonizing drawl to his basketball teammates and close friends, senior H. L. Brown and junior Bob 'Wings' Drake. The trio was on their way from their rooms in the basement of Vinson Hall and headed to the fieldhouse for some voluntary, but you best-show-up-if-you-want-to-play, preseason conditioning.

"Yeah," Brown, who was in his fourth year as starting point-guard, replied. "That coach sounds like a task master, a military drill Sargent."

Prochnau, a starter at forward when his ankles held up, groaned as he replied, "Some footballers mentioned Coach Covey being like that when he assisted with the team. Said they were glad the basketball team has him fulltime now.'"

"Bet so," added Drake, a standout starter in the middle from the moment he put on a Northwestern uniform.

"Yeah, lucky us," Prochnau responded in a sarcastic tone as they entered the fieldhouse.

The sounds of carpentry greeted them from the multipurpose gymnasium and, when they stepped inside, they saw workers busy, on the far end of the main court, building the stage for the big show after the Saturday homecoming football game. On the full side-to-side court at the near end, a five-on-five scrimmage of mostly underclassmen, transfers, and freshmen was underway. Of course, Coach Covey sat up in the bleachers, and watched his new squad of players compete for playing time.

"You're late!" a voice exclaimed.

"Huh?" Prochnau mumbled so low only Brown and Drake could hear, as they put a check by their name on the roster taped to the bench. "We're fifteen minutes early!"

Brown, who played for Covey in high school at Geary, Oklahoma and made all-state while leading the team to a birth in the state tournament, looked over the list of names, as the trio waited for the scrimmage to end.

Seniors: Ed Donnelly, H. L. Brown, Larry Prochnau, and Don Kawulok. Juniors: Bob Drake, Kenneth Hamilton a junior college transfer, and Bert Nichols. Sophomore: Henry Nickolson, Ron Frech, and Dale Ross. Freshmen: Mike Mitchel, Steve Wood, Ed Fisher, Dick Sonnenberg, and Bill Bixler

"We've got some good talent," Brown stated. "Just need to jell, get some shooting, defense, and play together."

"Yeah," Prochnau added. "Especially, if that other black guy is as good as you (Brown)."

Drake nodded in agreement, as the trio joined a couple other veterans for the next game against four of the freshmen and Hamilton. Covey stood to watch the performances.

The seasoned players, of course, had their way for the most part against the newbies, and one incident made that clear.

Freshman big man Bill Bixler gently moved his head side to side as the cobwebs cleared, and his vision began to focus. *Where am I?* In moments, he realized he was on the floor on hands and knees, and staring down at the baseline.

The last thing he remembered, he was in great position against veteran Bob Drake, just in front of the backboard and bucket to get a rebound and quickly throw it out to another promising newcomer, junior transfer Kenneth Hamilton, for a break to the basket at the other end of the court. Again, Bixler wondered, *What happened? How'd I get down here?*

A movement caught his attention, and he raised his head slightly. "Huh?" A pair of Converse All-Star shoes were almost touching, straddling his face. *What's this?*

He looked up into the face of Coach Covey, whose lips were pursed and arms were folded. Covey said something, and headed towards the bench. He motioned the players to follow.

Bixler staggered to his feet, and asked, as they started towards Covey, "What did he say?"

One of the players snickered, "He said something like, 'You may have been a big deal at Waynoka, kid, but you've got a lot to learn up here.'"

Other players snickered, too, and it came back to Bixler what happened. *I had inside position on Wings and one of his not-so-subtle elbows created space and sent me to the floor.*

As they walked, Wings patted him on the shoulder, and Prochnau told him, "Coach barks at everyone, but try to do what he says."

"Everybody in!" Coach Covey called out. "First, want to pass along news about Curtis Thompson, a player on the team last two years. As you veterans know, he was drafted by the military. I've learned Thompson was accepted this past August into Officer Training School. He's at Ft. Benning, Georgia. Not sure what's in his future. Korea? Vietnam?"

The question was indeed on the minds of young men. Certainly, Covey's upper classmen. *Where will I be after graduation?*

"Second, you know this is Northwestern's homecoming, and this gymnasium will be converted to host the big show this weekend. Tomorrow on we won't be able to use the floor, so we're going to do outside running and conditioning around the track and the football field. I want you to work out in groups of five. Push each other. Any questions? Okay, let's get to it!"

Preseason 1966–67 Northwestern basketball conditioning around the track and football field. Players (L–R): Fr Ed Ritterhouse, FR Bill Bixler, Sr Don Kawalok, and transfer Jr Kenny Hamilton. Sr Ed Donnelley was working out with them, but his image was just out of the picture frame. Courtesy of Northwestern.

63.

TOP NEWS OF 1966: VIETNAM, TROOP EXPANSION, PROTESTS, RIOTS, TEXAS TOWER SHOOTER, MIRANDA RIGHTS, SPACE RACE, MINI-SKIRTS

December 31, 1966, Top News Stories of the Year
National TV Studios, New York

Washington, D.C. — "The top story of 1966," a reporter's voice sounded, as scenes of soldiers and protestors faded in an out on the TV screen, "was, once again, the Vietnam War and the massive expansion of the United States military there."

Vietnam and U.S. involvement

"After the 161,000 soldier buildup and going on the offense in the 1965 'search and destroy missions' led by Army General William Westmorland, all to support the South Vietnam government against North Vietnam and its communist allies, China and Russia, the Johnson administration," the reporter added, "pursued peace talks in the first of 1966."

"Although seemingly successful in General Westmorland's strategy of attrition on North Vietnam supplies and manpower," the reporter pointed out, as scenes of South Vietnamese protesting against their own government scrolled

Devotion to cause: Protests and smoldering bodies!

across the screen, "the Johnson administration has been pressed in how to support a South Vietnam government where distrust and instability seems to increase daily from Buddhist opposition and student led unrest. And," the reporter paused to let viewers be impacted by the next scenes on the TV of individuals setting themselves on fire and, later, black smoke slowly rising from a smoldering, charred body. "There is no doubt to their devotion to cause."

"Every day it's been military buildup; protests here, South Vietnam, and other countries; war strategy meetings; peace talk attempts; self-immolations; search and destroy missions resumption of bombing in North Vietnam, more talks, radio and TV debates; congressional hearings; political opining from both parties; and 'State of the War' news reporting."

True Prediction "Certainly, President Johnson's 1965 prediction became factual: 'Vietnam would get worse… and many more troops will be sent.'"

"The U.S. military involvement in Vietnam increased in 1965 by 161,000 over 1964 to 184,300 troops, and jumped again by end of 1966 to 385,300." The reporter paused to let what those increases might mean to military draft age young men and their families. "The Johnson administration seems certain an increase is likely over the next few years.

Increase in war deaths! "Of course, a large increase in soldiers means the expected tragedy of higher numbers of soldiers killed. … Deaths increased to more than five times the year before to 2,342 total end of 1965 and to 8,692 total end of 1966."

"Sadly, the number of deaths is projected to increase, as the Johnson administration has given every indication of staying the course in it's

Disunity has reasons. policies regarding Vietnam and continued military expansion in the year ahead."

The reporter continued, "At home, the Johnson

administration has been unable to unite the country and, as the number of soldiers and deaths has increased, opposition has grown." … "Reasons include: conscientious objection to war, disagreement in how to stop communism or socialism or even try at all, objection to the Draft or to military service or to the perceived or real 'unfairness of the Draft process,' and political opposition to policies."

"It didn't help that some well-known figures, like Muhammed Ali and Senator Robert Kennedy, spoke publically against the Johnson policies. Kennedy has been outspoken of the resumed bombing in North Vietnam, even though Ho Chi Minh, expressed, 'We will not seek peace.'"

"'Muhammed Ali,' the reporter stated, as a scene of the boxing champion filled the screen, "Ali changed his name from Cassius Marcellus Clay, Jr., named after his father who was named after a white 19th Century staunch Republican abolitionist, also from Kentucky. Ali refused to be drafted into the military, pointing out his, 'religious beliefs and opposition to the Vietnam War.'"

Muhammed Ali, a.k.a. Cassius Clay

"Major backlashes occurred, though, from draftees, soldiers, families of those and of many who'd been killed, as well as some politicians, and veteran support groups."

Washington, D.C. — "Strong congressional debate continues in how best to oppose the sweep of communism across Vietnam and Southeast Asia. There doesn't seem, though, to be much consensus around which policies and goals can be implemented. And," the reporter paused as other scenes across the American landscape scrolled across the screen, "News headlines, like, *The Futility of Fighting in Vietnam*, and *President Johnson's frustration with Vietnam*, not only affirm these points of view in the public at large, but also places a heavier burden for the Johnson's administration to carry."

Will not withdraw!

The screen filled with a scene of Vice President Hubert Humphrey stopping to make a statement prior to entering the White House. "The United States will not withdraw. We will persevere until free elections in South Vietnam."

"Such statements," the reporter expressed in a less than hopeful tone, "sound like the Johnson administration is holding fast to policies of aggressive search and destroy missions in Vietnam and further military buildup. Yes, Johnson continues to speak of Peace, but North Vietnam President, Ho Chi Minh says, 'Will not seek peace. Will fight to drive U.S. out of our country.'"

The reporter added in a solemn tone, as the screen faded to black, "Seems the winner will be the one with the most will!"

* * *

Progress in Civil Rights?

Washington, D.C. — "Another top story of 1966 revolved around the question whether any improvements occurred with enactment into law of the 1964 Civil Rights and 1965 Voting Rights Acts?"

"Yes, according to some civil rights leaders!" exclaimed the reporter. "Some were eloquently described by Dr. Martin Luther King, Jr. in his comments to the Southern Methodist University faculty, students, and staff on the 17th of March: 'We have come a long, long way,' King said in reference to the centuries of black (and white sympathizer) struggles for freedom and human dignity, 'but we have a long, long way to go.'" "Dr. King," the reporter continued, as the screen faded to scenes in Dallas, Texas, momentarily panning, in a silent memorial, slowly around Dealey

"Yes," according to Dr. Martin Luther King, Jr. and others.

Plaza, zooming in on the sniper's window, and coming to rest on the tragic area in the bend of the street with the grassy knoll in the background—a viewer might even see pigeons circling overhead. Soon the screen filled with scenes of the Southern Methodist University campus.

"Dr. King expressed,'…I am happy to say as a native Southerner, as one who loves the South and lives in the South that by and large communities have complied…, particularly the public accommodations section… This reveals… changes are taking place. …We have moved through the wilderness of legal segregation and now stand on the borderland of integration…'"

"…have moved through legal segregation…".

"King also commented on the strides made in registering blacks to vote and, in some black belt Alabama counties, blacks would be elected for the first time in history. As King put it, 'We've come a long, long way since 1896.' Or," the reporter explained, "*Plessy vs Ferguson, separate but equal segregation, Supreme Court decision.*"

"Dr. King emphasized, though, 'We still have a long, long way to go if equal justice is to be a reality.' He pointed out, '…Civil rights workers are still being brutally murdered…. In the last

Dr. King, "… still a long way to go."

four or five years, some 26 Negro and white civil rights workers have been brutally murdered in the state of Alabama alone…. In most cases nobody has been convicted…. The same… in the state of Mississippi…. These things continue to exist… We still see homes bombed…. churches burned down. Over the last 18 months, more than 52 Negro churches have been burned in Mississippi alone…'"

"Dr. King noted conditions in the North as well. '…The ghetto in the North is being intensified. Segregation in schools in the North is increasing… In cities like Detroit and Chicago, the Negro is about 28 percent of the population. Yet the Negro is almost 70 percent of the unemployed…'"

"'These reveal," King stated, 'we have a long, long way to go if the equal administration of justice is to be a reality… If we are to have equal education and economic opportunities.'"

"These admonitions Dr. King pointed out," the reporter added, as a

Atlanta race riots!

highway sign, *Welcome to the City of Atlanta*, appeared on the TV screen, "seemed to be the same issues that fueled the Atlanta race riots last September in its Southside community of Summerhill. However, the hostile actions with students, Stokely Carmichael, and a fledgling Black Power movement involved seemed to settle down quickly."

"The latest civil rights legislation put forth," the reporter added as

A natural truth: We are all the same and one-on-one relationships are essential to solve differences!

the screen faded to a scene of President Johnson in the Oval Office and then to the front of the Capitol Building, "deals with issues of equal application of justice, and discrimination in housing on the basis of race."

"Dr. King reminded us of a natural truth of all being alike, '…Skin may differ but affection dwells in black and white the same.'"

"Thus," the reporter's voice changed to a philosophical tone as the screen panned back from the front of the Capitol to where the American Flag could be seen flapping in the breeze atop the building. "It seems legislation by itself cannot solve race problems. Rather, one-on-one relationships are the essential ingredient!"

Miranda Rights!

Washington, D.C. — "Another 1966 top story is the Supreme Court case, *Miranda v. Arizona*," a reporter expressed. "Apparently, it will have lasting effect in the judicial system."

"Ernesto Arturo Miranda signed a confession, was convicted, and sentenced. He was not informed, however, of his rights." … "Rights guaranteed to all citizens as part of the United States Constitution." … "Chief Justice Earl Warren of the Supreme Court wrote the opinion: *The person in custody must, prior to interrogation, be clearly informed he has the right to remain silent, and anything he says will be used against him in court; he must be clearly informed he has the right to consult with a lawyer and to have the lawyer with him during interrogation, and, if he is indigent, a lawyer will be appointed to represent him."*

Austin, Texas — "Another top story," a reporter stated, as scenes scrolled across the screen of many people, with books in arms, hurrying along sidewalks that seemed to go in all directions, "was the mass-shooting at the University of Texas campus in Austin on August 1st. Student Charles Joseph Whitman, who had just turned twenty-five, went on a killing spree that took sixteen lives this day, and the count may still rise."

University of Texas tower shooter!

"Whitman went to the campus, and took over a 28-floor tower with an observation deck that overlooked the campus. In doing so, he killed three people and, at the top, began shooting across campus. His firing lasted about ninety-six minutes, in which he hit forty people and killed nine of them, ten counting the unborn in a pregnant woman, before he was shot and killed by Austin police. It was discovered he'd killed his mother and wife before going to the campus." ... "It's a memory that will haunt his family and the University of Texas."

New York City — "Other stories emerged during 1966," the reporter expressed, as scenes that matched each one scrolled across the TV screen.

"President John F. Kennedy's 'space race' challenge to the Nation to 'land a man on the moon by the end of the 1960s decade' took another step forward as the Gemini 8 space mission was launched during the year. Astronauts Neil Armstrong and David Scott were the first to dock two spacecraft together in orbit, but soon the spacecraft began to tumble. Fortunately, they averted a catastrophe by stabilizing the crafts and save their lives. The rest of the mission was aborted."

Space race to the moon!

"On the international scene, World War II, twenty years later, still takes lives, as four people died while digging under the Berlin Germany wall to gain their freedom from communist East Germany. When will that wall come down, and war deaths end?"

Ronald Reagan elected California Governor.

"Ronald Reagan was elected as California Governor. *Sound of Music* was best picture, Julie Christie best actress, and Lee Marvin best actor."

"In health, cigarette packets in the U.S. must have the warning: Caution! Cigarette smoking may be hazardous to your health.

Notable accomplishments, the Salvation Army celebrated 100 years of service to mankind. ... Sports feats: the Baltimore Orioles swept the Los Angeles Dodgers in four games to win the World Series. ... Masters Tournament, Jack Nicklaus, age 26, won his third green jacket, and became the first back-to-back champion. Arnold Palmer's army could only pull its four-time Master's champion to a fourth place finish."

"In economics, costs keep increasing: a gallon of gas averaged 32 cents, up 7 cents since 1960; a full size car averaged $2,800 up about $300 since 1960); and annual salaries averaged $6,750 fortunately up $1,300 since 1960."

Costs rise, as does the 'Mini-skirt!'

"And in the fashion scene, the mini skirt, with the hem mid-to-upper thigh, has made its mark on the country!" The reporter expressed in a somewhat-humorous tone as the TV screen faded to black, "I'm sure guys love the looks, but wonder if—hope—it'll get shorter next year?"

64.

BASKETBALL COACH ENCOURAGES PLAYERS

February 1967, "Push yourselves! Finish!"
Northwestern Oklahoma State University

Exhausted, but delirious with joy, was how the Northwestern basketball players and coaches reacted as the buzzer sounded to the hard-fought overtime game with Panhandle OSU.

This was a game where an old coach saying– "Push yourselves! Push yourselves! Finish!"—was on display, as Northwestern came through with a thrilling two-point win, 69 to 67. Coach Keith Covey congratulated Kenneth Hamilton for sparking the team to victory. For the opponents, the agonizing loss would make the trip home seem longer.   Northwestern posted a

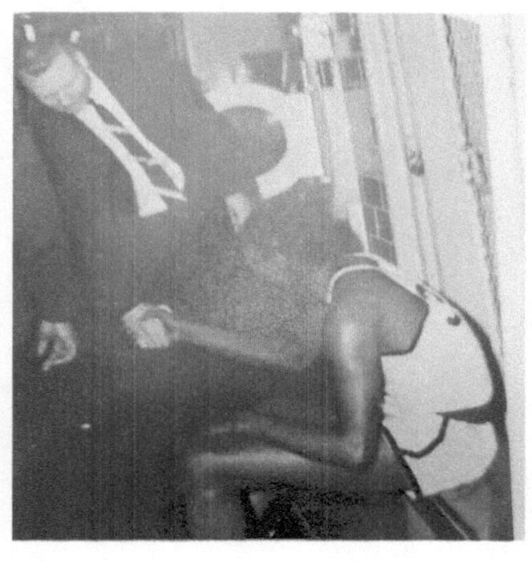

winning season of 15-10 but, unfortunately, didn't make the playoffs with its 9-9 conference record. Coach Covey also congratulated the team for a winning season, placing 2nd in the Top of the Nation Tournament at Adams State in Alamosa, Colorado, and for the three selections to the all-conference team: Bob Drake, H. L. Brown, and Ed Donnelly.

Never far out of mind, too, for the upper classmen was the expanding U.S. military involvement in the Vietnam War. *Will any of us from the 1966–67 Northwestern basketball team be drafted amd serve there?* They would soon learn the answers.

65.

ATHLETE REUNION AND REFLECTIONS
OF WHAT MIGHT'VE BEEN

Mid Spring 1967, What might've been!
Northwestern Oklahoma State University

Tinkering with things, taking them apart to see how they're made or work seemed to be an inherited trait of many males in the 1960s—maybe in all times. There were few things, possibly even girls, that would attract college age guys more than bringing life to an old junker.

It wasn't unusual to see a car or pickup with its hood up in the Northwestern parking lot between Vinson Hall and the fieldhouse. After all, some of those vehicles barely made the trip to campus and sat in the same spot for much of the semester until the return home or need to start for a special purpose. Now, an awesome set of wheels was a 'must see,' and a group would come and go between classes to hear, touch, smell, sit behind the steering wheel if possible, and dream.

"Sweet car!" I shouted into the powerful rumbling sounds of a big V8 engine to a group of guys whose heads were under the raised hood of the sharp looking 1967 Pontiac GTO hardtop. No one heard me, so I yelled louder, as I approached them, "Sweet car!"

Glen Smith was the first to see me. A look of surprise crossed his face, followed by a smile, as he stepped forward to greet me. Before he could say anything, I asked joyously, "Big Ben buy a new set of wheels with his Miami Dolphins money?"

"No," Glen responded with a laugh and a head nod towards his '55 Chevy across the parking lot. Its nearly flat tires affirmed it had been there since the Christmas holiday break, and life for him hadn't changed much since I left campus. "Ben's pro contract wasn't much," he said, "or he's holding out on me."

"Probably the latter," sounded a voice and snicker from under the hood. "Wheels belong to Chip Myers."

Myers? ... Thought he was out in California with the San Francisco 49ers. Before I inquired further, a familiar voice came from the other side of the GTO.

Signing Of Two Gridders

By JOHN ROWE

The signing of two football players to professional contracts plus winning seasons for four of the seven athletic teams highlighted the recently completed Northwestern sports year.

Footballers Chip Myers and Ben Smith were the individuals in the sporting news, and the football and tennis teams were the squads that stole the NSC headlines.

Total wise, Northwestern's seven teams had an overall winning record of 42-34-1, with the tennis team's perfect 14-0 regular season slate leading the way. Other records were as follows: football (6-3-1), basketball (15-10), golf (4-2), gymnas-

CHIP MYERS

BEN SMITH

Northwestern 1966–67 Oklahoma Collegiate All-Conference Football: Leon Stewart, George Chastain, Glen Smith, Clifton Savoy, Chip Myers, Ben Smith, Phil Reinking, Steve Russell, Doyle Mendenhall, John Estep, and Mac Branscum.

"Hey, Savoy," Myers shouted in a gleeful tone as he raised his head above the hood and tossed me a broad smile with a nod and a wave.

We simultaneously spoke the same words, "Thought you were gone from Northwestern."

I mouthed, "You, go ahead."

Myers continued, "After the pro football draft, we settled on a contract, and I reported for a short rookie camp."

"And bought the GTO," one of the guys added with a chuckle.

"Yeah, this, too," Myers responded with a sheepish grin.

"She's a beaut." I expressed, and walked slowly around her and admired the sleek curves and awesome look. … I probably drooled a little, too. "Congratulations on being drafted."

"Thanks. Back to you, too, on the conference (football) honors." … "Three times?"

"Thanks. Yeah. … Tell me," I asked as we continued to examine features of the car, "how does Northwestern football compare to those professionals?"

Chip's expression never changed. "Well, 'bout same." … "Just bigger, stronger, and faster."

As the stupidity of my question sunk in, we glanced at each other, and began to laugh. Slightly at first, then much louder—enough for others to wonder what they'd missed.

"What about you?" Myers asked. "Knew you'd finished end of December, but heard you'd accepted a graduate position at Oklahoma State University in my hometown, Stillwater. Is that right? What are you doing back here?"

"Yes, full time in June. Back here to thank Dr. Sterns Rogers for his assistance with the Oklahoma State position. Also, had to deliver some medical papers to Northwestern's football office. Docs at the Oklahoma City Orthopedic Clinic advised the knees should be surgically repaired. Same ones who removed the bone spur from my arm after our second season."

"That's a bummer," Myers replied.

"Yeah," Glen Smith added. Two other senior footballers and Vinson Hall roommates, Leon Stewart and Steve Russell, walked up. "Play four years and that's your reward."

All of us exchanged greetings and small talk for a moment, then I replied to Glen's comment. "Reward? Like you guys, it paid for my college. So, I'm good." I paused for a moment as a frustrating memory came to mind. "Well, would've liked our last couple of conference games to have been different. We did close the season with two wins—one over a tough Eastern New Mexico University team—and we did have a good year. And," glancing at Glen and then Myers, "I enjoyed our four years together."

"Me, too," Glen and Myers, both responded warmly.

"And," glancing at Stewart and Russell, "…these last two years with you guys, too."

They nodded and mouthed the same back to me.

"We had some outstanding performances this last season, too. I saw your names on the list of all-conference honors. Congratulations!"

Northwestern 1966-67 Oklahoma Collegiate All-Conference Football: Leon Stewart, George Chastain, Glen Smith, Clifton Savoy, Chip Myers, Ben Smith, Phil Reinking, Steve Russell, Doyle Mendenhall, John Estep, and Mac Branscum.

The normally quiet Leon Stewart spoke up, "In case you didn't notice," he teased, "three of the eleven—Ben, Glen and me—are from the same town (Crescent, Oklahoma)." … "A a year or so earlier, another outstanding player, Don Brooks, too."

Our eyes rolled in a 'yeah, yeah' expression. It was enough.

"Yes, 6-3-1 was a winning year, but…" I sighed, "I'll always remember how close to 8-1-1 or even 9-1 and in the playoffs—what might've been!" Heads nodded agreement, as I continued. "We could've had one, two, or even three more conference wins—just one play against the conference champs, East Central OSU, and an honest ref call in our homecoming against Central OSU. Win those, we'd be up for the third. Those memories hurt, and I'll never forget them."

Glen's body language revealed he was affected the same way. "Yeah, I know. Defense shut down East Central all game. Stopped them inside their twenty, but they scoop up a touched punted ball and run 80 yards for a TD—in one play." He paused for a moment and added, "What kinda luck is that? Their only score!" ... "They made only 86 yards the whole game against our defense... Thankfully, Lance Rollins recovered a fumble and Myers, you, were able to get open for a TD pass from Alan Zadorozny."

"I was thrilled when we tied the score." ... "Great throw and catch." ... "We deserved more than a tie, though."

Stewart spoke to how it impacted him, "The 7-7 tie was disappointing, but what's tough to stomach about that game, East Central took care of business and became conference champions."

"Puts a bitter taste in the mouth," I responded. "Win and we're 5-0 in conference and closer to being champs... But, at 4-0-1, we were still tied with them for the conference lead. Just needed wins in one or both of our remaining two games."

"Then the next week at our homecoming against Central Oklahoma State University, momentum had shifted to Northwestern down only 10-13. The referee called a fourth down measurement to be a first down for them. I couldn't believe it! The ball was several inches short of the chain pole! Should've been awarded to Northwestern!"

By the expressions of surprise, it was apparent these guys, except for Glen Smith, didn't know about this near-violence—mine—immediately after the ref call. "Defense had held Central on fourth down deep in our end of the field. The referee announced, though, 'First down.'"

"I was only a few feet from the measurement and observed the ball was at least a couple inches short of the pole. I questioned the ref's call, and he declared loudly, "First down!" I blurted out, "It's short!" He was adamant, "It was the ring connecting the chain to the pole, not the pole. It's a first down! Move the sticks!" I hotly yelled close to his face something like, "You're cheating us!" and I yelled to our coaches on the sideline. The ref commanded me to "Get back to your side of the ball!" My anger boiled over and I yelled, "I'm a team captain! (Who is chosen to represent and watch for the team.)."

"Later, someone said to me that Ben and Glen Smith forcefully nudged me away, as it seemed I was about to lunge at the ref."

More guys had now gathered around in the parking lot and were listening closely. "What happened in that game was all true! I had only seconds to decide what to do. Debate was flying back and forth in my mind. Only seconds to decide. On one hand, I wanted to do something—even physical—to get justice! I knew, though, if I touched the ref in any way, except accidental, I'd not only be ejected from the game, but probably from our last conference games. Maybe off the team! Yet, I thought of the thousands of hours our players had worked to get into position to win the conference. All to be lost maybe just because of one dishonest call!"

"Yet, I knew I should just walk away! Fortunately, Ben and Glen Smith settled the tormenting debate in my head. Northwestern might not have rallied to win, but momentum was on our side until that fourth down call. The action, much due to me, caused us to lose composure and Central scored in a few plays afterwards, and shifted the momentum… We lost 10-20."

The next few hours before I drove away from Northwestern were filled with goodbyes, well wishes and a few hugs to these teammates and others I visited that day in Vinson Hall and across campus. One person I regret not seeing was Northwestern defensive tackle, 6'4" 235 lb. Roger Smith, a senior from Hardtner, Kansas. I wanted to tell him it was an honor to play on the defensive team with him. ... Actually, with a whole bunch of others, too. At different times, each one performed like they were easily All-American. In Roger's case, described by a sports writer, like a 'wall.'

As I headed south out of town to a rendezvous with a scalpel, memories from four and a half years flooded my thoughts. When I passed the intersection leading to the old VFW Supper Club to the west, the World War II Nazi Officer Prison that was once around it and held some 5,000 prisoners, for some reason, popped into my mind... *Wow! Twenty years since then. Wonder where my teammates, classmates, and I will be in twenty years?* ... My thoughts soon included the actions of Big Ben and Glen Smith to notice me losing composure in our homecoming game... *If they hadn't moved me away from the heat of the moment, cared enough to act, what would've been my future?*

66.

1967 DRAFT NOTICES TOUCHED EVERYONE AT NORTHWESTERN

May 1967, It touched everyone!
Northwestern Oklahoma State University

A great hush fell over the Northwestern campus. It started slowly, in early afternoon in the men's dormitories a few days before the May 21ˢᵗ Sunday graduation. The hush spread rapidly from building to building, like a prairie fire from a spark and turns into a fast-moving inferno.

Mary Williams and some friends, who had walked with her from Oklahoma Hall to the student union for the evening meal, noticed it when they entered the building.

The quietness engulfed them, smacked them in the face, almost in a physical sense, like hot air does when it surges from an oven to greet anyone who opens the door to peep inside.

What is going on? Mary gazed around at the students waiting for the cafeteria doors to open. *Why is everyone so solemn, so quiet? Normally, this place in the evening is noisy with student chatter and laughter.* She noticed H. L. Brown, his roommate Glen Smith, Larry Prochnau, Bob Drake, and a few others bunched along the wall, saying little, almost stoic. Other students acted the same way. *Something is definitely up.*

She soon overheard the answer. "Yeah," a guy spoke quietly to a lady friend, "several in my dorm received draft letters, something about Orders to Report for Induction into the Armed Forces of the United States. Date to report was immediately after graduation. Others, soon. President Johnson said more soldiers are needed in Vietnam. Heard up to a half million. Lots of drafting to fill the number."

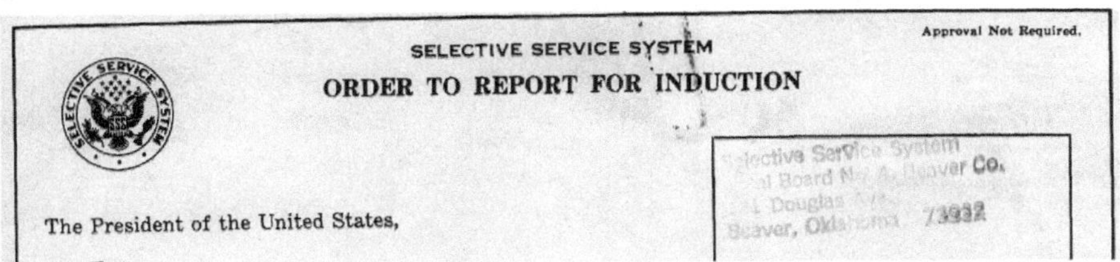

His lady friend looked up into his face, and asked. "Did you get one?"

"No, I didn't. I'm only a sophomore. They draft the ones who've had four years to complete a degree. Think also those not making progress, or who dropped out. Maybe also those who never went to college. There's other criteria."

"Who decides who is drafted and who stays home?"

"A local draft board decides who is on the list." He reflected on what he'd said for a moment and added, "A system where local influence could occur in whose son is on the list, how high up, and sent to military service; maybe to war and killed."

"Is that the reason for the draft-dodgers and those anti-draft protests on TV?"

"That, plus plain objections to war—the protests and violence."

The cafeteria doors opened and the students began to move. A guy close to Mary commented, "Heard Glen Smith, H. L. Brown, Larry Prochnau, and Lance Rollins received those letters. Not sure who else. Many of us, though, have Selective Service classifications of 1-A, and we'll be faced with the draft and serving soon."

"Yeah," another lamented, "Bob Drake on our basketball team is one of those."

A Vinson Hall basement bum added, "Heard Clifton Savoy also

received the letter and Orders to Report for a June induction physical, but it was deferred until December since he was in a full leg hard-cast from surgery on his football injured knee."

Mary mumbled softly, as she started down the food line, "Now I understand why H. L. Brown isn't lively as usual. I'd rather see him active with his dance moves."

Later, on the way back to Oklahoma Hall, Mary's mind was on the future. *Wonder how many will be sent to Vietnam? ... Hope nothing happens to them!*

67.

VIETNAM WAR: NORTHWESTERN GRADUATE, BENNETT, KIA

September 1967, News from the War Front!
Vietnam

Wisconsin was a long way from Oklahoma, but Ken Strunk, a 1967 graduate of Northwestern OSU, was finally moving ahead with his wife, Dian, in a career as a math teacher and coach. Every day was a new and fun adventure. Not this day, though! Not this day!

"Oh, my Lord!" Ken mumbled, as he slowly read: Northwestern 1965 graduate and U.S. Marine, 1ˢᵗ Lieutenant Jerry 'Frederick' Bennett, Killed in Vietnam Combat Action, 16 September 1967.

As Ken read, his body quivered from the emotions, like someone had sucker-punched him and then slammed a heavy blow into his gut! "It's Bennett's second Purple Heart… Was all set for a week leave to rendezvous with his fiancé in Hawaii and get married."

How tragic… Ken's mind then flashed back to Northwestern. *Saw Bennett just before I graduated. He was on leave shortly before shipping out to Vietnam. Said he wanted to "Visit friends and his beloved Northwestern once again."*

Ken remembered how Frederick beamed when he explained he'd enlisted after graduation, and then passed the rigorous training and background check of the Marine Corps for the officer position of Forward Artillery Observer.

Bennett had mentioned another recent Northwestern graduate: outstanding football and basketball athlete, 1st Lieutenant Carl Lemon, now in the Marine Corps. Lemon had just returned from Vietnam where twenty-five marines and five tanks were under his command.

"You gotta be out of your mind!" he exclaimed to Frederick. "Isn't that way out ahead of the front line where you see the shells land and report back—a dangerous position?"

Strunk recalled Frederick merely nodded his head slowly, and said calmly, "That's part of it. Someone needs to do it."

Those words stayed with Strunk the rest of that Wisconsin day, and sometimes through the years. *Wonder what Frederick would've become if he hadn't been killed? Husband? Governor? What happened to the fiancé? Why did he choose to be in such a dangerous spot?*

Author Note: While drafting the Northwestern story, I (Savoy) received a note from Bob Ferguson, a fellow Marine and close friend with Bennett. An excerpt from their Marine Corpse experience:

"Ben's death hit me hard. … I hoped my letter had reached him before he got hit. It was returned sixteen days later, unopened. Stamped in big, red letters on the back was the word "DECEASED." It cut deeply to know one of my best friends had not received my letter telling him how much his friendship meant to me. I opened it and read my last line, "Ben, when we get through this war, I'm expecting you to be in my wedding, so make sure you keep your sword sharp and your powder dry." … In September of 1967, Bennett was killed on Hill 66 in South Vietnam. He was as physically tough a Marine as I knew, but steel beats flesh every time. … I use his one-liners like they're mine, and my 2nd son is named Ryan Bennett Ferguson. Friends like Ben rub off on you so hard, memory warms for life." Bob Ferguson of Washington State.

This author, Clifton Savoy, had the pleasure of hosting Rt. Lieutenant General Lawrence Snowden, who served in WW II as well as the Korean and Vietnam Wars. He was speaking at a church sponsored Veteran Day Tribute about the assault on Iwo Jima. He was ninety, in his Marine dress uniform, trim and fit. "The Mt. Suribachi volcanic sands on the beach were so loose," he said, "neither soldiers or equipment could get much traction. Bogged us down! Thousands of our soldiers were killed and over the five weeks to take that small, eight-mile square Pacific island. Only a couple hundred of the 21,000 Japanese soldiers survived. Our casualties were as great." General Snowden, who was wounded in the Iwo Jima assault, was the highest-ranking survivor at the year of this Veteran Tribute. He went on to say. "A young Marine by the name of Ernest 'Boots' Thomas of Monticello, Florida and a couple of others fought to the top of Suribachi to put up our American flag to rally our soldiers below. This was the first American flag to fly

1ˢᵗ Lieutenant Jerry 'Frederick' Bennett, our friend and classmate, may our collective Northwestern legacy be worthy, in even the smallest way, of your ultimate sacrifice!"

over Iwo Jima, but it was soon replaced with a larger flag in the event captured in the famous Rosenthal photo." General Snowden paused and added softly, "Boots Thomas was killed in action not long afterwards." He paused again, and asked in a deeply emotional tone, almost in tears, "Where do we get such men… who'll sacrifice everything… even their lives to ensure our freedom… and what would they have become?"

I wasn't prepared to respond at the moment, but I could now:

"From places like Frederick, Oklahoma and campuses like Northwestern."

68.

TOP NEWS OF 1967: VIETNAM WAR LOSES SUPPORT, FIRST BLACK JUSTICE IS THURGOOD MARSHALL. DR. KING, "AGAPE LOVE IS THE SOLUTION."

December 31, 1967, Top News Stories of the Year
National TV Studios

*W*ashington, D.C. — "The top story of 1967 was a replay of 1966— the Vietnam War."

A person at a desk appeared. It was President Lyndon B. Johnson, with papers in hand and an anxious look like he was searching for an answer to one of the many issues at hand. "President Johnson and his cabinet have not waivered from the policy to support the South Vietnam government against North Vietnam and its communist allies, China and Russia."

"Opposition has grown, however, even though the President has pursued peace. And, in what way does the Johnson Administration support South Vietnam **Vietnam! Johnson searches for answers as opposition grows.** leaders whose distrust and instability increases daily?"

"Over the year, it's been more military buildup; anti-war and anti-draft demonstrations; peace attempts; more protests, violence, and self-immolations; resumption of bombing in North Vietnam, more talks;

radio and TV debates; congressional hearings and political posturing; and endless commentaries."

"A massive increase of soldiers occurred to 485,600 end of 1967, but the Johnson administration expressed that more troops are likely."

"Deaths of soldiers have increased each year, as well, to 20,055 total end of 1967. Sadly, this number is projected to increase."

"At home, opposition continues to grow. A new draft law has been enacted, but the anti-war and anti-draft movements flourish. Many flee to Canada to avoid being drafted, loss of more than 700 airplanes, and increasing numbers of prisoners of war, some speaking against the U.S. involvement, add fuel to the flame of opposition."

Deaths, and protests increase, and burden grows on military and soldier!

As the TV screen dimmed, the reporter concluded, "President Johnson's frustration with Vietnam is linked to this erosion of public support, and it place a heavy burden on the military and each soldier to produce positive results."

Washington, D.C. — "The other top story of 1967 was the progress in Civil Rights. That is, citizens being able to have a daily life with equality and freedom—the rights guaranteed in the U.S. Constitution."

"Dr. Martin Luther King, Jr., who has staunchly held to nonviolent in demonstrations and protests, has acknowledged, 'We have come a long way.'"

"One example is Thurgood Marshall, who was the first black person sworn in as justice of the U.S. Supreme Court. But, Dr. King pointed out, 'We still have a long way to go...'"

"However, there's pent up frustration in many places; especially, the hotbeds of big cities." ... "Demonstrators ask, 'Why is enforcement needed if these are also a constitutional right for colored people? Where's the equal protection under the law?' ... 'Why does legal racial discrimination still exist? Where's the equal access to education, housing, and public facilities? We've been told, 'We don't serve your kind here. The vacancy sign's wrong. We're full.' What about the right to vote? Why did it take a Supreme Court decision, *Loving v. Virginia* 12 June 1967, to rule, 'it's unconstitutional to prohibit interracial marriage?'"

"The Bible says there's no difference, '...made in the image of God... male and female.'"

"Not surprisingly," the reporter noted, "racial protests during the hot summer of 1967 ignited into riots. Fires were set in over one hundred forty cities, the deadliest of which occurred in Newark, New Jersey with 26 fatalities and Detroit, with 43."

Civil rights progress.

First Black Justice, but why does legal discrimination exist?

"Consider the violence, killings and bombings over the last few years alone to individuals who have sought equal justice and freedom. Danger and death lurks daily. A gun at the head of Dr. King was lowered instead of trigger pulled in old St. Augustine, Florida—just one example. Why would any civil rights advocate place their lives in the crosshairs of harm's way?"

Deadly riots in Newark and Detroit!

Danger and death lurks daily!

"Dr. King," the reporter added as a scene of King at Southern Methodist University in 1966 filled the screen, "spoke to the why, as he shared deeply held beliefs regarding solutions to the racial problems that have forever plagued mankind."

Agape love of God

"...We must see each other as brothers..."

... "not merely because the law says it. ...It's the redemptive goodwill for all men. ...Theologians would say it is the agape love of God operating in the human heart. On this level, he loves every man not because he likes him, not because his ways appeal to him, but because God loves him—loving the person who does the evil deed but hating the deed. I think this is what Jesus meant when he said, 'Love your

enemies...' God is not interested merely in the freedom of black men and brown men and yellow men, but God is interested in the freedom of the whole human race and the creation of a society where all men will live together as brothers.

As long as injustice is around, it will be necessary to bring it to the surface (in our nonviolent protests)... Some things are so precious, some things so eternally true, some things so right that they are worth dying for. If a man has not discovered something that he would die for, he isn't fit to live..."

"...something worth dying for." Dr. King's voice rang out as the TV screen faded to black, "Some things are so precious, some things so eternally true, some things so right they are worth dying for. If a man has not discovered something he would die for, he isn't fit to live."

69.

VETERAN RETURNS TO NORTHWESTERN, LBJ
ANNOUNCES WILL NOT RUN FOR PRESIDENT

March 1968, Back from military service
Northwestern Oklahoma State University

Veteran student-athlete but now with sports trainer responsibilities, Larry Don May mumbled to himself, "Glad to be back here," as he walked into the Northwestern fieldhouse. His mind was in Korea. A shiver came over him. *Too cold! How can anyone live there?*

May stopped in the hallway to familiarize himself to the pictures and names on the athletic bulletin board. *Just one Indian my freshman year fall of 1962, Bill Mitchell, and only one now, Bob Phillips, a Delaware from Woodward, Oklahoma.* May recalled there had been only two in between: Browning Pipestem and Lance Rollins. *Phillips doesn't look Indian. Linebacker? Wonder how he came to live in Woodward? ... Up to ten black players now: Tom King, Jim Cheeley, Maurice Hill, Dave Billups, (Clyde) Biscuit Jones, Kenny Jones, George Graham, Rudolph Preston, Ardell Smith, and Dale Diggs. How'd they come to Northwestern? ...* He noticed the ones with conference honors and the queen. *I'll have to remember to give 'em a late congratulations. Pam Washburn homecoming queen—a pretty choice.*

1967 Football Season: Record 4-6. Coach Bill Snebel. Honorees for the Oklahoma Collegiate Conference: Doyl Mendenhall OT, James

Wolff OT, and Paul Witwam DB. Ranger Homecoming queen for Fall 1967 Pam Washburn from Waynoka.

In another spot on the board, May noticed the picture and names for the just-ended Northwestern 1967-68 Basketball Season. *Fun team. Hmm, no conference honorees? Thought Henry Commodore had a chance— good scorer. Next year. ... Two athletes of color: Commodore and Kenney Hamilton. ... Wonder if Wings Drake will get another military deferment?*

Coach Keith Covey. Record 12-16. Players: Eddie Fisher, Bob 'Wings' Drake, Gene Valentine, Henry Commodore, Mike Mitchel, Henry Nicholson, Dale Ross, Mike Cook, Eddie Ritterhouse, Bert Nichols, David Taylor, Hank Ellis, Kenny Hamilton, Bill Bixler and Carl Moxley.

L–R: Hank Commodore, Bill Bixler, Tommy Griffin

Suddenly, a ruckus sounded from around the corner and the courts. "Come on!" exclaimed the voice. It sounded like Hank Commodore. "Give me another chance!"

"Sorry," Teammate Bill Bixler replied. "Make it. Take it. I'm the champ!" he exclaimed with a teasing laugh back over the shoulder as he hustled off the court where a frustrated Commodore stood with basketball in his hand. "Yep, I'm the champ!" It might have been the only time Commodore ever lost this one-on-one competition.

"You won't be if you give me another chance," came the rebuttal.

About that moment he noticed Larry May peering around the corner. "Make him play me, coach."

"Can't do that." May responded with a chuckle. "I'm the trainer, not coach. Besides, didn't Bixler win fair and square?"

"Yeah, but…"

"It was fair and square," Bixler teased again with a chuckle. "Fair and square."

Moving on, May replied, "By the way, you'll have another jumper and shooter next year. That Northern junior college guy from Oklahoma City Douglas, Tommy Griffin, contacted us that he's accepting the Northwestern student-athletic scholarship for the next two years. Comes in next fall 1968. Good rebounder, too. Supposedly has a 42" vertical jump. He's 6'3" and that jump puts his head near the rim. Certainly, a dunk and rebound. Also, track guy—javelin, discus, high jump, and pole vault. Probably good at football, too, since played in JC and recruited by TU, but promised he wouldn't play. So, bear down. Help's coming."

70.

March 31, 1968, Sunday, Johnson Stuns the Nation
Washington, D. C.

White House — The TV screen was immediately filled with the figure of President Lyndon B. Johnson behind a desk. "Good evening, my fellow Americans," he spoke in his characteristic solemn tone peppered with a Texan drawl. "Tonight I want to speak to you of peace in Vietnam and Southeast Asia…" He pointed out Hanoi had denounced the peace offer, and savagely assaulted the people of South

Special address to the Nation!

Vietnam and its allies during the Tet holidays. "If more heavy attacks occur, Hanoi, North Vietnam, will not destroy the fighting power of South Vietnam and its allies, but many men will be lost. And the war will go on…"

Johnson's Chief of Staff, likely followed along with a copy of the speech from off camera. Would Johnson include the recent crash in Greenland of a B-52 carrying hydrogen bombs and how it triggered a nervous search for the weapons? … Would he say anything of North Korea seizing the USS Pueblo and crew, with accusations of spying? … Mention Senators Eugene McCarty (D-MN) and Robert Kennedy (D-NY) challenging Johnson for the democratic nomination for the presidency? … Would the President actually include what would be his stunning announcement? … Every moment would have been a nervous one.

Cost of war!

Johnson spoke about the cost of war, "To meet our responsibilities in Vietnam and Korea, we need additional expenditures.The estimate is \$2.5 billion this fiscal year and \$2.6 billion the next… Yet, Congress has not acted."

He reminded those watching, America has kept the compact of President John F. Kennedy's pronouncement: "…willing to pay the price, bear any burden, meet any hardship, support any friend, oppose any foe, to assure the survival, and the success, of liberty." … Johnson affirmed, "…We shall keep it."

"It is true," Johnson expressed in a somber tone, "a house divided against itself by the spirit of faction, party, region, religion, race, is a house that cannot stand. A division is in the American house now. There is divisiveness among us all tonight. And holding the trust that is mine, as President of all the people, I cannot disregard the peril of the progress of the American people and the hope and the prospect of peace for all peoples, so I would ask all Americans whatever their personal interest or concern to guard against divisiveness and all of its ugly consequences."

Guard against division

"With American sons in the fields far away, with America's future under challenge right here at home, with our hopes and the world's for peace in the balance, I do not believe I should devote an hour… to any duties other than the awesome duties of this presidency of your country."

"In unity… America will be a stronger nation, a more just society, a land of greater opportunity and fulfilment because of what we have done together. What we won when we were united must not now be lost in suspicion and distrust and selfishness and politics. Believing this, I have concluded I should not permit the Presidency to become involved in the partisan divisions that are developing in this political year."

"Accordingly, I shall not seek, and I will not accept, the nomination of my party for another term as your President.

Thank you for listening. Good night and God bless all of you."

The screen faded to black.

"…will not accept nomination…"

71.

1968: RE-CONNECTION WITH L'ZAR, DR. KING ASSASSINATED, CHARACTER NOT COLOR!

Thursday April 4, 1968, Memories
Oklahoma State University, Stillwater, OK

I was mesmerized by the microbial world taught by Dr. Anna B. Fischer at Northwestern. Its minute characteristics grabbed the attention of this country kid whose youth was chiseled out of the rugged outdoor life of a horse, cattle, and crop farm in the Oklahoma Panhandle. Now, this day, at Oklahoma State University, as a graduate student, I'd see even smaller components in this fascinating sub-cellular world using an electron microscope. Yet, before day's end, other unimaginable events would be the ones forever embedded into my memory.

"Be back by 7:30," the lab director warned in an or-else tone. "I'll be free by then to look at your research samples."

Two hours — enough time to grab a bite. In seconds, I was headed towards The Strip, a street of food vendors next to campus and south of the Student Union and Conference Center.

"About a twenty minute wait," the waitress said to the four students in line ahead of me at a popular quick food and suds place named The Coachman.

Reality struck as I pondered my options. *Not sure have enough time to wait. Didn't want a hotdog, but better grab one on the way back.* It's not my nature to toss in the towel so easily, though, and I glanced around to see if any of the red booths were about to be vacated. I was shocked to see someone I met once back at Northwestern, and he was eating alone.

It was L'Zar who had asked for my autograph five years ago, spring of 1963. I debated for a moment. *Do I want to eat bad enough to sit with him and maybe create an impression with anyone here at Oklahoma State who might know his preference for guys and spread the word among the thousands of students—few whom I knew? ... Or do I just walk out the door?*

Now, I have no idea what might attract a person to the same gender. Absolutely no romantic —eros—attraction to me of those sweaty bodies of athletes after practice or games. Hugs? Yes, friendly ones, like when I finished at Northwestern. But more? ... Puke!

I motioned with my hand, and told the waitress, "I'm with that person over there." She looked his direction, then quickly back at me, with a sizing up gaze and puzzled look, but I walked on by without an explanation. She must've known something about L'Zar (anonymous name), as I felt her stare burning my back.

He didn't notice me until I stood at his table. "L'Zar, mind if I eat with you?" I asked, and slid into the other side of the booth without waiting for his reply. The startled look on his face softened as I added. "Remember? Northwestern. You asked for an autograph."

A slight smile appeared as he replied in that melodic tone I would never forget, "Yes! Clif...ton, right?"

I nodded, and then noticed in the dim light his swollen cheeks, bruises on his face and the remnants of a black eye. "What happened to you? Been in a car wreck or accident?"

"Felt like it," he shuffled slightly in the booth seat and explained in an anguished tone as he remembered. "Was to meet a guy, and it was an ambush. Bunch of his buddies came along. Beat me up. Bruises all over my body."

I asked as I turned in my food order, "Does that happen very much?"

"Mostly just harassment, but a couple times over the years."

"How do you handle them? Call cops or somebody?"

"No, don't want notice. Might be exported back to my country."

"Where you from?" I asked in a quizzical tone.

"Persian country. My treatment there would be far worse."

"Huh? What do you mean?"

"People like me there disappear or somehow have an accident that kills us. Don't want to go back. I love your country. It's freedom. Everyone looks different. Lucky you're born here."

"Never thought about things like that or my country that way," I mumbled between bites of my hamburger. I began to ask whatever came to mind. "Bet girls don't like you."

"Not true!" he exclaimed in a vigorous way. "They do. Some of my best friends are girls. Even compare notes."

"You're joking," I responded with a laugh.

"No, seriously." As he gestured, he subtly laid a hand on the table almost touching mine.

"Not so close, L'Zar! Remember what I warned I'd do?"

With a slight grin, he moved his arm back, and said, "If don't try, never know."

Soon, I finished my burger and fries, and stood to leave, "Thanks for sharing your booth." Over my shoulder I added, "And, be careful with who you meet up with in the future."

I heard a faint, sort of sad, reply, "Thanks for eating with me."

As I neared the exit, I suddenly realized a good number of the booths were empty and no one was standing in the wait line. "What's going on?" I mumbled. I'd find out within minutes.

72.

April 4, 1968, Memories
Oklahoma State University, Stillwater, OK

Minutes after leaving L'Zar and walking back to the lab, I noticed a small group of people on the sidewalk peering into the display window of a store. They seemed to be in a trance. A few steps more, I saw a TV. The scenes and commentary sucked me in as well.

Memphis, TN—Walter Cronkite of CBS News was reporting, "…Dr. Martin Luther King, the apostle of non-violence in the civil rights movement, has been shot to death in Memphis…"

Dr. King assassinated!

"Wow!" I exclaimed under my breath. "How? Who?" Others in the group must've asked the same, and responses filled the air.

"Heard shot at 6:01 p.m. Central, and died at a hospital about an hour later."

Another added, "…on his room balcony at the Lorraine Motel. From across the street."

"Leading protests for striking sanitation workers."

It struck me that I didn't realize Dr. King was such a beloved leader in the civil rights movement. Hadn't given much thought to him or the protests that often received violent resistance. The breadth of my world was pretty small, but I don't recall in my teen or young adult years of any protests and riots or violence in the middle of the country—at least, the western plains of Oklahoma and Kansas and Northwest Texas where I grew up.

Cronkite continued as related scenes faded in and out on the tv screen, "…the mayor reinstated the dusk-to-dawn curfew… Four thousand national guardsmen were called out… President Lyndon B. Johnson expressed, "America is shocked and saddened by the brutal slaying…" In

Shot, standing out on a balcony in Memphis, TN!

People filled streets, dazed and crying!

Riots and violence!

Harlem, the nation's largest Negro community, reacted in shock when word of King's murder reached them. Men, women, and children poured into the streets, and appeared dazeds and many were crying…" Scenes of riots and violence in other cities appeared, too.

I personally never witnessed someone, because of their color, be denied service or lodging or any of those types of things. Eventually, heard such comments by some of the black student athletes at Northwestern, but what was shared were experiences from their youth or family history handed down from a parent. No, the ugliness of the human denigration didn't hit me broadside until I learned the Northwestern basketball team walked out of a restaurant because it would not serve H. L. Brown, a black player on the team. (Author Note: Years later, it made me angry to learn Big Ben and Glen Smith, the first two black athletes to play at Northwestern, had to eat outside on a park table while the rest of the team—one I was on—ate inside. Had I known at the time, I hope I'd taken my plate and eaten outside with them. I am deeply sorry for not knowing of their agony.)

Big Ben Smith was right!

Upon hearing of Dr. King's assassination, I unconsciously blurted out, "Big Ben was right," as a memory from back at Northwestern flashed through my mind. *Ben was the first black person I met in life. Lived across the hall from each other, played collegiate sports together, and we became good friends.*

It was spring 1966. He was in his room in a very unpleasant mood as excerpts of a Dr. King speech were bumping the pro baseball games off the

radio airways. I stepped into his room to check out the loud ruckus and he exclaimed, "That fool's going to get shot one of these days!"

My thoughts sidetracked momentarily, *Does Ben remember that day?* Back to the present, *Wonder how he felt when he learned Dr. King had been shot and killed? Probably like everyone who wished for the day King's dreams would come true.*

"...fool's going to get shot one of these days!"

A guy on the sidewalk asked, "What'd you say?"

"Oh, nothing," I replied as I glanced his way. At that moment, I remembered. *Oh no! Missed my time to use the electron microscope.* It was late, so I headed to my apartment. The six block walk seemed extra-long this day, as my mind wandered.

Big Ben, I now realized, didn't think Dr. King was a foolish person—

"No fool, just constantly in harm's way!"

one who would chase any cause without concern for the risk. No, Ben probably knew that sooner or later being shot and killed likely was in King's future because the causes King chose to champion—willing to die for—placed him constantly in harm's way.

As I walked, site of the Cowpoke football stadium brought more reflection, *Where is Ben now? Too bad he wasn't in physical shape when he reported to the Miami Dolphins. Might've made the season roster. Needed a mean friend like me to push him to get in shape.* A feeling, something like a consolation, rushed over me. *At least, Chip Myers, of the five players who played four years at Northwestern, made a pro roster.*

Where's Glen, Ben's brother? Last heard, drafted and trained as an interrogator. Sounds like for prisoners of war. His muscular build and size would certainly be intimidating.

H. L. Brown, too? Ben and Glen's roomie. Where did he wind up after being drafted? Someone said, "Being trained in artillery." Sounds like a quick ticket to Vietnam.

And what about Curtis Thompson? Know he finished officer training school, but will he receive orders to Korea, Vietnam, or some other hot spot?

... No one knew at the moment, but a tragic day — one that would shock the nation—was only a few months into his future.

As I opened the door to my apartment, I wondered if anyone else from Northwestern had orders to the war zone? If yes, I hope no one comes home in a body bag.

TV that evening had updates of the King assassination and some highlights of his life. I was especially attracted to his "I have a Dream" speech he passionately delivered 28 August 1963 in the March on Washington, D.C. for Jobs and Freedom. The words, their collective meaning, registered with me for the first time. I was awed by the scene of King speaking on the steps of the Abraham Lincoln Memorial, with the Great Emancipator's statue towering behind King and the vast crowd of 250,000—including 50,000 or more white supporters—in front and along the reflection pool and seemingly all the way to the Washington Monument. The crowd roared approval at times to King's points.

Exhausted, I hit the bed, but sleep didn't come as I replayed parts of the day in my mind. This time, though, the Lincoln Memorial scene had only Dr. King and the statute of Lincoln, but no crowd even though its roars of approval still sounded. The loudest seemed when King proclaimed,

"...I have a dream that my four little children will one day live in a nation where they will not be judged by the color of their skin but by the content of their character."

That's what I want for my children, too—judged by their character instead of color of their skin. "It's what everyone would want," I mumbled as the scene faded away in my sleep. "Character instead of color." ... *"Character instead of color."* ... *"Character..."*

73.

JUNE 1968: ROBERT F. KENNEDY ASSASSINATED. A MEMORY FOREVER

June 4-6, 1968, Forever a Memory!
Los Angeles, California

Lieutenant Curtis Thompson had orders to ship out to the Korean war zone, but had a few days leave in the Los Angeles area. He was enjoying a visit with his uncle Troy Henderson and family, who lived in Compton, when a life-taking event, of national impact, forever was embedded into his memory.
R: Curtis Thompson

"Thanks for getting our tickets to the Dodgers and Pirates baseball game," Thompson expressed in an adrenaline-charged tone to his uncle who was behind the wheel for the late-night drive back to Compton. "It's been a great day. ... Really great!"

"Yeah, glad it worked out we could go," he expressed and glanced at Thompson. "Dodgers won and big crowd. What size did the announcer say?" He reached to turn on the radio before Thompson could respond. "Just after the hour. There's probably a box score summary of the game." The radio sounds squawked as he quickly moved the dial around. "There it is..."

Dodgers Win! "Wrap up of the Tuesday, June 4th Los Angeles Dodger game against the Pittsburgh Pirates," a voice on the radio sounded. "Dodgers 5 and Pittsburgh 0. … Dodgers had 8 hits. No player had more than one. … Don Drysdale was the winning pitcher. Gave up only 3 scattered hits, had 8 strike outs, and no walks. Even had one of the Dodger hits to help his cause. … Night game and a large crowd of 30,622 attended. … The Dodgers have a long way to go, though, to catch the National League leader, the St. Louis Cardinals.

Thompson and Uncle Troy exchanged further comments in a giddy tone like it was gift-opening-time on Christmas morning, even though the midnight hour had just struck. "Yep, a win, and the big crowd made the game all the better. … Drysdale had his stuff, and getting that hit seemed like he was telling 'em, "I'm more than a pitcher!" … Yeah, don't think he wanted to come out for that pinch-runner."

Minutes later, the radio voice was replaced with shocking news that changed forever their memories of this day and time.

Another Kennedy shot! "This program is interrupted," the voice on the radio sounded, "for a special news update… "A few minutes ago, a little after midnight, a gunman shot Robert F. Kennedy!"

The news had special meaning for them, and Thompson's mind and body snapped fully alert, as did Uncle Troy's. They simultaneously glanced at each other and asked, "What did it say?" Before either replied, the radio voice continued…

Life changes in a heart-beat! "Kennedy was in the Ambassador Hotel in Los Angeles and learned he'd won the democratic party primary in California for the presidency of the United States. More details to come…"

Thompson was stunned at what they'd heard. *Kennedy shot?* Scenes of the afternoon, just hours earlier, flashed through his mind. *The motorcade of Kennedy, who was wrapping up his California democratic party campaign, was coming through Compton on the way to Los Angeles. Thompson and uncle decided to go to the motorcade route, in hope of seeing Kennedy.*

They stood on a corner where the motorcade would turn, and the crowd noise grew louder and louder. The first car came into view, then another, and another. The crowd moved our way, too, along the street. Then, all at once, there was Kennedy—in a convertible with top down. He was sitting on the top of the back seat, far more exposed to danger than his brother, President John F. Kennedy, when he was assassinated.

The car, everything, moved slowly, actually barely crept along, as it turned the corner. We were just a couple of feet away on the edge of the curb. Kennedy looked at me, stuck out his hand, and shook mine, as one or both of us said something.

Thompson looked over at his uncle, who seemed in deep thought too, and asked in a broken, solemn tone, "Do you remember what Kennedy said," … "or what I said to him?"

"…Kennedy shook my hand!"

Uncle Troy glanced sadly at his nephew, shook his head, and said, "No."

"Seems something like, "Good luck," … and I think I said, "Hello."

"Maybe he recognized your military look—short hair, trim, and physically fit."

Thompson searched his thoughts for an answer, and a puzzled look filled his face. *A crowd had gathered around them quickly. Maybe Kennedy's comments were to all of us? … Just as suddenly as Kennedy's motorcade appeared, it disappeared down the street. The day was off to a great start. Now, Dodger Stadium and ballgame, here we come!*

Wednesday passed with little news of Kennedy's condition. Even another Dodgers win over Pittsburgh, 2 to 1, drew little interest. A few hours after midnight, though, news came…

"Robert F. Kennedy was pronounced dead at 1:44 a.m. PDT on June 6th. He was mortally wounded shortly after midnight of June 5th. He'd just learned he won the California democratic primary for the presidency of the United States. At the moment of the shooting, he was shaking the hand of Juan Romero, a 17-year-old busboy at the Ambassador Hotel.

As the last comment repeated in his mind, Thompson looked down at his hand. *"At the moment of the shooting, Kennedy was shaking the hand of..."*

Thompson looked at his hand...

Author Note: Lt. Curtis Thompson served in Korea and then in the Vietnam war zone as a boots-on-the-ground embedded U.S. officer adviser to a 500-soldier unit of the South Vietnamese Army. After full service, he remained active with the military and retired as a Lt. Colonel. Yes, he also returned to Northwestern OSU to finish his degree in math, and pursue his dream of mentoring youngsters as a teacher and coach. A girl's basketball team was his first opportunity, and he continued coaching girls. His teams have been in the Oklahoma State Tournament ten times, in the championship game four times, and champions twice. The journey was made possible when a young AWOL Thompson met the President of Northwestern, Dr. Jesse Martin, who gave his full attention and arranged opportunities for Thompson to pursue his dreams. Thompson and family reside in Oklahoma City, and still sharing his dreams.

74.

FALL 1968: TOUGH RACIAL QUESTIONS.
"BEING BLACK WAS NEVER . . ."

Fall 1968, "Being Black was never..."
Northwestern Oklahoma State University

"Wow! Where did those first two years go?" Mary Williams mumbled as she set her books down on her work desk in the rear of the library. Her junior year activities and classes were well underway, and, of course, being outgoing and with Northwestern having a compact campus, and most of the women living in Oklahoma Hall, it didn't take long to meet everyone. Soon, Mary's path crossed that of Jane Nagle, a 105 pound by 5'1" stick of dynamite who lived on the same floor but opposite wings. Their lives were never the same.

Jane was a junior transfer from Pennsylvania, by way of a brief work time in the State Department in Washington, D.C. Whenever asked how she came to Northwestern and Alva, in the western Great Plains, she'd often say something like, "Oh, too long a story." On the personal level, Jane didn't mince words, and spoke direct to the point in a way that seemed, at first, an interrogating manner. Her questions to Mary were spontaneous, tough and, as their friendship grew, increasingly with an air, "If you can't handle them, you don't deserve my friendship."

"I'm white," Jane Nagle expressed to Mary, "so it's no big deal for

A black woman to a white university?

me to be at Northwestern, but how is it you came, a black woman, to a mostly all-white university?"

"President Martin," Mary replied in a teasing tone and without hesitation as she'd been asked the same question a number of times already, "wanted more color on campus."

Jane rolled her eyes. "Come on, be serious."

"I am," Mary replied. "Mr. Floyd Alexander was Principal of Oklahoma City Moon Junior High. Many of the Douglas students had been at Moon. He and President Martin knew each other when both taught at Nowata, Oklahoma. Dr. Martin asked Mr. Alexander to bring a car load of Douglas students to visit Northwestern and Alva. I was one of them, liked what I saw and could attend with a work scholarship starting Fall 1966. About ten other black students, five or six from Douglas, attended that semester with me."

"Ever been called, uh..." Jane uncharacteristically hesitated, not sure how to ask.

"Ever been called a..."

"...a nigger?" Mary added as she anticipated the question.

"Yeah."

"Couple of times. Once here at Northwestern..."

Jane interrupted. "Really? ... Here at Northwestern?"

"Yes," Mary replied with an anguished look and hesitation in her voice as the memory returned, "...and the other was in 1964. ... Remember it well. My mother and I traveled to the area where she grew up in Texas just across the Southeastern corner of Oklahoma."

"Tell me about that Texas time first."

"We were excited. Mom was the youngest of ten children. We were visiting her childhood home area and reliving some of those memories. As we drove around, Mom chatted about so many things: her Dad being a minister—an African-Methodist-Episcopal Circuit Rider for fifty-two years—a site where they lived, and how the family lived off the land and hired out for field work to make a living. In town, we stopped at an eating place for lunch. Guy behind the counter as we walked in the door, took one look, and exclaimed, 'We don't serve niggers here!'"

"That's terrible!" Jane exclaimed in a disgusted voice.

"Yeah, I was shocked, as this had never happened to me anytime into high school. And bear in mind, Mom placed me in all sorts of classes across Oklahoma City over the years, where I interacted with all types of people and color, including white."

"How did you react to him?"

Mary grinned as the moment came back to her. "Mom kept her composure, but was quick with a response, "Well, we don't eat them either!" I never had the chance to see the expression on his face, as we turned immediately and left."

"Good for you."

"Mom and I should've known we'd be treated that way, though, because a sign outside town had the words, '…where the whitest people live and blackest dirt exists.'"

"Oh, my. … Now tell me about the time at Northwestern."

A sad look filled Mary's face. "It was the most disturbing face-to-face negative racial experience I've had anywhere in life. I was visiting a white friend in her room on a different floor than mine in Oklahoma Hall." Mary looked momentarily into Jane's eyes and continued, "You know how two rooms shared a bathroom, one on each side. Well, the doors to each room were open into the bathroom. A white girl, who lived in the room opposite my friend, saw me through the open doors, and exclaimed loud enough for me to look at her, "I can't believe a nigger is in my room!" My temper flared, and I retorted something about how plain she looked, and immediately left my friend's room."

"No? For real? Ever see her again?"

"Yes. Once. On the sidewalk in front of the library where I worked."

"Punch her in the nose?"

"No," Mary replied with a slight laugh. "We were walking towards each other. After she saw me, she purposely stepped off until I passed.

"Ever been denied food at a restaurant?" I grinned and held my head high, of course. Never saw her again, and never experience anything like it in my life."

"Only that time visiting Mom's childhood area in Texas. Mom did say her and family had some, though. Heard a few of the Northwestern black athletes had a couple of them, too."

Will Rogers "How come your relationships with people are much like that guy, uh… what's his name, the famous Oklahoman, oh yeah, Will Rogers, who never met a person he didn't like?"

"You're funny, Jane," Mary replied with a laugh. "Yes, I've interacted well with most people all my life. Color didn't seem to matter, and was seldom on my mind. Same at Northwestern, downtown in Alva, and the Methodist Church. All mostly white. I even sang in the church choir and played the piano. No issues except the one I mentioned. That's it."

"So, you were just born this lovable and loving way?" Jane asked in a doubting tone. … Then she added a little spice to their exchange, "lucky you."

"You're teasing," Mary replied quickly. "You know a baby doesn't walk right away. It has to learn. Each of us is a collective result of those around us."

"I'm a product of Biblical truths…" Jane nodded agreement and Mary continued, "I'm a product of the biblical truths and inspiration passed along from my Grandparents to me through Mom. Life challenges and anxieties didn't bother me so much after I learned, *From one man, God made all the nations, that they should inhabit the whole earth; and He marked out their appointed times in history and the boundaries of their lands. (Bible, Acts 17:26).*"

Mary paused to let the words sink in with Jane, "As a believer, those words—*"From one man, God made…"*—has been a powerful security blanket for me.

Mary grinned at her friend, "Plus, I'm special because God made me this way. Mom knew this truth, but took me time to learn it. Until I did, she wouldn't allow the color of our skin to keep us from reaching for the stars. No chip on the shoulder. No blaming someone else or excuses when I stumbled. When I did, Mom would pick me up, set my feet in the right direction, and presented a positive vision of what's possible. With that truth and security, if I failed while giving my all, then it probably wasn't a path God wanted me to travel."

"God made me! I am special. … wouldn't allow color to keep from reaching for the stars!"

Jane probed Mary from another direction, "There has to be someone or something that irritates you. Who, what is it?"

"What, who irritates you?"

"Yes, there is," Mary replied with a hint of anger.

"Ah, ha. Hit a nerve. Tell me."

Grouped JUST because of color!"

"It's when I'm included in a group just because of my skin color." Mary took a deep breath to let her dander subside.

"Don't get me wrong. I care deeply for black people—all of them, but I also care about all people, no matter their color. And, I try to live and interact with all people the same. But for me and grouping, I'm an individual. I want to be identified by my name, performances, accomplishments and, like Dr. Martin Luther King said, 'character and not color.'" Mary paused again. "Don't treat me any different than any other person. Dr. King said it eloquently in his lead-in comment to a speech at Southern Methodist University, "Skin may differ, but affection dwells in black and white the same." That's me!"

Mary wasn't finished. "Understanding what it means to being born with dark skin has been a life-long learning journey. I'm sure it's the same for every person of color.

"I am an individual. I want and expect others to see who I am— my character and accomplishments!" Most often, I'm labeled with a group identity—Negro, black, minority, person of color—instead of seeing me as an individual; seeing who I am; and my thoughts, dreams, and accomplishments. I don't see a teacher as a black or white teacher; just a teacher. I don't see a gifted musician as either minority or non-minority, but just a gifted musician. I expect and want to be seen that way, too!"

"Never dawned on me, Mary," Jane expressed in an apologetic tone, "that the mere mention of blacks or people of color had the grouping effect you describe."

"The group-mentality kills individual initiative!" "It kills initiative, too," Mary added, "And, to our detriment, government programs identify us with a "persons of color" tag, and breaking out of that grouping isn't easy. For those of us who try and do, we're often met with repercussions from those, whites as well as blacks, pushing the group mentality. Fortunately, Mom kept me on the track of individual initiative, with expectations of high performance, always dreaming and reaching for the stars."

"You mean blacks, too?"

"Yes, even from blacks. Breaking away from the group to follow an individual journey, to follow a dream is not easy."

"Congratulations on being elected Northwestern's 1968 Homecoming Queen, but…"

"Thank you," Mary responded without realizing Jane was setting her up for a knockout question as they walked to the university cafeteria. "I feel blessed to have been chosen by the students to represent them and Northwestern in its 1968 Homecoming events. The two runner-ups—Shirley Gibson from Beaver, Oklahoma and Lee Ann Turner from Liberal, Kansas—are beautiful. Same for Linda Patterson from Woodward, Oklahoma, the 1966 winner, and Pam Washburn from Waynoka, Oklahoma, the 1967 winner ... All really beautiful."

Northwestern's 1968 Homecoming Queen, Mary Elaine Williams, and runnerups, Shirley Gibson (L) and Lee Ann Turner, Courtesy Northwestern

"...you sure," Nagle continued with her question and flattened Mary's feel-good disposition, "...you sure the students didn't vote for you as some type of tokenism—whites trying to somehow make up for historical injustices to blacks?"

Mary stopped in her tracks, as the mental wheels kicked into high-gear. Back walking, she quickened her pace to catch Jane a few steps ahead and replied, "That point of view might've had some weight, but look at it this way. It's been a life-long journey for me to understand what it means to be born with dark skin. ... So, it would be natural for white individuals, ones who grew up in areas like the western Great

Plains where few blacks lived, to have a learning journey, an innocence, too. If true, they wouldn't have much understanding of any "historical injustices or who committed them" for which to make amends."

"The group mentality kills individual initiative! Blacks as well as white sympathizers have paid a historical price!"

Nagle started to respond over her shoulder, but Mary said more. "Plus, history, what I know, reveals that a lot of white Christians have been supporters and sympathizers of the black struggles in slavery, through every conflict, up to the present, and many have been killed for their actions. It's black people and those whites who have paid a historical price."

"Points made," Nagle conceded.

But Mary wasn't finished. "Did my dark skin help me get elected homecoming queen? Maybe, but I think, no, I hope, the students saw me as an individual; knowing who I am and talking to me. Finding out who I am; and my thoughts, dreams, and accomplishments. Plus," Mary added in a wishful expression, "I hope my looks competed favorably."

Nagle stopped walking and turned to look at her friend. "Okay," she said, but followed in a 'don't give an inch' attitude as she resumed walking, "but why did the Northwestern Student Senate stop the election, and resume the next day? Was that racism?"

"Don't you ever let up?" Mary yelled to her friend through a blustery Oklahoma wind that suddenly swept in from the prairie and whipped her head scarf about her face.

"Was it some type of color bigotry?"

"No. Answer the question? Was it racist?"

"Might've seemed like it but, actually, it was confusing. I was one of seventeen candidates, and was on my way to vote, when a student told me, "The polls had been closed." It was early, so I asked, "Why?" The reply stunned me, "Because you were winning!" I wasn't sure how anyone would know without opening the ballot box but, granted, the attendants could've deducted it from voter comments.

I learned the voting process was discussed that night by the Student

Senate, which conducted the election. Others were there. I also heard that Randy Murrow, the Senate President, asked, 'Why change the rules because she's black and winning?' Based on his question, my color had an impact in the discussions. That, dear Jane, might make it seem racism was involved.

"It could've also exposed a weakness in the process. That is, there's a difference in getting more votes than any other candidate, compared to getting a majority of the total. The number had a bearing, as the next day, only the top four vote getters were left on the ballot. Didn't matter, though, as students chose me to represent them as queen. That was quite an honor!"

Mary took a breath and continued, "Think of it. How many other almost all white universities or colleges have ever elected a black woman as its queen, and she was subsequently recognized and honored by the faculty, staff, and administration as well as by the local community?" Mary answered her own question, "I'm not aware of any."

"Repercussions to a kiss by a white guy?"

"Well," Nagle shouted back at Mary now through a fierce wind, "what was it like to have a crowning kiss by a white guy and in front of all that half-time, almost all white crowd?"

"Went off as usual. I remember how windy it was more than anything. Just like now." At that moment a gust pulled Mary's scarf and she hollered at her friend, "Hold up!"

Nagle of course responded over her shoulder in her give-no-quarter personality sort of way, "Just keep walking, Mary," she shouted, "just keep walking!"

———————

Author Note: Jane Nagle returned to the East coast with her teaching degree, but she and Mary Elaine Williams remained good friends throughout life; even talking weekly by phone. Shortly after the interviews and permission for this chapter, Jane passed away May 2020. Yes, she remained true to the end to her stick of dynamite, explosive personality.

Mary's life journey was much the same as at Northwestern: always busy, focused, moving forward and, yes, never meeting a person she didn't interact well with. *Color was never allowed to be a roadblock to reaching for the stars.* Many noteworthy accomplishments mark her trail, and honors include: Northwestern Alumni Humanitarian Award 2000, National Eagle Forum Award, Appointment to the Oklahoma State Board of Education by Governor Frank Keating, Gallery Assistant for the Smith-Mason Art Gallery and Museum in Washington, D.C., and Artist in Residence for Oklahoma City Public Schools. "I'm blessed to have a great marriage, forty-seven years in 2020, to Ralph Nichols, who also has an accomplished career, and two talented daughters. And, yes I'd still go to Northwestern if I did it all over again."

The 1968 election and homecoming honors bestowed upon Mary Elaine Williams by Northwestern is historically significant, on a national scope. This involved not only being elected by the students to be queen over all homecoming events; but also, being subsequently honored by the faculty, administration, and community at large. Besting sixteen other candidates was quite a feat by itself. But, for a mostly all-white public university or college and in the year, 1968—one of the most divisive and violent years in the history of the United States, the result was phenomenal. It is historically unprecedented as Mary Williams was one of the first, if not the very first, black woman to have been elected and honored by such a university or college of the United States. Adding to the historical significance, there doesn't seem to be many others in a predominately white public institution over the next few decades.

75.

TOP NEWS OF 1968: SIMILAR TO 1967 WITH ADDITIONS OF ASSASSINATIONS OF DR. KING AND BOBBY KENNEDY. RICHARD M. NIXON ELECTED PRESIDENT. NORTHWESTERN OSU, A MOSTLY ALL-WHITE PUBLIC INSTITUTION OF HIGHER LEARNING ELECTS BLACK WOMAN AS HOMECOMING WEEK QUEEN. A FIRST?

December 31, 1968, Top News of the Year
National TV Studios

Washington, D.C. — "The top stories of 1968 are much as in 1967, except mor violent and bloodier," A reporter's voice sounded as scenes gave way to ones of protests, riots, and buildings burning in Washington, D.C. and other cities across the country. "1968 will go down as one of the most divided and violent in the history of the United States—second only to the early Civil War 1860s a century ago."

"Why?" The reporter asked as the TV camera panned slowly across a large area of burned out buildings. Pieces of paper, kicked up by gusts of wind, tumbled down the deserted street. "What caused so much violence, destruction, and death?" Similar scenes in Chicago, Baltimore, Memphis,

1968, one of most violent and bloody since Civil War Days!

Kansas City, Los Angeles, Detroit and other cities scrolled across the screen.

Vietnam—Deaths, and World-wide Anti-war Movement.

Civil Rights

Presidential Election

Assassinations

Violent Protests and Fires

"Vietnam involvement increased, and the number of soldier deaths grew. Adding to the violence at home in the form of war protests, was the continued issues of the civil rights movement for equality and freedom. Protestors took to the streets, sometimes in the tens of thousands, to influence authorities in decision-making. Many turned into riots and violence.

"It also was an election year for the presidency of the U.S., and protests against campaign positions stoked the fires of destruction."

"The assassinations of civil rights leader, Dr. Martin Luther King, Jr., and Senator Robert F. Kennedy, who was one of those at odds with President Johnson's Vietnam War policies and campaigning to replace him, added fuel to the flames of violence. Upon hearing of Dr. King's murder, riots of large numbers of people broke out in over one hundred cities across the country with buildings burned and deaths occurring. In Washington, D.C. alone, tens of thousands of protestors took to the streets over a four-day period, with many buildings burned, businesses destroyed, and thirteen deaths."

———

"As the year began, the Johnson administration was adamant the Vietnam War was being won, which meant, the South Vietnamese army was beginning to perform at the level necessary to defend its country. The Johnson administration pointed out, 'The 60,000 Vietcong into South Vietnam in late January—the Tet Offensive—was repulsed with 15,000 Vietcong casualties compared to 400 U.S. and 900 South Vietnamese soldiers.' The administration also claimed, 'There was progress towards peace talks," and President Johnson has not waivered from his pledge of "Peace with honor in Vietnam.'"

"But escalation of the war required a greater number of college students being drafted, some occupations and teaching specialties would lose deferment, and reserve units activated for the first time." The scene faded to scenes of protests on campuses, at political rallies, and draft board or military recruiting offices. "Changes in the draft laws made increases possible, and the outcomes were not well received by those who were against being dragged into fighting for one reason or another. The saying, 'Make love, not war,' gained popularity."

"Make love, not war!"

"At the same time, political campaigns for the U.S. presidency were heating up, and major opposition was being voiced to President Johnson's war policies. Senator Robert F. Kennedy, in Johnson's own democratic party, was one of the most vocal. Ironically, Robert was a close confidant to his brother, President John F. Kennedy who initiated buildup of the U.S. military in Vietnam. Such criticism, coupled to major disunity and civil strife, three months into the year, March 31, Johnson announced, 'I will not seek reelection, and devote all my time to winning the war and addressing other issues of the Nation.'"

"Nonetheless, the anti-war movement escalated, with thousands of draft dodgers fleeing to Canada and others locked in prison. By mid-year, 700 draft resistors were in U.S. prisons and more than 4,000 had fled to Canada to avoid being drafted."

Draft dogers flee!

"There seemed to be protests every week. These often turned into riots of destruction, fires, and deaths. Over the year, like 1967, it's been military buildup, anti-war and anti-draft demonstrations, peace talk efforts, more protests and violence, bombing on and off in North Vietnam, radio and TV debates, congressional hearings and political posturing, assassinations, and endless commentaries."

"Johnson had said, "Vietnam would get worse and more soldiers would be needed." He was right! A massive increase has occurred to 536,100 by end of 1968. But, consider," the reporter said in a sad tone,

"More and more soldiers, deaths, and injuries!" "Unless peace talks are fruitful, new recruits will be needed to replace the ones being rotated out of the war zone."

"Increases tragically mean higher numbers of deaths and injuries. These jumped in 1968 to 36,954. Sadly, they will continue as long as there is war."

————

Presidential election. "… consider moratorium on criticizing war." "Leading into the 1968 presidential campaign, President Johnson asked the American people to, "consider a moratorium on criticizing the U.S. and its Vietnam War policy." Other administration officials supported Johnson: Vice President Hubert Humphrey advocated the war was being won and peace talks will prevail. … Clark Clifford expressed how the South Vietnamese Army would soon "take over for themselves." … Dean Rusk spoke to the "dangers of deescalating the war."

"Still, the voices of opposition grew. Among them were: Senator Robert F. Kennedy until being assassinated. … General Sharp expressed being against the Johnson Vietnam policy. … Senator Morse urged withdraw from Vietnam. … Former Vice President Richard Nixon asked for a cease fire. … Dr. Ralph Abernathy, filling the void left by the slain civil rights leader, Dr. Martin Luther King, Jr., proclaimed against the war. … Others speaking out included: Senator Eugene McCarthy, Senator Edward Muskie, Nelson Rockefeller, George Wallace, and Congressman Joseph Pesnick."

Reasons cited by critics "Reasons cited by critics included: increasing numbers of military, casualties, prisoners of war, draft policies — more than half college students and guard for the first time, draft dodgers and deserters, peace proposals are fruitless, and the cost of war—3,400 planes lost through mid- year which was more than all of Korea conflict."

"Robert Kennedy was one of the front runners for the Democrat Party nomination, but an assassin removed him from the picture the night he learned he'd just won the California democratic primary—a mere two months before the August Democrat Party convention in Chicago. More than 10,000 protestors descended on the convention, and were met by 23,000 police and national guard.

Different groups rallying to protest included: The National Mobilization Committee to End the War in Vietnam, the Youth International Party or Yippies, the Students for a Democratic Society, and Black Panthers. Gasoline was tossed on their protest fires when Chicago Mayor, John Daley, refused them any permits to protest in the streets, and when he stated, "no thousands will come to our city, our streets, our convention." A number of riots occurred during the days of the convention, and several protestors were later convicted of "inciting a riot."

"The election was won in a landslide by **Nixon wins big!** Richard Nixon and his running mate for Vice President, Spiro Agnew, over the democrat nominees of Hubert Humphrey and Senator Edward Muskie, and over George Wallace, the American Party nominee."

Memphis, Tennessee — Scenes of the civil rights movement in the 1960s scrolled across the TV screen with the year superimposed over each one, as a voice sounded in the background.

"1960—student sit-ins across the South for equality and freedom. ... 1961—black people cars riding for freedom and to end segregation in inter-state travel. ... 1962—explosive enrollment of James Meredith at University of Mississippi. ... 1963—black people in nonviolent demonstrations with Dr. Martin Luther King, Jr, and other leaders in Birmingham, "We shall overcome...," and confronted with water hoses and dogs. ... 1963 August—Dr. King on the Lincoln Memorial steps in Washington, D.C. with 250,000 people, "I have a dream…" … 1964 Civil Rights Act … 1965—march from Selma, Alabama to state capitol,

Some of the civil rights movement in the 1960s!

"We shall overcome…" … 1966—Dr. King in Dallas at Southern Methodist University, "We have come a long, long way, but have long way to go…" and … 1967 hot summer—civil unrest "ignited riots and fires in over one hundred forty cities with many fatalities."

"The other top story of 1968 was the assassination of Dr. Martin Luther King, Jr., the beloved leader in the struggle for equality and

Dr. King assassinated!

freedom for all people of America." The reporter paused for a moment as a scene of a *Memphis, Tennessee* highway sign filled the screen. "Dr. King was shot the evening of April 4th while standing on the outside balcony of his motel room. He died shortly afterwards."

"Dr. King was giving leadership to a sanitation worker strike. The evening of Wednesday April 3rd, he spoke at the Church of God in

The previous evening…

Christ. "Support the brothers and sisters," he encouraged, and identified economic actions which could have an impact if carried out. … Regarding protests, he emphasized, "Peaceful demonstrations were the best way to be heard," as violence would be the focus of those looking on and the injustice ignored."

"When news of King's assassination reached the people of the United States, though, riots and violence broke out across much of the country," the reporter added sadly. "Fires and massive destruction occurred in over 100 cities. Deaths as well. Many believe these riots to be the greatest demonstration of social unrest the United States had experienced since the Civil War. In Washington, D.C., they lasted four days, with over 10,000 rioting, massive destruction, buildings burned and at least thirteen deaths."

"Interestingly," the reporter pointed out, "President Lyndon Johnson signed another Civil Rights Act, 1968, also known as The Fair Housing Act, legislation pushed by King and the civil rights movement, into law during these riot days, but it's unclear if they influenced him to do so."

Photos of Dr. King began to appear on the TV screen. Among the most notable, was the "I have a Dream…" speech delivered on the steps of the Lincoln Memorial, with the statute of the Great Emancipator, Abraham Lincoln, in the background.

"Dr. King, closed his Memphis church comments with a reflection of his life journey and what he perceived ahead."

Civil Rights March on Washington, D.C., August 28, 1963.
National Archives and Records Administration.

"Perhaps, while standing at the podium, thoughts of how close death had come flashed through his mind like: the near puncture of his aorta upon being stabbed with a knife in New York City, or the gun to his temple after a would-be assassin kicked down the door in St. Augustine, Florida. From that Memphis podium, Dr. King spoke of threats against his life, and of the possibility of an untimely death. But Dr. King ended his strike worker speech like he was confiding only to a close friend that he was not afraid to die."

'I don't know what will happen now. We've got some difficult days ahead. But it really doesn't matter with me now, because I've been to the mountaintop. And I don't mind. Like anybody, I would like to live a long life. Longevity has its place. But I'm not concerned about that now. I just want to do God's will.

"I have seen the Promised Land and we get there!"

And He's allowed me to go up to the mountain. And I've looked over. And I've seen the Promised Land. I may not get there with you. But I want you to know tonight, that we, as a people, will get to the Promised Land. So, I'm happy, tonight. I'm not worried about anything. I'm not fearing any man. *Mine eyes have seen the glory of the coming of the Lord.'"*

"Next day, Thursday April 4, 1968, Dr. Martin Luther King, Jr. died from an assassin's bullet!"

"Dr. King had spoken, in a prophetic sort of way, using the biblical Moses who led the Israelites out of four hundred years slavery and then forty years in the wilderness on their way to the land promised by God. Moses, though, did not enter the Promised Land, but he could see the whole land from the top of Mount Nebo. *Bible, Deuteronomy 34:1–4.*"

"Moses climbed Mount Nebo… The Lord showed him the whole land… "This is the land I promised on oath to Abraham, Isaac and Jacob when I said, 'I will give it to your descendants.' I have let you see it with your eyes, but you will not cross over into it." And Moses the servant of the Lord died there in Moab…" *Complete text: Bible, Deuteronomy 34:1-8 (NIV).*

———

Alva, Oklahoma — The TV screen filled with a map of the Southwest Plains. After a moment, the view focused inward to the northwestern border of Oklahoma, and a reporter's voice sounded, "Within six months of Dr. King's Promised Land proclamation of "equality and freedom," his prophetic vision became reality six hundred miles to the west at Northwestern Oklahoma State University located in Alva, Oklahoma."[AD]

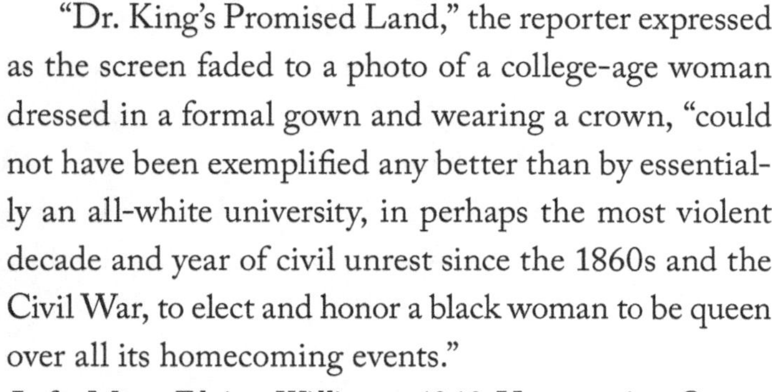

"Dr. King's Promised Land," the reporter expressed as the screen faded to a photo of a college-age woman dressed in a formal gown and wearing a crown, "could not have been exemplified any better than by essentially an all-white university, in perhaps the most violent decade and year of civil unrest since the 1860s and the Civil War, to elect and honor a black woman to be queen over all its homecoming events."

Left: Mary Elaine Williams, 1968 Homecoming Queen. Courtesy Northwestern.

The reporter explained, "Mary Elaine Williams, the only black candidate of seventeen total, was elected by the student body as queen over all Northwestern homecoming activities. She subsequently was honored by the full university, local town, and feeder communities across the western Great Plains, which also were essentially all-white."

The scene faded to one of Mary Williams sitting in front of the university library on the ledge of a water fountain, and responding to reporter questions.

"Yes, this is quite an honor. ... I am excited." ... "My election shouldn't be a surprise. History reveals thousands of white Christians have been involved in the black struggles to end slavery, through every obstacle to the present, and many were killed for their actions. It's black people and these whites who have paid a historical price."

"Did my dark skin help me get elected homecoming queen? ... Maybe, but I think, no, I believe the students saw me as an individual; knowing who I am and talking to me. Finding out my thoughts, dreams, and accomplishments. Plus," Mary added in a wishful tone, "I hope my looks competed favorably."

"The students chose me to represent them as queen. That was quite an honor! Think of it. How many other almost all-white universities or

An unequaled legacy? colleges have ever elected a black woman as its queen, and she was subsequently recognized and honored by the faculty, staff, and administration as well as by the local community? … I'm not aware of any."

As the interview ended, a crowd of Mary's classmates gathered around her, and Dr. King's voice rang out: "…I have been to the mountaintop, and seen the Promised Land! I know we, as a people, will get there! … Not by the color of our skin, but by our character!"

————

Author Disclaimer: The queen-election story of Mary Elaine Williams is true; however, she was neither interviewed by a reporter nor included in the national Top News Stories of 1968. Her Promised Land story should have been, though, as it has a significant place in the national civil rights movement. Its historically significant, on a national scope. This involved not only being elected by the students to be queen over all homecoming events; but also, being subsequently honored by the faculty, administration, local community, and the numerous feeder-towns.

For a mostly all-white public university or college and in the year, 1968—one of the most divisive and violent years in the history of the United States since the Civil War and the 1860s, the result was phenomenal. *It seems historically unequaled* as Ms. Williams was one of the first, if not the very first, black woman to have been elected and honored by such a university or college of the United States.

The historical significance seems even greater when looking back from the year 2020. It seems not until 1991 did another predominately white public university do what Northwestern did in 1968. That's when the University of South Alabama elect an African-American, Kalyn Chapman James, to be its Miss University. For certain, Northwestern was well ahead of the times!

76.

REFLECTIONS OF 1967 AND
END OF THE SIXTIES

March 1969, End of the Sixties
Northwestern Oklahoma State University

"Don't want to be charged for those," commented Northwestern basketball player, Bill Bixler, as he handed his uniforms to the equipment manager. He'd stopped by the player dressing rooms in Percival Fieldhouse to make sure they had been returned.

Mission accomplished, he paused by the entrance doors and looked over the athletic bulletin board. A disappointed look crossed his face. "Not a good season for the football or basketball teams," he mumbled. … A long sigh followed with a grimace. "At least Darrell Caldwell, Ardell Smith, and Jerry Garrison made the football conference team and Hank Commodore and Dale Ross in basketball." … He read the names on the football roster. *Hmmmm, didn't realize that many black guys on the team: James Cheely; Maurice Hill; Clyde Jones and Kenny Jones from Slickville, PA; George Graham and Ardell Smith from OKC; Dale Diggs from Wichita, Kansas. … The two on the basketball team were really good: Hank Commodore and Tommy Griffin. … Mary Williams was a good choice, too.*

1968 Northwestern Football and Homecoming: Record 1-7-2. Coach J.W. Cole. Players… Honorees for the Oklahoma Collegiate Conference: Darrell Caldwell at OT, Ardell Smith at DE, and Jerry

Garrison at DB. Northwestern Ranger Homecoming Queen for Fall 1968 was Mary Elaine Williams, a junior from Oklahoma City, Douglas High School.

Bixler looked again at the team picture and information of the just-ended basketball season.

BASKETBALL: Scoring Record Set

1968-69 record: 12-16, Front (L-R): Coach Keith Covey, Hank Dowell, Ed Fisher, Henry 'Hank' Commodore, Dale Ross, Mike Hargrove. Second: Don Hart, Mike Mitchel, David Taylor. Back: Henry Nicholson, Tommy Griffin, Bill Bixler, and Billy Drake. … Oklahoma Intercollegiate Conference Team: Commodore and Ross. Courtesy Northwestern.

He noticed the record again. *Played great at times. … Third in the preseason conference tournament and broke our game scoring record of over a hundred twice, but… should have had a better record.* He re-read the conference honorees. *Only Commodore and Ross? Thought Griffin had a chance. Maybe next year. Anyway, fun team to be around.* Bixler sighed deeply, headed towards the exit, and made a promise to perform better next season.

He paused momentarily in the bright Oklahoma day, as he walked out of the fieldhouse, and reflected on the where abouts of buddies who were on the team the previous season. *Wonder if Wings Drake was shipped off to Vietnam like H. L. and Thompson and the other guys? ... Hope they come back safely.*

———

Author Note: Several players on the 1968-69 Northwestern basketball squad—Mike Hargrove, Henry 'Hank' Commodore, and Tommy Griffin—were honored later as inductees into the university's Sports Hall of Fame. It was unique they were all on the same basketball team. Further details are provided later in the Appendix section to this book.

77.

1969 LETTER FROM VIETNAM. "WE'RE ALL JUST SHADES OF COLOR. START OUT IN LIFE, INNOCENT, LIKE THAT KID WHO RUBBED MY HAND TO GET THE COLOR OFF. THAT WAY UNTIL TAUGHT SOMETHING DIFFERENT. THANKS FOR BEING MY FRIEND."

June 1969, Letter to Larry Prochnau from H. L. Brown
Hunkered down in a bunker in Vietnam

"Dear Proc,

Wish you were here. Well, not really. I wouldn't wish this on anyone, but I miss you and the Northwestern Vinson Hall basement guys. Those were the best days.

Not sure you heard where I've been since we had to report for the draft right after Northwestern graduation day (spring 1967). Fun getting our diplomas, but a bummer to have to go to Oklahoma City for the induction physical. All on the bus were students. 'Member any?

Hard time for me when heard you didn't pass. Counted on a friend being with me. Thought be together, like the 4 years at Northwestern. Next day, shipped off to Ft. Polk Louisiana for basic training. Felt like our basketball teams in early season—cattle prodded to market. Advanced Infantry Training in artillery at

Ft. Sill, Oklahoma. Sent to Germany, but orders changed in air. Rerouted to Vietnam with 44th Artillery Division. Base called, Dong Ga. Hostile fire, RPGs, moment we landed at Camron Bay. Scrambled to foxholes along runway until firing cleared. Think a lot about things while over here. Sometimes have lots of time. Remember the young kid at Panhandle OSU before our basketball game? The one I spoke about on the bus back to Northwestern? I'll never, never forget how he acted toward me. He really didn't know about black people. Innocent like a child. Thought about that over and over. More even since heard about Martin Luther King killed last year. Think about life a lot, too, over here.

Shocked me when he came up to me, stood for a moment, stared up at me, and then rubbed the back of my hand. Rubbed and looked. Then rubbed some more. Didn't know what he was up to. Then, looked into my eyes, and asked that question, "How do you get it off?" It stunned me!

Proc, think you mentioned there's no difference between us—all the same. Start out in innocence, like that kid, until we're taught something different.

Other Northwestern guys maybe here. Heard Ben Smith is no longer with the Miami Dolphins. Always had trouble getting in shape. Too bad. They would've protected him. His brother, Glen? Not sure. Last knew, he was drafted, March 1968. Ft. Polk, like me. Advanced training at Ft Bragg. Interrogator for military intelligence. Heard now in Nam. Think Curtis Thompson was in Korea, but now here, too. Lance Rollins and Wings (Bob Drake) maybe here somewhere. Know of any others?

Our anti-aircraft group is most always with Marines. When fighting, we're right there. We'd take an area, lose it next day. Sometimes gave it. Some guys just seem to lose it after a while and go crazy. Our an anti-aircraft fires downrange. Never see if hitting target. Forward observers tell how to adjust. Same kind of action in which Frederick (Jerry Bennett) was killed. Get hostile fire all the time, but don't talk about those things here much. Look to time after military and Nam.

Doesn't matter over here what you look like. I have your back and you have mine. Let's survive together. No color in these bunkers or foxholes. Watch out for each other. Don't care whether black or white or something else! We're a mix, just shades of the same color. Everyone's blood is red. What I like about Oklahoma. You live, you live like me. You die, you die like me. I don't care what color you are! Everybody in the foxhole's the same. You got my back. I got your back. Way I live my life. Got Mom and Daddy back home. We fight for them. A lot like what we were at Northwestern. Wasn't a black or white thing. It was an 'us.' Yes, that's right.

Thanks for being my friend,"
H. L.

APPENDIX

to

SHADES OF COLOR

INNOCENCE OF A CHILD

———

AN UNEQUALED LEGACY

INTRODUCTION TO THE APPENDIX

The information within this Appendix provides further details to the body text, and consists of: 1) Further questions and a commentary by the author; 2) biographical profiles with information not previously presented; 3) sports accomplishments of several individuals not presented in the text; 4) the two summaries of how the book title originated; 5) a brief profile of Northwestern OSU, and 6) a short piece about the author.

Questions and Author Commentary

What happens when history is 'never learned, forgotten, or purposely ignored?' Are we left to be tossed to and fro by whomever controls the 'soapbox?' And, if the history presented is untrue, how do we make correct decisions on an individual or collective basis? Was it Spinoza, the philosopher, who expressed? "if we just walk on by the library and never go in, we'll never know we don't know." ... What was the method that Hitler's 'spin' agents utilized during World War II? Something like, "Tell a lie often enough, and the people will believe it." Subsequently, millions were killed. ... Are there 'spin' agents today, or do they really believe what they push out to what has heretofore been an unsuspecting society? ... Whichever the case, do we lose our freedoms?

World viewpoints and 'spin' seem to impact us every moment of the day. Someone or group in a position of power takes a 'knows what's best, superior attitude, and believes they have the authority to speak for others 'who they consider less informed.' Time after time a law is passed, a rule implemented, a tax or fee enacted, on and on, to which a large percentage of society did not want or support. But, when forced upon all, everyone is stuck with the cost of paying for it. Even worse, though, blamed for bad, unpopular consequences. If you think this doesn't happen, just look at the actual history leading up to, during, and after slavery and abortion. There are other examples, too. ... Knowing the truths of history helps to stop some of these evils, and mitigates others.

Pushed to the front burners today are the hot issues of race and the history of slavery in the land of what would become the United States. Some questions were identified previously and covered by the true stories within *Shades of Color*. Others are given below:

When did slavery begin? Was it present among the Indian tribes? If so, why? Who started it in the Colonies? Did blacks own slaves, too? Is it correct to say, "racial," when all are of the 'human race?' Why did the British government allow it? How did 'free' blacks exist at the same time as black slaves? Were there white slaves? Ones of other color? How did black slavery of 1619 and mid-1600s mesh with the established British Endentured Servant System? How many years did slavery of any group exist in the colonies under British rule? What were those British laws? Was it against British law to set slaves free, and why did Ben Franklin and Benjamin Rush, two white signers of the Declaration of Independence, start the Abolition Society in 1773 if they and others were for slavery *(David and Tim Barton, www.Wallbuilders.com)*? How many years did slavery exist in the British colonies before the Independence in 1776? Who created the Ku Klux Klan, when, and why? Who kept it active over its many years of existence? What political party controlled the appointment of the Supreme Court justices in the 7-2, 1857 *Dred Scott v. Sanford Decision* that reaffirm the existence of slavery in the U.S.? Who were the white sympathizers that joined with 'Free blacks' to push back against slavery, KKK intimidations, create a new political U.S. party, and elect Abraham Lincoln as President? When were the first blacks elected to Congress? Which was their political party? Which present-day political party has a continuous history linked to slavery, the KKK, affirmation to slavery, opposition to election of

Abraham Lincoln and the Emancipation Proclamation, opposition to the 13th (end of slavery), 14th and 15th (due process and voting rights) Amendments to the Constitution? Opposition to civil rights, push for segregation, eugenics, and even the movie "Birth of a Nation" in the White House?' … How many blacks were lynched by the KKK? How many white sympathizers? Which political party watered down the enactment provisions of the Civil Rights Acts of 1957 and 1960? What senator was the leader? Which party led the longest filibuster in congressional history against the 1964 Act?

On and on up to the present day to even both of the 2021 White House occupants, the list of questions can be expanded easily. The truths of history have definitive revelations! No 'spin' is necessary to understand them. Just present the true facts! Quickly, it is seen that whites, blacks, and others of color have been on both sides of this evil. History reveals many—black as well as white and other colors—have been killed opposing the evil. So, is it lazy or just plain ignoring history that some in the present day purport the issue is strictly a color versus white issue? … Or, are there other sinister motives and objectives?

Why, if so? What's the benefit to gain by being adamant to a false history that results in a strict 'black vs white' division? What's to gain? Who's to benefit? … Could the fear be when each person knows the truths of history, they will align their future with better decision-making. In the voting block patterns now seen, will blacks and whites and other colors align themselves with a different party? But, will allegiance remain the same as long as they are taught a false history which divides? Which one—learning the truths of history or false information and 'spin'—moves each person closer and closer to the evils of the Biblical '666?' … The choice is ours. I choose 'Freedom!'

Clifton Savoy, Ph.D.

———

Author Note: A couple of the historical sources for photos, etc, for this Northwestern writing project are: 1) the National Archives, and 2) the American historians, David and Tim Barton (www.Wallbuillders.com). The National Archives has numerous historical materials, which are not copyrighted, but acknowledged. Wallbuilders, under the direction of the Barton's, has "a national pro-family focus into America's forgotten history and heroes, with an emphasis on moral, religious and constitutional heritage. It's a name from the Old Testament writings of Nehemiah, who led a grassroots movement." Wallbuilders is purported to have over one hundred thousand historical documents in it's repository, and includes much about black history before and after the 1776 Revolution and Declaration of Independence from British rule.

Another excellent source of the black perspective, history, and stability of the family is the organization called 1776 Unites, www.1776Unites. com, a project of the Woodson Center and leadership of Bob Woodson.

TURNER BEAR, JR.

Northwestern OSU Fall 1951 – Spring 1953

Great Seal of Muscogee "Creek" Nation I.T. Approved by the Nation for use in Turner Bear, Jr.'s biographical profile October 2016. Turner Bear, Jr., October 2019, in Northwestern sweater awarded second year of lettering in 1952.

I was born in 1933 and named after my Dad, Turner Bear, Senior. I have two sisters and two brothers. My family lived in Checotah, Oklahoma, a town of about 2,500 people.

Our Indian ancestors were known as the "Muscogee." They lived in northern Georgia and Alabama and western Carolina. They also were called "Creek" because they lived along certain creeks where game and fish abounded.

Although, they occupied those lands for hundreds of years, treaties didn't protect them, and they were driven west to Oklahoma Indian

Territory by the U.S. Government (army) in 1836-1837. Thousands died along the harsh trail to Fort Gibson, where survivors had to pull themselves up, literally, with nothing more than each other. To top off the injustice, a new way of life—agriculture and farming—was thrust on them. Some made the transition in how they valued their self-worth and prospered, but many did not. The loss of our lands in the East, loss of life during forced relocation, and forced into a new way of life fueled bitter memories. This dimmed, though, over the years, as each generation rolled up their sleeves to succeed. Although unspoken, accomplishments have been recognized as outward honors to our Creek ancestors who lost all—many, even their lives.

The Turner Bear Family learned the ways and the character of the Creek Indians, and I was taught and spoke that language in my formative years. When I was about six, just as U.S. patriotism was unifying the country due to the onset of WW II, Mom and Dad said, "We need to learn how to live and do business with non-Indian people. So, from now on, only English will be spoken in our house." This commitment included attending public schools, too.

My Dad was active in many organizations that affected the socio-economic conditions of the Muscogee (Creek) Indians, and in 1957 President Dwight D. Eisenhower appointed Dad to be Chief of the Muscogee (Creek) Nation. Dad served as Chief from 1957-1961. Dad also served on the National Congress of American Indians, and he was President of the Inter-Tribal Council of what has come to be called 'the Five Civilized Tribes.'

I came to Northwestern as a result of my Checotah high school basketball coach, Wesley Kenney, who had gone there. He took a car-load of senior players to visit. I was the only Indian. Northwestern would give me the opportunity to continue playing sports, and my parents would help with finances. So, I enrolled Fall 1951.

At Northwestern, I played quarterback in football, point guard in basketball, and centerfielder in baseball. Dick Highfill was head coach of all three, and Walter Johnson was his assistant. The Newby football field was so plush, as Coach Highfill worked hard to keep it that way. We ran the spread formation. Called it the "Saltfork Spread," named after the Saltfork River nearby.

I started the Central Oklahoma game, and Northwestern beat them for the first time in 31 years. Score was 26 to 21. I passed for our first touchdown—a 37 yarder. Remember the game and play sixty-five years later, like it was just taking place. Was 20 degree weather, wind 10-15 mph from the northwest. We were going towards the East goal. Third down and only a few inches. Coach said, "Fake a power dive, and then hit the end." Sure enough, the whole defense must of figured we wouldn't dare throw in that wind and cold, and every one crashed the line to stop the run. I can see the ball in the air, Ben Koop (our end) breaking free, catching the ball, and running in un-touched. I still have a news clipping of the game. My 1952 team photo shows our uniforms. Also, there's the names of the players. I wasn't big, but I was fast—10.3 seconds for 100 yards. We passed and ran the option. I punted, too.

We didn't have facemasks back then, but football at Northwestern wasn't as rough as a similar sport the Creeks played. Fifteen players from one tribal town would be on one end of a rectangular field, and fifteen from another tribal town would be on the other half. There were goalposts on each end, and players had to hit or kick the ball to score. Players had two hickory sticks with an end hollowed out and the ball was made from leather wrapped around a small rock or something hard. A medicine man threw the ball into the game, like a hockey puck, to start it. He also was the scorekeeper.

Not uncommon to be clubbed with the stick. I recall times where a player would get knocked out, and rolled off to the side so play could continue. There were prizes and side-wagers. Some of these could be interesting. There also was a game on a circular field, where both men and women played. It wasn't as rough, but women sometimes ganged up on a man player if he was too rough. Had to hit a target high on a pole in the center of the field. A medicine man also started this game and kept score.

My first year at Northwestern I lived on campus in a dorm. Never had any issue with anyone on the team or campus or town. I didn't go into town much, though, since didn't have a car. Socially, I was accepted all around and was in a small fraternity as a freshman since there was no cost. I hitch hiked most of the few times I went home to Checotah. Same thing when I returned. Parents took me as far as Sand Springs. Once to Highway 64, I'd be able to hitch-hike the rest.

A person of color attending an all-white school, like I did at Northwestern during that time—Fall 1951 through Spring 1953—might have been viewed as a breakthrough against "Separate but equal education," as it was before 1954 when the Supreme Court overturned it in Brown v. Topeka Board of Education. In reality, though, the decision didn't much impact Indians, as our schools were under the federal government. Didn't matter for me at Northwestern anyway.

Going into my second year, I married a girl from back home, and we lived off-campus. No problem renting or buying anything downtown. She wanted to be closer to home, though, so we transferred to Northeastern OSU at Tahlequah end of year. However, I never played sports there.

Although I only attended Northwestern two years, I have special memories of the place. My last sports days were there. A grin always came when I'd see the Central OSU exit sign at Edmond on the highway. It would remind me of our 1951 game where we (Northwestern) beat them, running the spread formation.

The spread is popular, now, fifty years later at schools like OU and OSU and across the country. Northwestern was ahead of them all! Also, my first year of marriage was at Northwestern. And, sometimes I'd later on meet other Indians who've attended Northwestern, like Benny Smith (1962) and Wayne Postoak (1962), at Haskell Indian Nation University events at Lawrence, Kansas. My wife, Joyce Ann

(Childers) Bear, Creek Indian, graduated from Haskell and served on the Board of Directors. I also traveled to Northwestern years later just to visit with retired Coach Highfill. He was ailing some, but it was a great renewal and memory.

I used my degree in social studies and coached football at Sequoyah high in Tahlequah, Oklahoma. I obtained a Masters at Oklahoma University. Then was at the Seminole Reservation at Brighton, Florida 1956-59, and was with the U.S. Bureau of Indian Affairs for 28 years.

I'm retired now, but I occasionally relive the memories of my youth and sports days. Northwestern is a warm part of them. Sometimes I've even put on my Northwestern letter jacket or sweater. A few moth holes are there, and they're a little tight, but I enjoy yelling,

"Go Rangers!"

BENNY SMITH
Λ. Ꮷ. Ꮐ (DO TSU WA)

Northwestern OSU Fall 1959 – Spring 1962

*Seal of the Cherokee Nation Approved for Use in Benny Smith's
Bio-Profile 17, August 2016; Benny and Cheryl Smith Family*

My ancestors arrived in Oklahoma Indian Territory in several ways. Some on their own, like Sequoyah, who invented the Cherokee alphabet. He settled near Sallisaw in 1829. However, thousands of others were relocated by force in 1838-1839. They were rounded up by the U.S. government from homelands in the Appalachians of northern Georgia, Alabama, and North Carolina. It occurred even though the U.S. Supreme Court ruled in 1832 in favor of the Cherokees' keeping their homeland. Nonetheless, thousands died along the trail from the harsh conditions, disease, and famine. Survivors described the trail as "The place where they cried."

My Grandfather, Redbird Smith, and Father, Stokes Smith, were medicine men and served as Chief in the original Keetoowah Society of the Cherokees. Grandfather is recognized for reviving all the old traditions and customs, which I learned, too.

Many came to them for treatment, including Black people living nearby. Few become Cherokee medicine men, though, as, it's a spiritual calling. Life-learned information is passed to the next generation. This passage, however, is only permitted to one who has demonstrated the highest human values and self-initiative to learn and allow the spirit to be manifested in life.

Although I was raised in these old traditions—honored ways and culture of the Cherokees, I would never claim to be a medicine man. I had the honor, though, to learn prayers, rituals, and blessings for various events. I also learned how to read, write, and speak the Cherokee language, using the system developed by Sequoyah and adopted by the Cherokees in 1825. Each of the 86 letters represents a distinct sound in the Cherokee language. I'm still fluent in the language, and I understand my 1962 Master's degree thesis, *Keetoowah Society of the Cherokee Indian*, is still requested from the library at Northwestern OSU.

My Cherokee name is, Do Tsu Wa. In Cherokee, it is spelled, "Λ. d. G." I'm named for my Grandfather Red Bird. However, the name doesn't mean red or bird. Rather, it's a title given to red bird, the cardinal, which means "Of real beauty." … My Father's name in English is "Stokes." In Cherokee, it's, "Ꮥ. Ᏸ. Ꮯ." It sounds like, "Ga Ge Di," and means "heavy." … When Indian land allotments were enacted in the Oklahoma Territory by the 1887 U.S. Dawes Act, Indians were required to have a surname. Our family took "Smith," as we had blacksmith skills.

In my youth, I was constantly on the go. I played Indian stickball and enjoyed all types of competition. And, no, I didn't scream with blood-curdling yells—or dress in buckskin pants, go bare-chested, and wear body length head-feathers! Rather, it was blue jeans, a plain shirt, and a flat top haircut—like most other guys. Don't get me wrong, though. I've always been proud of and honored my Cherokee ancestors and heritage.

My basketball and softball teams in junior high at Gore, Ok, were undefeated over 2-years. In my 9th and 10th grades, I played guard and shortstop on the high school basketball and baseball teams. Gore didn't play football, so I transferred to Vian High School my junior year. First game against the Sequoyah Indians, Coach Benny Kiger started me at quarterback. We won, quarterback was my position my junior and senior years, and I was selected to the All-District Team both years. I was also a 2-year starter at guard in basketball and shortstop in baseball.

At Conners State Junior College, three Vian teammates played two years of football with me, and we all started. I played both ways, and never came off the field. Played OE, LB, and all special teams. The four of us also started in baseball 2 years. I was at 2nd base.

At Conners, Wesley Keeney was the basketball and football defense coach. He was a Northwestern OSU alum and encouraged me to go there. Coach Art Parkhurst recruited me for football, but he made it clear I could play basketball and baseball. I also ran track Spring 1960, but this Cherokee learned distance running *isn't* his sport! I also helped to initiate the rodeo team at Northwestern, where I attended Fall 1959 through Spring 1962.

Most of the time in football at Northwestern, I played offense LE and defense LB. Couple of games, I played both ways. I also played on all special teams. Had good games at both LE and LB positions. In the 1959 Homecoming game vs Panhandle State, I had 2 interceptions, and we won. A year later in our 1960 Homecoming game vs Central Oklahoma State, I caught a TD pass—and we won that game, too. … I played guard in basketball two seasons, 1959-60 and 1960-61, but mostly as a reserve. In baseball, I played 2nd base, left field, and right field.

My football eligibility expired at the end of Fall 1960 and, in the 1961 season, I helped the coaches on the sidelines and in practice, much like a graduate assistant coach. The experience was a valuable springboard to my high school coaching career. Also, after my football eligibility expired, I helped start the rodeo club at Northwestern. Eight seconds on a bull or bucking bronco is an eternity! A memorable competition was the Tonkawa College Rodeo, where I placed 2nd.

My being an Indian didn't seem to matter at Northwestern, playing sports, in the classrooms, or socially on campus. My roommates—Larry Weiser, Gary "Wogie" Wolgamott, John McCoy, and Berry Brown—and I were just plain guys. We had the same purposes: get an education, have fun and, of course, chase girls—none of whom were Indian—even on weekend visits to their hometowns. I spent time with Wayne Postoak (a Choctaw and only other Indian at Northwestern), Veldon Zollinger, and Kenneth Blue. Worked one summer on a wheat harvest with some of these guys. The white contractor only cared if we could do the work.

I didn't experience any negative issues in the town of Alva, either. I did my practice teaching in the local school system. Before that, I refereed basketball games in those schools. Yes, coaches and fans yelled in the heat of competition, but they were pointing to a call made. Not personal. Most important of all, my wife of 54 years is Cheryl Faye (Parks) Smith. She's a blue-eyed blond and 100 percent "paleface," and she grew up in Alva.

I had a double major, Physical Ed. and Industrial Arts, and graduated from Northwestern with a Master's degree Spring 1962.

My professional career covered forty years, that included teaching/coaching positions at Keyes, Oklahoma, in the far west of the Panhandle, and in Waynoka near Alva. The Keyes and Waynoka folks didn't care if I was Indian or not. Their interest was their children performing at their best on the field and in the classroom. … My last 32 years have been spent at Haskell Indian Nation University, where Indian students come from hundreds of tribes. I've had the pleasure coaching, teaching, and mentoring these students. I've served as coach, Dean of Students, Director of Guidance and Counseling, Athletic Director, and whatever else was needed. Lifting each student up was my passion. Been a long time since my Northwestern days—sixty years. As I reflect back to the relationships I had, and how I was treated, a couple of old Cherokee sayings come to mind.

Ꮥ ᏣᏓᏁᎰᎯᏂᎨᏍᏗ

De tsa da do yo hi ni Ge s do

"All to hold hands no matter how far we have to reach."

ᎬᏩᏟᏨᏗ ᏣᏓᎰᎯᏍᏗ. ᎢᏤᎮᏍᏗ

Gu wa Li tsv Di tsa da yo hi s di e tse he vdi

"We cannot find reasons to let others go as in giving up or turning your back on them."

No color litmus test existed there either. Rather, the quality of our lives was inextricably linked to all others, even the weakest among us. This life philosophy was integral to my coaching, teaching, and mentoring:

ᎦᎦᏢᎪᎡ ᎠᏂᏩᎦᎷ ᏆᏍᏉ ᏧᎦᏑᏂᎩᏓ

(E ga Li go Sv Wa ni ga lo Sv Na s quu Yi ga dla ni Yi da)

"We're only as strong as the weakest teammate!"

BEN AND GLEN SMITH

Northwestern OSU Fall 1963 – Spring 1967

"We don't serve 'Coloreds' here!" Would it be like that at Northwestern? My brother, Ben, and I didn't know what to expect when we reported for two-a-day football practice that hot, muggy August 1963. "First blacks to play a sport here," we were told. "Only one other black student, Dorothy Dodson, here first—Spring 1963. She worked in the cafeteria, and I met her on a recruiting trip. She flashed a smile when I said, "I'll be back in the Fall." H. L. Brown, a basketballer, joined us when the Fall classes began. Curtis Thompson, arrived in January 1964, and made it four black athletes in 1963-1964.

Ben's and my life journey began in the 1940s on an 80-acre farm 8 miles west of Crescent, Oklahoma, a small rural town a short distance north of Oklahoma City. It was a time when "coloreds" weren't welcome in some businesses, at least at the front door. Signs for "coloreds restroom and water" were normal. Some had an arrow pointing to back of the building to a water hose or to a smelly outhouse full of flies and located back in the trees or bushes. Also, happened up through high school. At fairs, portable potties had signs for "Whites" and "Coloreds."

Even into our early twenties, the 1960s and before the 1964 Civil Rights Act had teeth, Ben and I've stepped into some cafés and immediately were told loudly where everyone could hear, "We don't serve coloreds here." … My stomach would cramp, and I'd want to double over, and cry out, "Why?" Made us feel like a half man! God didn't make no junk! … As we walked out, they'd quietly say, "Come to the backdoor," 'cause they wanted our money.

There were four girls and seven boys in our Smith Family. I was next to youngest and Ben was a few years older. Poor, and all had chores to scrap out a living on a 80 acre farm. We raised chickens and some cows; and grew cotton, wheat, and alfalfa. Had a garden. Couldn't survive without any of those. We traded labor for things, mowed lawns, and watched over a neighbor place for a rich man living in Oklahoma City, so we could fish and swim in his ponds. As I got older and bigger, I often did heavy farm-work for other farmers. Must have lifted thousands of alfalfa bales onto trucks in the field and then again into barns. Can still feel the itchy, scratchy stuff. The work did build my muscles and strength. Ben wasn't in shape when we reported to Northwestern football like me since he worked away from the house at the time.

Our Smith Grandparents and Dad came from Topeka, Kansas and Mom from around Paris, Texas. Grandparents scrapped together enough to buy the 80 acres in the early 1900s. Not sure what our slave history before Oklahoma was like, as Grandparents, Dad, or Mom didn't talk about those things. Just kept telling us, "Don't get into trouble."

We plowed with a mule, then a small tractor after we could buy one. Milking cows built strong hands. Yes, I was squirted by my brothers. Was a good shot, too. We attended a black country school, Booker T.

Washington, a couple miles from Dover, a small town about 500. Met a white player, Leon Stuart, in a basketball tournament in 4th grade. Both jumped center, and shook hands to start game. Good friends ever since. In 1956, after 1954 school segregation ended, we went to Crescent schools. Leon played football with me, and again later at Northwestern with Ben. The three of us—all from Crescent—made All-Conference our last season, 1966.

Coach Art Parkhurst recruited Ben and me to Northwestern to play football, but we also played basketball and baseball my first year. It was only football after that. Could jump pretty good. Dunk if had some stick'um. One of my fondest memories was my game when football coaches told me I was starting. Happiest man in the world, as never ever thought of that.

The memory I cherish most, though, was a road trip to Central OSU in Edmond our first season 1963. The team stopped on the trip for a pre-game meal in a café where Ben and I had been turned away to eat just a few months prior to being at Northwestern. We had the biggest grins, as we walked in with the team, sat down, and ate without being told, "We don't serve coloreds here." Never forget that experience. Money talked!

First year, Fall 1963, played only offense Tight End. No defense cause coaches said didn't want to risk getting us hurt. (laughing) "Okay for guys like you, Savoy." Couldn't do pushups very good as had deformed elbows and couldn't straighten them out. Shortened my reach to catch the ball. … I had a good year at TE my 2nd year, and made the 1964 all-conference team. My 3rd and 4th years, Played safety on defense, but subbed in sometimes for passes on offense. Made all-conference as safety both years—overall, my last three years.

Ben played several positions his first two years, while he gained weight from his skinny 6'5" 230lbs. Soon, teams didn't like a 265lb FB running at them. His last year he blossomed as a defensive lineman, made All-Conference, and signed with the Miami Dolphins Spring 1967.

Ben or I never had any issue with anyone on our team or lost our temper in practice. The Indian players before us, probably made our experiences easier. It did bother me about passes over the middle. I seemed to be the one who got most of those, but concluded I was the toughest receiver.

On athletic road trips, roomed with Ben, but sometimes others too if room big. And our experiences mostly were without issue. There were a few hostile experiences, though. At one place, a player hit me dirty from the back. I started after him and about to deck him when a ref grabbed me. He never flagged the other guy, but gave me a stern warning. Couple other times something like that happened. Thought maybe my color, but knew if I charged back, I'd probably be ejected, so didn't do anything. Ben said he experienced similar stuff, too.

On another road trip east of here, Ben and I had to eat outside on a park table. Makes you feel like the low end of a dog—like there is something wrong with you. Useless. Sick in the stomach. Didn't think much of my team for allowing this, but learned years later, only a couple knew. No experiences like these at Northwestern or in Alva. Never had any racial issue the whole time Ben and I were there. Nothing in the classes either. Again, the Indians before us probably helped pave our way. The only incident might have been not getting into the VFW Club at first until Marvin Miller and Darral Inman explained we were their Northwestern basketball teammates.

Lived in Vinson Hall basement, same room, all four years with Ben and H. L. Brown. Lived across the hall from some jocks: footballers, Ken Strunk and Clifton Savoy; and basketballer, Jim Schroeder. Ben and Clifton became close our last two years. ... Didn't have much in our room. Ben had an old radio he'd found. It's case was broken, and you could see the tubes glow. Loved baseball. If wind was blowing right, could get the L.A. Dodgers. If not, listened to St. Louis Cardinals with Harry Carey. Could get them about every night. Ben knew player stats.

I cut roomies hair with some hand clippers and a knife comb, but a cousin at home cut mine. Too poor to go to a barber in Alva. Washed our clothes in the bathroom sinks. Mom taught us how to iron to make the crease in them. … Drove a 2-tone pink '55 Chevy, but no money, so it was parked all the time. Didn't go into town much. Watched sports and a few programs and hung out in the TV lounge. Didn't go home much either, unless caught a ride with someone.

Some pranks, like the one on Ben and me at the morgue but, for social life and entertainment, spent most time at the church student unions playing games and things like that. Then back in the room. Played Pinochle. Competition was heated, with double and triple deck. Ben, H. L., me, and guys who'd join us. Leon Stewart came a few times. … Never tried to date any of the white girls on campus. Yes, hugs after games from cheerleaders, but took it as an athlete being hugged.

Four black girls were at Northwestern Fall 1963. Had class with one, and talked all the time, at least, until boyfriend came to visit. On homecoming, all of us went to the VFW, and danced a lot. They didn't return after the school year. No black girls around after this until Ben and my last year in Fall 1966, several other black students enrolled. Mary Williams, a Velma, Linda Foster, Ruby, Bill, Richard Lowndes, and others I can't remember their names. No, Ben and I weren't Ladies Men, but probably thought we were. Just knew all the black students on campus. Guess, 'cause we had color and some of those gut-wrenching experiences in common.

Spring 1967, Ben was off to the Miami Dolphins. I needed a few hours of course work. My degree was in sociology. No teaching degree. Also, needed the English Proficiency test. Drafted March 1968. Notices began 1965-66. Foot soldier at Fort Polk Louisiana, then advanced training at Ft Bragg, NC, as an interrogator, military intelligence. Off to Vietnam for 14 months and then 5 months states-side. Used GI Bill to go back to Northwestern January 1970 to complete my degree. I really enjoyed my time at Northwestern, and would go there all over again.

Ben, after a short football time with the Dolphins, worked with

Kerr-McGee plant just south of Crescent. There until his heart attack and death in 1993. I've had joy through the years from comments by our Northwestern teammates how much they liked Ben and me.

Moved to Los Angeles in 1971. There ever since. Married a girl from Pensacola, FL. Have three sons. Worked in medical field; hematology. We'd run the tests, analyze the results, and send to the doctor. Retired now, and I am looking forward to reading the stories of Northwestern.

Northwestern Sports Hall of Fame
The 1968–69 Basketball Team

(L–R): Mike Hargrove; Henry 'Hank' Commodore; Tommy Griffin

Win-loss records sometimes don't reveal the true sports worth of a team. It didn't for 1968-69, as three players were later inducted into Northwestern's Sports Hall of Fame—Mike Hargrove in 1993, Henry 'Hank' Commodore in 1996, and Tommy Griffin in 2006. A brief profile of their careers follows. ... Others on the squad excelled in their own way with outstanding lives as well.

Mike Hargrove earned letters in football, basketball, and baseball. Twice, he was an all-conference selection. Drafted by the Texas Rangers, his performance earned the 1974 American League Rookie of the Year. In 1975, he was voted to the AL All-Star Team. Hargrove spent six seasons each with the Rangers and the Cleveland Indians, and his .396 career on base ranks among the top-100 in Major League Baseball history. Hargrove's playing days ended, and he became manager of Cleveland 1991-99, and led them to five-straight division titles and two trips to the World Series. Next, Hargrove guided the Baltimore Orioles from 2000-03 and Seattle Mariners from 2005-07 before wrapping up his pro career.

Henry 'Hank' Commodore had a super star basketball career at Northwestern, and was selected three times as an all-conference honoree—a distinction of what appears to be only one of three Northwestern student-athletes so honored over the twenty-year period of the fifties-sixties and maybe years before and after those decades (others were in football). Commodore came to Northwestern from Ford City, PA, and played basketball from 1967-1971. At the time of his induction, Commodore was its all-time male scoring leader at Northwestern, and held six other records. These included: most field goals in a game, single game field goal attempts, career field goal attempts, game free throws, and career free throws. He was named to the Oklahoma Conference Team his last three years. He also was selected on the NAIA All-American team after his senior season, and drafted into the National Basketball Association by the Philadelphia 76's. After his pro career, Commodore used his Northwestern education to teach and mentor youngsters as a high school counselor in Leechburg, PA.

Tommy Griffin's journey was somewhat different. His dad passed when Tommy was ten but he acknowledged, in addition to the influence of his mother and God, mentors played a key role in his life. These were at every educational level. Key ones were: Mr. Roger Pierce at Moon Junior High and later at Douglas High in Oklahoma City, advisor Jimmy Foster at Tulsa University, Coach Cecil Perkins at Northern Oklahoma Jr. College, and the late President Dr. Joe Stuckle at Northwestern. Griffin also attributed positive direction from national leaders like President John F. Kennedy and Dr. Martin Luther King, Jr. Griffin expressed, "It was a loss when such people were assassinated."

In choosing Northwestern, Griffin expressed, "I was attracted to the high rating given to its teacher\educational program. I wanted to be a teacher and coach, because of the ones who helped me. While at Northwestern, I played with some good athletes, like Henry Hank Commodore. I also had many good memories. One was being selected as an Outstanding College Athlete of America in 1970." Griffin also was chosen for his senior year performance to the Oklahoma Collegiate Conference basketball team.

As far as racial issues, Griffin noted, "If there were any on the Northwestern team, I couldn't tell. I never experienced any from the teachers, coaches, or administrators. Students? Maybe, but they were probably more a male competition or rivalry. Off-campus or downtown in Alva, I never experienced anything either. Many knew my name, 'Tommy.'"

After graduation, Griffin taught math and social studies and coached in high school. "I tried to help individuals reach their goals. My reward has been them reaching them." Over the years, Griffin has been a head coach in swimming, track, basketball, and baseball. "I've been blessed to have such a great and supportive wife, Gail, who also is a teacher. We have two sons, Taylor and Blake, who both later starred in basketball. Griffin never became a head coach in high school football, but was an assistant coach in the sport for twenty-nine years. He describes his overall coaching journey this way: "Here's the beauty of it. God has a plan, and you have to keep your eyes and ears open to see and hear it when it happens."

Griffin served as head basketball coach for twenty-seven years in the greater Oklahoma City area, and won the state championship game eight out of nine times: Two each at Classen and John Marshall High Schools, and four at Oklahoma Christian School—two with his son Taylor and all four with his other son Blake. Griffin stated, "I've been blessed to have success."

INNOCENCE OF A CHILD!

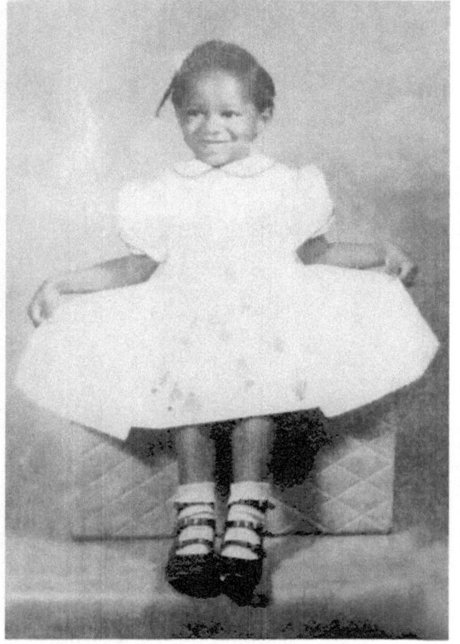

L-R: Gary and Judy Wolgamott, 1948; Mary Elaine Williams

"We're all the same. Start out innocent until we're taught something different."

"Don't care whether black or white or something else—just shades of the same color! Everyone's blood is red."

—*H. L Brown, 1969, hunkered down in a bunker in Vietnam Northwestern Class of 1967*

Sierra, Virginia, and Hannabah, daughters of Ken and Charlene Blue

Mary Elaine Williams with Oklahoma City friends
Courtesy of Mary Williams

Clifton and Billie Jean Savoy, 1947

AN UNEQUALED LEGACY!

"… I have a dream that my four little children will one day live in a nation where they will not be judged by the color of their skin but by the content of their character." Dr. Martin Luther King, Jr. August 28, 1963, Lincoln Memorial in Washington, D.C.

"… I have seen the Promised Land and we get there!" Dr. King, Jr. April 3, 1968, at the Church of God in Christ, Memphis, Tennessee. (*Bible, Deuteronomy 34:1-8)*

Northwestern's 1968 Homecoming Queen, Mary Elaine Williams, and runners-up, Shirley Gibson (L) and Lee Ann Turner, Courtesy Northwestern

The election of Mary and subsequent honor by the students, faculty, and staff by essentially an all-white university for all its homecoming events in 1968 was a major milestone in the Civil Rights movement. Northwestern was one of, if not the first public university or institution of higher education in the United States to have set this monumental point in history—an unequaled legacy!

1992: Lt. Colonel Curtis Thompson.

After tours in both Korea and Vietnam, Thompson returned to Northwestern and graduated with the class of 1973.

And, it all began when a white college-age girl gave an AWOL hitchhiker a ride to the campus of Northwestern, a mostly white university, and place he'd never been and received an opportunity to share his dreams in person to the President of Northwestern, who in turn gave young Thompson an opportunity. … Events, simply, not easily explained!

Northwestern Oklahoma State University
www.nwosu.edu | (580) 327-1700

Hello,

We are pleased to read the heart-warming, stories in this book. It is an honor Northwestern was mentioned over and over. The expressions, "I would attend there again," attests to not only the friendly one-on-one relationships but, also, to the quality of our educational offerings and family-oriented environment. Northwestern succeeds only when you reach your purpose in life. We have long felt this university is unique in many ways, as these stories reveal—even seemingly unequaled across this Nation by any other public institution of higher education and maybe private ones as well. And, some icing on the cake, at one of the lowest cost. You'll find more information below and further details on our website. I look forward to welcoming you personally.

Sincerely,

Dr. Janet Cunningham, President

ORTHWESTERN IS A UNIQUE UNIVERSITY where students feel at home, and the community welcomes them with open arms. Students gain experiences that will last a lifetime. While we provide an incredible education, our rates are affordable for many to obtain their degree. As you will see in the stories in this book, our university has created a place where students and their families are accepted and welcomed. These heart-warming stories show the relationships made at Northwestern, but also demonstrates what Northwestern is all about—student success. We welcome you into a glimpse of our home, and invite you to come tour our campus anytime.

Now, a little about Northwestern Oklahoma State University. We have a physical presence in three campus locations, the primary one in Alva, Oklahoma, is located in the former Cherokee Outlet, which was also known as the Cherokee Strip. The Cherokee Outlet was located in Oklahoma Territory prior to Oklahoma's statehood in 1907. The other two are Woodward and Enid, Oklahoma. We are a hardy bunch, as most of our early history revolved around the Great Plains spirit. Although we no longer ride horses through town, Northwestern does have one of the best and largest collegiate rodeo teams in the country with many of the cowboys and cowgirls being the best in their events.

Northwestern's unequaled legacy wasn't planned or forced. It just naturally occurred because of the cohesiveness, the oneness among our students, faculty, staff, local communities, and feeder-towns throughout these Great Plains. At Northwestern, we know you by your name, and your true story waiting within will be given every opportunity to bloom, to live, to be successful—much like the young African-American whose story is in this book, who was AWOL from the military, hitchhiked to get to a place he'd never been, to Northwestern, got an almost immediate audience with the President, got to live out his dream of playing collegiate basketball and becoming a teacher\mentor and coach with several state championships, and retired, after tours in both Korea and Vietnam, as a Lt. Colonel instead of being taken to prison.

Northwestern was established in 1897, ten years before Oklahoma Statehood. Students became teachers in rural areas, primarily one-room schoolhouses. Today, a proud tradition still stands where "Rangers" receive an outstanding education, for a fraction of the cost.

Northwestern offers bachelor degrees in a number of fields from education and fine arts, to business and natural sciences, as well as a doctoral program in nursing practice. There are also several master level degrees offered in education, psychology, heritage tourism and conservation, and American studies.

Yes, Northwestern is a place where special dreams become reality. We have had marvelous stories of real people time, after time, helping others bloom themselves and succeed. One of our recent graduates finished medical school first in the class. Another student became one of the richest persons in the world. A number have been drafted into professional sports. One was honored as the rookie MVP of the Major Leagues and, later, he coached, winning multiple pennants. Others have gone on to both the NBA and NFL, and chosen for the pro-bowl and as coach. We've won a national football championship and have individual rodeo champions, while other students have excelled in business, the health services, arts, and professorial positions. In every academic program, success stories abound.

To learn more about Northwestern, please visit:
www.nwosu.edu

ABOUT THE AUTHOR,
CLIFTON SAVOY, PH.D.

Clifton Savoy on Miami South Beach, Florida

Clifton was born and raised in western Oklahoma, called the 'Panhandle,' an area once known as 'No Man's Land' before statehood. He's a graduate of Northwestern OSU, class of 1967. He and wife, Judith, now live in Tallahassee, Florida, but he has never forgotten those roots. Now, he is following his passion—to bring life to stories that deserve to be resurrected, to live, be remembered, and not altered with time. … *Shades of Color* is one of them, and it's an honor to bring these heart-tugging memories back to life. Check his author website for information of other stories, or just send a 'Howdy.' Or, come, sit a spell by his campfire, and share your stories. Coffee's usually a perk away.

www.CliftonSavoy.com
CFSavoy@Nettally.com

Author Note: Please return to page 353 to learn more about my alma mater, *Northwestern Oklahoma State University.*